CW01203703

SPIRITUAL LIVES

General Editor
Timothy Larsen

SPIRITUAL LIVES

General Editor
Timothy Larsen

The *Spiritual Lives* series features biographies of prominent men and women whose eminence is not primarily based on a specifically religious contribution. Each volume provides a general account of the figure's life and thought, while giving special attention to his or her religious contexts, convictions, doubts, objections, ideas, and actions. Many leading politicians, writers, musicians, philosophers, and scientists have engaged deeply with religion in significant and resonant ways that have often been overlooked or underexplored. Some of the volumes will even focus on men and women who were lifelong unbelievers, attending to how they navigated and resisted religious questions, assumptions, and settings. The books in this series will therefore recast important figures in fresh and thought-provoking ways.

Titles in the series include:

Woodrow Wilson
Ruling Elder, Spiritual President
Barry Hankins

Christina Rossetti
Poetry, Ecology, Faith
Emma Mason

John Stuart Mill
A Secular Life
Timothy Larsen

Leonard Woolf

Bloomsbury Socialist

FRED LEVENTHAL
AND PETER STANSKY

OXFORD
UNIVERSITY PRESS

OXFORD
UNIVERSITY PRESS

Great Clarendon Street, Oxford, OX2 6DP,
United Kingdom

Oxford University Press is a department of the University of Oxford.
It furthers the University's objective of excellence in research, scholarship,
and education by publishing worldwide. Oxford is a registered trade mark of
Oxford University Press in the UK and in certain other countries

© Fred Leventhal and Peter Stansky 2019

The moral rights of the authors have been asserted

First Edition published in 2019

All rights reserved. No part of this publication may be reproduced, stored in
a retrieval system, or transmitted, in any form or by any means, without the
prior permission in writing of Oxford University Press, or as expressly permitted
by law, by licence or under terms agreed with the appropriate reprographics
rights organization. Enquiries concerning reproduction outside the scope of the
above should be sent to the Rights Department, Oxford University Press, at the
address above

You must not circulate this work in any other form
and you must impose this same condition on any acquirer

Published in the United States of America by Oxford University Press
198 Madison Avenue, New York, NY 10016, United States of America

British Library Cataloguing in Publication Data
Data available

Library of Congress Control Number: 2019939510

ISBN 978–0–19–881414–6

To Jean from both of us

Preface

The authors of this biographical study have shared an interest in Leonard Woolf for many years. They first met when Fred Leventhal was an undergraduate and Peter Stansky a graduate student, and they lived in the same Harvard House. They both received Ph.D. degrees in modern British history, having done so with the same splendid mentor, David Owen, and they have remained close friends ever since, even though they have lived miles apart on the opposite coasts of the United States since 1968. Over the years they have both approached Leonard Woolf from different perspectives. Fred has written studies of various political figures on the British left as well as several articles about Woolf, while Peter has been interested in Leonard as a member of the Bloomsbury Group. They were both privileged to have brief encounters with Woolf himself. It might be of interest to mention them here.

Peter met him in the summer of 1962. He and William Abrahams were just beginning a study of Woolf's nephew, Julian Bell, for their book *Journey to the Frontier* and went to see him in his tiny cold office, a cubicle off a passage at Chatto & Windus, the publishing house with which the Hogarth Press had become affiliated. He himself, with his white hair and skin, conveyed a sense of colorlessness increased by the fact that the room was skylighted, and all was bathed with a certain arctic light on a cold June day in London. His attitude towards Julian, his wife's beloved nephew, who had been killed in the Spanish Civil War, was characteristic. Clearly he cared for him, but was not about to abandon his critical sense. His view of Julian's virtues and defects, although premised on the affection due to a nephew, was truthful and hard-headed. For the very reason that individuals were so important, the perception of them was not to be clouded by any false sentimentality. In effect, his conversation was like his autobiography: it gave the appearance of being discursive, but as it went on, each touch added up to a picture of Julian as he remembered him. The comments were put in what seemed to be an erratic way, much as a painter might daub on his color, but it was the best way for him to create a portrait. Having begun by saying he had little to say, he ended by saying a good deal. We were never to meet again, but we corresponded. His letters were succinct and to the point, and always sent in used envelopes, in what one imagined to be a sign of Gladstonian parsimony but may actually have come from the habit of saving paper during the Second World War. In these exchanges he revealed a keen editorial sense along with the shrewdness of a man of business. We had wanted to use extensive quotations from Virginia Woolf's then unpublished memoir of Julian; he allowed us to use only about half of what we had originally asked for. He was right, editorially, for he forced us to rely on our own words, and not on another's, to gain the effect we wanted. Also, by limiting the amount of hitherto unpublished material by his wife to appear in print, he was, as he pointed out, protecting the economic value of her words. After *Journey to the Frontier* was published in 1966, he sent a warm, but brief note of praise, and listed a few, as is inevitable, errors. He also paid us the supreme compliment of praising the book in his autobiography, writing that he would not write much about Julian in it as we had provided a good account of his life. Our meeting was brief but supremely valuable, and I was lucky to have had the experience.

Fred met Woolf in August 1968 at the start of research for a biography of Henry Noel Brailsford, the journalist and writer on international relations, with whom Leonard had close ties in the world of weekly journalism and on the Labour Party Advisory Committees on International and Imperial Questions. He replaced Brailsford on the staff of the *Nation* in 1922 and worked with him on the *New Statesman* during Kingsley Martin's editorship. Their attitudes were generally similar, although Woolf's antipathy to Soviet Russia emerged earlier than Brailsford's. Both were staunch advocates of Indian independence. An author's query for information on my part elicited an invitation to visit Leonard at Monks House on a summer afternoon. He cordially welcomed my wife and me, provided tea, and later accompanied us on a walk to the banks of the Ouse, where Virginia had drowned herself. He was forthcoming with recollections of Brailsford but failed to locate any correspondence. During our brief visit, Leonard, then nearly 88, seemed to go up and down the stairs with alacrity, looking in vain through some of his files. He promised to continue searching after our departure and corresponded only a few months before his death expressing regret that nothing further had been found. In July 1990, during a brief foray into Leonard's papers and those of Kingsley Martin in the University of Sussex collections,

Preface

I had the pleasure of spending an afternoon with Trekkie Parsons, who was helpful in illuminating Leonard's political ideas and moral values, as well as providing the photograph that accompanied my essay on Leonard in the volume *After the Victorians: Private Conscience and Public Duty in Modern Britain* (1994). These memories, and my long friendship with Peter, who essentially introduced me to the Bloomsbury Group, have informed my understanding of Leonard and facilitated the writing of this biography.

These personal connections, however tenuous, may have been the stimulus for our decision to refer to our subject throughout the biography as Leonard, not as Woolf (potentially causing confusion with Virginia). To her he was Leo, to his family he was Len, but to us and to those who have heard us talk about him, he was and remains Leonard.

In this collaboration Peter Stansky has been mainly responsible for Part I and Fred Leventhal for Part II of the book.

Acknowledgments

We are grateful to the following for permission for quotations.

For Leonard Woolf

The University of Sussex and The Society of Authors as the Literary Representative of the Estate of Leonard Woolf.

For additional quotations from Labour Party memoranda and reports written by Leonard Woolf: Labour History Archive at the People's History Museum, Manchester.

For Virginia Woolf

From *The flight of the mind: The letters of Virginia Woolf: Volume I 1888–1912* by Virginia Woolf published by The Hogarth Press. Reproduced by permission of The Random House Group Ltd. ©1975.

From *The question of things happening: The letters of Virginia Woolf: Volume II 1912–1922* by Virginia Woolf published by The Hogarth Press. Reproduced by permission of The Random House Group Ltd. ©1976.

From *The diary of Virginia Woolf: Volume I 1915–1919* by Virginia Woolf published by The Hogarth Press. Reproduced by permission of The Random House Group Ltd. ©1977.

From *The diary of Virginia Woolf: Volume II 1920 – 1924* by Virginia Woolf published by The Hogarth Press. Reproduced by permission of The Random House Group Ltd. ©1978.

From *A reflection of the other person: The letters of Virginia Woolf: Volume IV 1929–1931* by Virginia Woolf published by The Hogarth Press. Reproduced by permission of The Random House Group Ltd. ©1978.

From *Leave the letters till we're dead: The letters of Virginia Woolf: Volume VI 1936–1941* by Virginia Woolf published by The Hogarth Press. Reproduced by permission of The Random House Group Ltd. ©1983.

From *The diary of Virginia Woolf; Volume IV: 1931–1935* by Virginia Woolf published by The Hogarth Press. Reproduced by permission of The Random House Group Ltd. ©1982.

From *The diary of Virginia Woolf: Volume V 1936–1941* by Virginia Woolf published by The Hogarth Press. Reproduced by permission of The Random House Group Ltd. ©1984.

Excerpts from *The diary of Virginia Woolf*, Volumes I, II, IV and V, edited by Anne Olivier Bell. Diary copyright © 1977, 1978, 1982, 1984 by Quentin Bell and Angelica Garnett. Reprinted by permission of Houghton Mifflin Harcourt Publishing Company. All rights reserved.

For Lytton Strachey

Paul Levy, the Strachey Copyright Holders, and the Trustees of the Strachey Trust.

We are grateful for brief quotations from other sources which we have included under the doctrine of fair usage.

Cover picture

Alfred Harris (1927), Lebrecht Images

Picture Credits

1. Barbara Strachey (1938), National Portrait Gallery
2. Photo Gisèle Freund/IMEC/Fonds MCC (1939)
3. Mary Evans Picture Library/Sigmund Freud Copyrights (c. 1945)
4. *Jewish Chronicle*/Heritage Image/age fotostock (c. 1965)

We would like to express our appreciation for the help provided by librarians at the following institutions: Bodleian Library, University of Oxford; British Library of Political and Economic Science; Churchill College Library, University of Cambridge; Houghton and Widener Libraries, Harvard University; Labour Party Archive, People's History Museum; Stanford University Library; University of Sussex Library.

We would also like to thank the following individuals for their assistance and encouragement: Ian Britain, Arianne Chernock, Jamsheed Choksy, Marjorie Garber, Jean Leventhal, Peter Mandler, Laura Mayhall, the late Trekkie Parsons, and Darren Treadwell. We are grateful to Timothy Larsen and Tom Perridge for inviting us to undertake this biography.

Contents

List of Illustrations — xv
Abbreviations — xvii

Part I. The Personal Journey

1. Youth — 3
2. Cambridge — 15
3. Ceylon — 30
4. Virginia and After — 50

Part II. The Political Journey

5. International Government — 83
6. Anti-Imperialist — 109
7. The Wars for Peace — 133
8. Socialism and Civilized Society — 161
9. Journey's End — 188

Select Bibliography — 203
Index — 207

List of Illustrations

1. Leonard Woolf by Barbara Strachey, 1938 (National Portrait Gallery) — 79
2. Leonard and Virginia, 1939 (Photo Gisèle Freund/IMEC/Fonds MCC) — 79
3. Leonard Woolf with pipe, *c.*1945 (Mary Evans Picture Library/SIGMUND FREUD COPYRIGHTS) — 80
4. Leonard with dogs, *c.*1965 (*Jewish Chronicle*/Heritage Image/age footstock) — 80

Abbreviations

ACImpQ	Advisory Committee on Imperial Questions
ACIntQ	Advisory Committee on International Questions
Barbarians	Leonard Woolf, *Barbarians at the Gate* (London: Left Book Club/Victor Gollancz, 1939)
Beginning	Leonard Woolf, *Beginning Again: An Autobiography of the years 1911–1918* (London: Hogarth Press, 1964)
Colonial Empire	Leonard Woolf and Charles Roden Buxton, *Report to Labour Party Annual Conference on the Colonial Empire* (London: Labour Party, 1933)
Co-operation	Leonard Woolf, *Co-operation and the Future of Industry* (London: George Allen and Unwin, 1919)
COS	Charity Organisation Society
Deluge	Leonard Woolf, *After the Deluge* (London: Hogarth Press, 1931, 1939)
Diaries in Ceylon	Leonard Woolf, *Diaries in Ceylon 1908–1911* (London: Hogarth Press, 1963)
Downhill	Leonard Woolf, *Downhill All the Way: An Autobiography of the years 1919–1939* (London: Hogarth Press, 1967)
Economic Imperialism	Leonard Woolf, *Economic Imperialism* (London: Swarthmore Press, 1920)
Empire	Leonard Woolf, *Empire and Commerce in Africa* (London: Labour Research Department/George Allen & Unwin, 1920)
Empire in Africa	*The Empire in Africa: Labour's Policy* (London: Labour Party, 1920)
Glendinning	Victoria Glendinning, *Leonard Woolf: A Biography* (New York: Free Press, 2006)
Growing	Leonard Woolf, *Growing: An Autobiography of the Years 1904–1911* (London: Hogarth Press, 1961)
Hotel	Leonard Woolf, *The Hotel* (London: Hogarth Press, 1939)

ILP	Independent Labour Party
Imperialism	Leonard Woolf, *Imperialism and Civilization* (London: Hogarth Press, 1928)
International Government	Leonard Woolf, *International Government* (London: George Allen & Unwin, 1917)
Journey	Leonard Woolf, *The Journey Not the Arrival Matters: An Autobiography of the years 1939–1969* (London: Hogarth Press, 1969)
LW	Leonard Woolf
LSE	London School of Economics and Political Science
Mandates	Leonard Woolf, *Mandates and Empire* (London: League of Nations Union, 1920)
Modern State	Leonard Woolf et al., *The Modern State*, ed. Mary Adams (London: George Allen & Unwin, 1933)
Principia	Leonard Woolf, *Principia Politica: A Study of Communal Psychology* (London: Hogarth Press, 1953)
Quack	Leonard Woolf, *Quack, Quack!* (London: Hogarth Press, 1935)
Socialism	Leonard Woolf, *Socialism and Co-operation* (London and Manchester: National Labour Press, 1921)
Sowing	Leonard Woolf, *Sowing: An Autobiography of the years 1880–1904* (London: Hogarth Press, 1960)
Spotts	*Letters of Leonard Woolf*, ed. Frederic Spotts (London: Weidenfeld and Nicolson, 1990)
TLS	*Times Literary Supplement*
UDC	Union of Democratic Control
VW	Virginia Woolf
War for Peace	Leonard Woolf, *The War for Peace* (London: George Routledge & Sons, 1940)
WCG	Women's Co-operative Guild
Wise Virgins	Leonard Woolf, *The Wise Virgins* (London: Edward Arnold, 1914)

PART I
The Personal Journey

1
Youth

Leonard Woolf was born on November 25, 1880, on West Cromwell Road in the Kensington district of London. As he remarks in *Sowing*, the first volume of his autobiography,[1] he emerged from non-existence at that point, and he anticipated returning to non-existence at some latter point. This struck his characteristic ironic, bleak, and amused note: how he approached his life. He was determined to make the most of it, but he was also aware that in so many ways it was an exercise in futility: "I cannot truthfully say that my future extinction causes me much fear or pain, but I should like to record my protest against it and against the universe that enacts it" (*Sowing*, 11–12). Here, at the very beginning of his autobiography, he rails against a deity in whom some believe, though he certainly did not, yet who seems to have arranged the world very badly:

> I resent the stupid wastefulness of a system which requires that human beings with great labour and pain should spend years in acquiring knowledge, experience, and skill, and then when at last they might use all this in the service of mankind and for their own happiness, they lose their teeth and their hair and their wit, and are hurriedly bundled, together with all that they have learnt, into the grave and nothingness.
>
> (*Sowing*, 12)

His maternal grandfather, Nathan de Jongh, a Jewish diamond merchant, and his wife, Henriette, came to London in the 1860s from Holland. With the discovery of diamonds in South Africa, London had increasingly become a center of the diamond trade. Considering his later anti-imperialism, it is ironic that Leonard's family should have benefited economically from the empire. His paternal grandparents, Benjamin and Isabella Woolf, grew up in the East End of London, Ashkenazi Jews, whose forebears came to London in the late eighteenth century. Benjamin Woolf was a successful tailor, opening shops in the fashionable West End of London. Raised as an orthodox Jew, he became a member of a Reform congregation in London. His son, Sidney, became a very successful barrister. This emulated a common English progression, from trade to the professions, with the significant difference that these particular families were Jewish. Jews were being increasingly accepted, up to a point, in English society—perhaps best symbolized by their being able to sit in parliament as of 1858. They were, it might be said, "in but not of," not "one of us." Leonard's mother, Marie de Jongh, had been married before but was widowed when very young. Her future husband was an executor of her late husband's will; the two families were also intermarried. Though the de Jonghs were somewhat grander than the Woolfs, both families were financially prosperous, and both had had homes in the Bloomsbury district of London. In the opening of his autobiography, Leonard struck the theme that would be so much part of his life, that he was both an "insider" and an "outsider." As he points out, he is writing looking out upon the Sussex countryside with which he deeply identified, in the parish where he served as its hard working clerk as well as many other local posts. But he was also a Londoner. Through his education he strongly identified with the classical tradition, "the Greece of Herodotus, Thucydides, Aristophanes, and Pericles" (*Sowing*, 13). Yet his actual ancestors so many years before had come from Persia or Palestine.

Another question to be considered in a study of his life is the position of Jews in English society. Jews had been expelled from England in 1290 and were readmitted in 1656. They occupied, it is fair to say, a somewhat ambiguous position in English society and to a certain degree still do. This was certainly reflected in Leonard's life and is particularly striking in his relation to the Bloomsbury Group and his wife, Virginia. Like other religious groups over time, notably Roman Catholics and those Protestants who were not members of the Church of England, not to mention middle-class and working-class English men and eventually women, Jews were granted political rights and would appear to have become full members of the English nation. But not quite. This is strikingly encapsulated in the life of Benjamin Disraeli, the great nineteenth-century prime minister. Jews could not be members of parliament until 1858, when MPs were allowed to take their oath swearing on either the Old or the New Testament, not just the New. As Disraeli had become a Christian in his early teens, his own political career was not restricted by his having been born Jewish. He was the beneficiary of English legalism. At the same time, that did not prevent him from being perceived as Jewish, and attacked as such. Although Leonard never converted to Christianity, being a non-believer, he was completely non-observant from an early age. That did not preclude others, including those closest to him within the Bloomsbury Group, as regarding Jewishness as being an important part of his character and not necessarily in a positive way. And he himself felt that being Jewish was a central factor in shaping his character.

Jews were a little bit apart, perhaps more likely to be identified as such than members of other religious groups, whether or not the particular individual was religious. What has been called "civilized intolerance" or what one might characterize, paradoxically, as benign anti-Semitism can be seen as an abiding characteristic of English society, although it became less so in reaction to the rise of the Nazis. Although Leonard was an atheist from an early age, he was always known as a Jew. This was true, even though, as far as we know, he was neither involved with Jewish issues, nor influenced in his opinions because he was a Jew, although towards the end of his life, perhaps somewhat to his surprise, he looked favorably upon Israel.

By chance, he was born at the time that Jewish issues were coming more to the fore in English society. In the course of his life he does not seem to have been much concerned with these questions, even though they may have affected how he was viewed by others. His forebears had established themselves before the great migrations that took place from Eastern Europe in the latter years of the nineteenth century. At the time of his birth there were approximately 35,000 Jews in England. Previously immigration to England had not created a problem. But, starting in the 1880s and for the rest of the century, there was an influx of approximately 150,000 East European Jews. In reaction to this, parliament in 1905 passed the Aliens Act imposing some restrictions on immigration. The growth of the Jewish population presented something of a dilemma for the existing Anglo-Jewish community. On the one hand, many of them wanted to be helpful to their co-religionists. On the other, as the recent arrivals were poorer and far less assimilated than themselves, the older residents were deeply concerned that the immigrants would cause problems in the relation of the English Jews to the wider community. The newer arrivals tended to be more politically radical, a position for which Leonard might have had some sympathy, although his politics did not move particularly leftwards until he returned from Ceylon at the age of 30. But as far as one knows he had little connection with any Jewish political groups. He certainly became socially concerned and involved with questions of poverty, particularly under the influence of Sidney and Beatrice Webb. But there is no indication that he took any special interest in the situation of his co-religionists. Although Jews tended to congregate in the same areas, the poor in the East End, the better-off in Golders Green, the Woolfs themselves at the time of his birth lived in fashionable Kensington. Unlike their European brethren, Jews had never been restricted as to where they might live when they returned to England in the seventeenth century. There may not have been any official anti-Semitism, but that did not mean there was no discrimination against Jews. Consequently it is frequently hard to comprehend how deep anti-Semitism is in England. The Jews of England almost seem to have made a contract with the state. In return for being allowed to get on with their lives without restriction, they pledged themselves not to make trouble and agitate against perceived discriminations. Those who had arrived before the 1880s had to a considerable degree integrated themselves into English society.

In a somewhat negative way, Leonard was deeply concerned with spiritual questions. He points out at the beginning of his autobiography that he totally lacked a sense of sin, despite his awareness that the object of the Day of Atonement was to seek pardon for one's sins. He found it very difficult to apologize for anything he had done, although he fully recognized that at times he may have behaved badly. In terms of religion, the family was observant; his mother regularly attended religious services on the Sabbath, but his father went only on major holidays. He also served as a warden at the Reform West London Synagogue. His sons received tutoring in Hebrew from an apparently incompetent teacher. A year after Leonard was confirmed at the Synagogue in 1893, he informed his mother that he would have nothing further to do with religion, that he was an atheist. This caused some tears on his mother's part but not profound upset. Nevertheless, in subsequent years he did occasionally go to synagogue, perhaps in the interest of family peace, and he kept in fairly close contact with his family, particularly his mother, often to Virginia's irritation. His mother was a powerful figure who did much to keep the family together after her husband's early death. She was a conventional yet strong-minded woman, and Leonard did not depict her in a favorable light in his novel *The Wise Virgins*. Leonard and his siblings all married non-Jews. (Only his brother Cecil, who was killed in the First World War in his twenties, did not marry.) He never denied being Jewish and was, despite being a non-believer, continually referred to as Jewish, which sometimes made him self-conscious. But, as far as he could tell, he was never discriminated against, although he was occasionally the target of anti-Semitic slurs by some of his closest friends, as in letters Clive Bell wrote to Lytton Strachey. In his autobiographies he did not record any anti-Semitic incidents. He may have suppressed these memories, for certainly at his secondary school, St Paul's, Jewish students were bullied even more than other pupils. He wrote amusingly about God, noting that, if he existed, his position had become much less powerful, having shifted from being an absolute to a constitutional monarch. From an early age he was committed to the idea of rationality, that one was a free agent, not hobbled by any idea of sin. It was not through any sense of atonement or duty that he felt obligated to do good in the world.

Sidney Woolf died of tuberculosis and heart failure in 1892, at the age of 48, leaving nine children ranging in age from 3 to 16. Leonard, the third eldest, was only 11. The eldest was Leonard's sister Bella, to whom he would be closest and who was the most literary of his siblings, publishing children's books and guides to Ceylon. Sidney Woolf's death was a terrible blow and helped to influence Leonard's pessimistic view of life. His father had become a very successful barrister, a Queen's Counsel at a young age, one of only 175 bearing that distinguished title when he was appointed. But he left a comparatively small estate. Despite Leonard being so young when his father died, Sidney was important in shaping the person he became. The family income was much reduced, and they moved from Kensington to Putney, a modest London suburb. In memory of their former glory, their new house was called "Lexham," the street on which they had lived in Kensington. Leonard had been born into the higher levels of the middle class, but now he would need to win scholarships in order to maintain his class position. While class position in England does not depend entirely on income, money obviously plays an important role. In his reduced economic circumstances it was necessary to reinforce that position through education. The family was under strain, but even in Putney they still employed three servants, in contrast to the many they had had in Kensington. In a way the experience encapsulated what was to happen to middle-class families in the course of the twentieth century as the number of servants they could afford to employ declined. In *Principia Politica*, Leonard, citing the nineteen family servants in Kensington, provides a rich picture of the luxury of upper-middle-class life in England before the First World War, the hierarchy of servants running from governesses and tutors to boot blacks. Equally surprising, considering how involved his life was to be with political questions, was how unaware of politics he was when he was growing up. Yet his experience of the intense class hierarchy of his early days may ultimately have informed his later commitment to socialism, even though those in his family's employ were treated well. He felt very secure in his nursery world, and that solid early upbringing helped to build a sense of assurance, combined, paradoxically, with insecurity because of the family's later financial situation. Even so, when quite young he observed some working-class processions in the local streets. Occasionally a derelict or mad person, emerging from a poorer part of London, would misbehave in a neighboring street in Kensington and instill fear in Leonard, some sense of the abyss that might exist beneath the security of late-nineteenth-century England. But, on the whole, he was in a cocoon of middle-class life, even after Sidney's death, when the family was far less well-off and had to watch its expenditures carefully. He was old enough to be aware of the seriousness of the situation.

His father's death inadvertently led to the forming of his central belief system. "From that moment a kind of unchildlike seriousness came into my life, a sense of responsibility and of the insecurity of material things, like houses, food, money. It did not make me unhappy or, after the first shock, worry me" (*Sowing*, 84) Yet within a few years, influenced by the family's reversal of fortune, he acquired a rather grim

> sense of fundamental insecurity, and a fatalistic acceptance of instability and the impermanence of happiness. This fatalism has given me a

> philosophy of life, a sceptical faith which stood me in good stead in the worst moments of life's horror and miseries. For just as, though I believe passionately in the truth of some things, I believe passionately that you cannot be certain of the absolute truth of anything, so too, though I feel passionately that certain things matter profoundly, I feel profoundly in the depths of my being that in the last resort *nothing matters*. The belief in the importance of truth and the impossibility of absolute truth, the conviction that, though things rightly matter profoundly to you and me, nothing matters—this mental and emotional metaphysic or attitude towards the universe produced the sceptical tolerance which is the essential part of civilization and helps one to bear with some decency or even dignity the worst of Hamlet's slings and arrows of outrageous fortune. (*Sowing*, 86)

It was part of what he called his "carapace," his defense against the blows that the world might inflict upon him. On the other hand, perhaps because he was a non-Christian, he lacked a sense of sin, a sense of guilt. Like his father, he was capable of judging himself as well as others rather harshly. In a significant way, his carapace might also have served, almost unconsciously, as his way of deflecting, indeed virtually ignoring, anti-Semitism.

He enjoyed the traditional education of his class. From 1892 to 1894 he went to a prep school, Arlington House, in Brighton, which his elder brother, Herbert; also attended; the headmaster kindly admitted the two boys, and the other brothers in turn, at lower fees to compensate for the family's reduced circumstances. There Leonard excelled at sport and acquired a permanent love of games, and doing them with style. His interest and ability in sport compensated for whatever unpopularity his braininess and Jewishness might have caused him. Looking back, he found his early education tedious and anti-intellectual. But, as at home, he reveled in the experience of reading for pleasure.

In 1893 he became a pupil at the eminent London public school St Paul's. John Colet, friend of Erasmus and Thomas More, founded the school in 1509. Though obviously Christian-based, named for and physically next to the great cathedral, it was also somewhat secular. It was administered by the Mercers, one of the great livery companies of the City of London. Along with Eton, Harrow, Winchester, and Westminster, it was at the time Leonard went there, and has continued to be, one of the best-known and most highly regarded schools in England. It had been willing to admit some non-Christians and has had notable Jewish pupils. The decade after Leonard, the publisher Victor Gollancz and in subsequent years Isaiah Berlin, Oliver Sacks, and Jonathan Miller among many others attended the school. Nevertheless, there was anti-Semitism at St Paul's that was even more vicious than the appalling bullying that seems to take place at so many schools. The novelist Compton Mackenzie, a contemporary of Leonard's, would write admiringly about him in their school days, yet he nevertheless recorded how he tormented his Jewish fellow students:

> It was my delight to put drawing pins with the sharp end up on the seats of Semitic school-desks. It was my delight to stick the lids of these desks with gelatine lozenges and watch the way the lid would come up with unexpected force and strike a Semite chin. It was my delight to be a unit in two lines of exuberant young Nordic companions lined up on either side of a corridor in St Paul's School and when some timid, book-laden young Jew passed along on the way up to his class-room to push him from side to side all the length of those grinning rows of boys until his books were scattered on the floor.... I thought it extremely funny when some much admired athletic seniors plunged a young Jew head foremost into a tub of butter rashly left outside the school tuckshop. I derived a warm feeling of patriotism from seeing a young Jew bounced up and down on one of the drums of the Cadet Corps until the parchment burst and was left to explain, without sneaking, to the authorities what had happened.... Looking back on that silly anti-Semitism manifested with all the crudity of savage boyhood, I recognise that the fundamental cause of it was resentment at the way our Jewish schoolfellows used to sacrifice everything to reach the top of the class.[2]

The ultimate aim of an English public school was to produce an English gentleman, a position that in the view of most at the time a Jew would have a considerable challenge to achieve.

In Mackenzie's 1937 novel *The East Wind of Love*, the central character terminates his friendship with Emil Stern, based on Leonard, in part because he is a Jew and his schoolfellows taunt him about the friendship. Mackenzie depicts Stern as having the looks and athletic skills that would have made him very popular had he not been Jewish. The religious atmosphere of the school in its rather superficial nature is captured in Mackenzie's description of school prayers, from which the Jewish students, along with the few Catholics and some others, were exempted:

> As a Catholic [Fitzgerald waited] outside the swinging glass-panelled doors together with two or three of his co-religionists, some fifty Jews, and about half a dozen members of the more rigid Nonconformist sects while the Latin prayers were read by the Captain of the School to the six hundred odd members of the Anglican Communions mustered in the Hall. So far as any religious atmosphere existed at the official Prayers, the Catholics and the Jews and the Plymouth Brethren might have joined their schoolfellows without the slightest religious offence, since it would have been safe to wager that not one boy in the Hall could have said what the special prayers for the day were for, albeit by sheer repetition over hundreds of days, the Pater Noster and the concluding Gratia Domini were imprinted with meaningless verbal accuracy on their memories. The masters standing in the aisles looked over their mortar-boards with countenances that aimed at expressing a courteous piety, a kind of *noblesse oblige* towards Almighty God; the boys stared blankly before them save where here and there an irrepressible youth convict-wise murmured through motionless lips a witticism or a criticism to his neighbour.

It is here that Mackenzie introduces Stern, who is befriended by the central character, Ogilvie, presumably based on the author himself:

> Stern was the nearest creature in St James's to a prodigy. He was not yet sixteen, and small for his age.... He was not yet developed enough physically to be called a handsome boy, though to proclaim him pretty were an insult to that finely carved pale face more Greek than Semitic, to those heavy-lidded large lustrous eyes and scarlet upcurving bow of mouth. His skin seemed nearly translucent like fragile porcelain, his hands white and light and trim as feathers.... A Gentile half as attractive as Stern would have won the glances of every ambitious young amorist in the school, but being a Jew he was disregarded. As for his cleverness, there were clever and industrious Jews at the top of every form on the classical side of St James's, and Stern's ability to write Greek Iambics ... was attributed by his class-mates to the capacity for unlimited swotting that every Jew possessed and not at all to the inspiration of poetic genius.[3]

The third main character in the novel is Fitzgerald, a Catholic of Irish descent. It is intriguing that Mackenzie would have made the three into something of outsiders, a Jew, a Scot (Ogilvie), and an Irish boy. For a while Ogilvie terminates his friendship with Stern in part because he is a Jew and his schoolfellows taunt him about the friendship, but by the end of the volume they are very good friends, Ogilvie having spent some weeks with the Stern family in France. Mackenzie alters some details, making Stern 15 in 1899 when Leonard was 19, giving him just one sibling, a brother, Julius, who is a musical prodigy. Stern is depicted as very much the intellectual, argumentative and strong minded and while in France very much, as was Leonard, a supporter of Dreyfus.

It is not clear why and how St Paul's was selected, but presumably it was both more congenial and less expensive than a boarding school, as he could live at home. Also he secured a scholarship, traditionally one of the 153 available reproducing the number of Jesus's "miraculous draught of fishes." The school had moved in 1884 from being next to St Paul's to a sixteen-acre site in Hammersmith; Leonard would bicycle there the three miles from Putney. He found the school, as shaped by its High Master, F. W. Walker, limited in its intellectual depth. As with the other prominent public schools during the century, the schools had become national institutions designed to train young men for successful careers in banking or family businesses or the military or the Church, but also frequently in ruling the state and the empire as civil servants. Walker's aim was to create brilliant classical scholars. The brightest boys were groomed to win major scholarships at Oxford and Cambridge colleges, preferably Balliol at Oxford and Trinity at Cambridge. Benjamin Jowett, the famous Master of Balliol, had been a student at St Paul's. Particularly after the civil service was opened in 1870 to a meritocracy, admitted to its ranks by examination, members of the middle class could become highly competent servants of the state at home or abroad. It was firmly held that the study of the Classics was the best way to train the mind and the character for such work. It is striking that, although it was at this time that Leonard had renounced Judaism, he characterized himself during his St Paul's years as a bristly Hebrew character, a combination of Jekyll and Hyde. He also became aware of himself as an intellectual; he enjoyed using his mind, on mathematics and the Classics, and deriving aesthetic pleasure from poetry, art, and increasingly music. But he also became more aware of what might be considered a paradox. In his view, the chief culprit in the denigration of the mind was where the most prominent boys in the country were trained, the public school. This was because of its philistinism, its hatred of the "swot," even though it was their accomplishments that gave the school prestige through the scholarships they won at Oxford and Cambridge. Leonard's ability at and love of games largely protected him from bullying. As Mackenzie reveals, he was probably taunted at times for being Jewish. He does mention being called a "dirty Jew." Then, and for many years after, English people were not reluctant to make derogatory remarks about Jews, and more often than one might think when Jews were present. Nonetheless, Leonard maintained, perhaps accurately, that being Jewish did not act as an impediment to his career.

He did feel that at the school the masters, despite teaching academic subjects, had a philistinism deeply ingrained within them. There was an exception: one of his teachers, A. M. Cook, took a special interest in him, encouraged him intellectually, and treated him as a fellow adult. With his encouragement, Leonard read Montaigne, Sterne, and Ibsen, and jotted down in his notebook quotations from such authors as Tolstoy and Meredith. Cook gave him as a prize for being first in writing a grandly bound copy of Francis Bacon's essays. Mackenzie recalls conversations with Leonard bemoaning the school's philistinism, but he himself does not mention this in his own autobiography. He also met young writers, notably G. K. Chesterton and E. C. Bentley, both of whom had recently been at St Paul's and who invited him to join a small political debating society consisting of recent graduates of the school and a few current pupils. Both Chesterton and especially his younger brother, Cecil, an exact contemporary of Leonard's at St Paul's, were later known as prominent anti-Semites. Yet in Leonard's time, three of the four current students in the debating society elected with Leonard were Jewish, with Cecil as possibly the one Christian. He did not overlap with another prominent St Paul's socialist, G. D. H. Cole, who was nine years younger. Duncan Grant was at the school for two years, but, being five years younger, even if they had been there at the same time, they would not have known one another. They would eventually be virtual brothers-in-law.

Leonard's classical education shaped his lifelong commitment to truth and justice. In many senses he was having the not-uncommon experience of some rebellious members of the middle class, educated at public schools, learning the knowledge and skills that enabled them to become reformers, to fight the system that the schools themselves so clearly represented. Probably more than at Cambridge, it was at school that his idealization of classical Greece was acquired. One might say that the spiritual ideas for his entire life were developed at St Paul's, a fusion of his Hebraic principles with Hellenist cultural values. Despite its many palpable defects, English private education could perform valuable work in providing the tools that would support a rich intellectual life. Leonard went on to become a prolific and adept writer, skills that were formed in the relentless translations and essay writings that took place at school and would continue at university, most particularly in the papers that he would present to the Cambridge discussion society, the Apostles. In March 1899 he sat the scholarship examination at Trinity College, Cambridge. He had not taken the exam the previous autumn, when other Paulines had done so. He had been ill, and the spring exam was mostly for students already at the college. He felt isolated; it was one of the worst experiences of his life, entering a totally new world alone and miserable. He did not win the major scholarship that Walker expected of him and for which he had been crammed by Walker's son. But he was awarded an exhibition, a smaller scholarship, and he could then afford to become an undergraduate member of Trinity College. The following March he managed to win a full foundation scholarship. He had to be careful with money, but he had enough to get along at Cambridge. He was set on a standard path to have a successful career, whatever he might choose to do. Cambridge would change his life but not in anticipated ways.

Notes

1. The biographical details presented in this book are largely drawn from Woolf's five volumes of autobiography.
2. Andro Linklater, *Compton Mackenzie* (London: Chatto & Windus, 1987), 38, quoting Mackenzie's unpublished and undated essay "How I Learned Not to Hate the Jews."
3. Compton Mackenzie, *The East Wind of Love* (London: Chatto & Windus, 1949), 6–8.

2
Cambridge

Despite the anguish of his first encounter with Cambridge, when he took the entrance exam on his own and no one spoke to him, Leonard felt well prepared for the new adventure:

> I had intense intellectual curiosity; I enjoyed intensely a large number of very different things: the smooth working of my own brain on difficult material; playing cricket or indeed almost any game; omnivorous reading and in particular the excitement of reading what seemed to one the works of great writers; bicycling and walking; work and the first attempts to write. (*Sowing*, 97)

He knew practically no one, as most St Paul's scholars went to Oxford. Whether intentionally or not, Cambridge proved a better fit for him, being less worldly and more Puritan in tradition than the somewhat Cavalier Oxford, with its stronger ties to London and the government and civil service, reinforced at Oxford by that old Pauline, Benjamin Jowett. So too, being at Trinity rather than King's at Cambridge, the other college closely associated with Bloomsbury, reinforced a more stringent way of thinking. Trinity was the largest and most intellectually distinguished of the Cambridge colleges. Shortly after arriving, Leonard met the strange, brilliant, and eventually the more or less "unknown" member of the Bloomsbury Group, Saxon Sydney-Turner, with whom he would share a set of rooms in college for three years. Even so, they did not necessarily see that much of one another, as they had very different schedules. Yet they certainly became great friends. Leonard was obsessed by the Book of Job. As he wrote on March 20, 1901 to Lytton Strachey: "The more I read it the more certain I feel that it is above the first class, that it is absolute perfection and *can only* rank with Plato & Shakespeare."[1] His siblings rather casually abandoned Judaism, as did Leonard, but for him it may have been a more agonizing decision. One has the feeling that he may have been the sort of person who, despite his denials, yearned for a faith, yet at the same time strongly believed that having a faith was an impossibility.

He also became close friends with a few others who had come up to Trinity at the same time: Lytton Strachey, Thoby Stephen, and Clive Bell. In the style of the time, they called one another by their last names or possibly nicknames but not by their first names. That would be a great change in usage some years later among these friends who began using first names—ironically in Leonard's case, since they were generally referred to at the time as "Christian" names. Adopting first-name usage is seen rightly as a significant change in the early years of the Bloomsbury Group, emphasizing its belief in the importance of friendship and personal relations. Thoby Stephen was the brother of Vanessa and Virginia. He eventually introduced his friends to his beautiful sisters when they came to visit. Thoby was the son of Sir Leslie Stephen, the eminent late Victorian man of letters, who also came to Cambridge from time to time. He had resigned his fellowship at Trinity Hall when he decided he no longer believed in God. Thoby's nickname, based on his imposing physique, was "the Goth." Leonard writes about the family with some awe on first meeting them. He comments on their great beauty but also that they, like all of the family, were in his word "monolithic," formidable in both their talk and their silences. When the sisters came to have tea with their brother, the seriousness of the occasion was enhanced by the necessary presence of a chaperone in the person of their cousin, Katherine Stephen, the Principal of Newnham. Leonard wrote of their beauty as a fine amalgam of their mother's Pattle ancestry and Stephen strength.

> It was almost impossible for a man not to fall in love with them, and I think I did at once. It must, however, be admitted that at that time they seemed to be so formidably aloof and reserved that it was rather like falling in love with Rembrandt's picture of his wife, Velasquez's picture of an Infante, or the lovely temple of Segesta. (*Sowing*, 186)

Lytton Strachey was known as "the Strache," and Leonard, notably, as "the Rabbi." Clive Bell, apparently without a nickname, became a friend, as he lived on the same staircase. He had aesthetic interests, but he was much more in the "huntin', shootin', fishin'" mold of the

English country gentleman. In the classic English way, his family had fairly recently become gentry, enabled to do so on the basis of money made from coal.

Other Trinity men eventually associated with Bloomsbury were Desmond MacCarthy, who had already received his degree, having arrived in 1894, and Adrian Stephen, Thoby's younger brother, who entered the college in 1902. Several figures who would become part of Bloomsbury Group were affiliated with King's College. They were the somewhat older E. M. Forster and Roger Fry, but they became closely associated with Bloomsbury not at its inception in 1904 but rather in 1910. Both were members of the Apostles. But, most importantly, there was a contemporary Kingsman who became a close friend both of Leonard's, but even more of Strachey's—John Maynard Keynes.

The Trinity group studied either History or Classics, Leonard doing Classics. Their education consisted mainly in their endless conversations with one another and their wide reading, but it was not necessarily closely tied to their studies. They were not all that successful academically in terms of exam results, Leonard falling below expectations. In Part I of the Classical Tripos in his second year he did earn a First but in the Third Division, and then, in Part II the next year, a Second. After that he spent a fifth year in Cambridge in order to prepare for the civil-service examination, in which he also did not score very highly. He did well enough to qualify for a post in the colonial service though not in the highest ranks, nor distinguished enough for the Treasury, the grandest level in the competition. On the other hand, he won several college academic prizes, an English essay prize by examination, a second place for an essay on the poetry of Byron, which he disliked, and another Trinity prize for a study of mystics. For this group of friends, and perhaps for most of the students at Trinity, the official academic requirements hardly seemed to be a major factor in their existence or their education. Academic achievement was not necessarily the major reason they were there; the ancient universities might be seen as more of a finishing school to prepare one to enter successfully the outside world. Leonard and his friends were very serious and devoted scholars, but not necessarily of the subjects they were officially studying. It was the focus neither of much of their reading, nor indeed of what seemed more important than anything else, their conversation. Sydney-Turner, the most academically brilliant of the Trinity group, ironically went on to a routine career as a civil servant. He was, however, as we shall see, largely responsible for what may have been the first publication of the group.

Leonard certainly enjoyed a rich intellectual life at Cambridge. This was more important to him than working on his writing of Greek and Latin, which might have made a difference in his examination results. His autobiography makes little mention of academic work, of attending supervisions or lectures. Much of it, in any case, was repetitive of what he had studied at St Paul's. A long list survives of the numerous classical authors whom he read as an undergraduate, as well as his extensive reading texts in English and French.[2] It was a superb education for its own sake, but it did not concentrate enough on doing work that would pay off academically. This had also been true at St Paul's, where Walker regarded him as a disappointment who did not fulfil his brilliant promise.

The Trinity philosophers were crucial in his education but not as his teachers. In his autobiography he fails to mention the Classics dons, some very distinguished, such as R. C. Jebb and James Frazer or the Apostles Henry Jackson and A.W. Verrall or indeed Jane Ellen Harrison, whom the Hogarth Press later published. Except for Harrison, they were at Trinity and may well have taught him and certainly would have known him. Their progressive approach to the Classics should have been congenial to Leonard. But they do not appear in his account of his Cambridge years, so important to him in so many ways. He preserved quite a few of his Cambridge writings, papers on Byron, Browning, Lucretius, and Theocritus. S. P. Rosenbaum, in his *Victorian Bloomsbury*, cites his essay on mysticism, which may have earned him the Trinity English essay prize in 1901. As Rosenbaum writes:

> The essay is valuable for its indication of the general direction Bloomsbury's non-theistic, mystical impulses would take. Mystics are defined by Leonard as those seeking to explain man's relation to the Final Cause through the soul rather than through reason. The two types of mystics were thinkers who consciously reflect on the soul and poets who unconsciously recognize its beautiful workings. Plato and the neo-Platonists were the greatest mystical thinkers; among the moderns,

Swedenborg, Novalis, and Emerson stand out. Maeterlinck is the latest of the true poetic mystics, not Symbolists like Rimbaud with their meaningless assemblages of words. Leonard's view of mysticism is thus secular but not modernist. He argues characteristically that skepticism rather than belief is the natural result of the mystical questioning of rationality and sees this borne out in Christianity's persecution of mystics such as Eckhart and Boehme.[3]

Leonard even proposed that he and Sydney-Turner edit a book on mysticism, with Strachey and Bella Woolf as contributors.

At Cambridge Leonard was a member of several of the reading and discussion societies that were so characteristic of the university world. These societies and his friendships at Cambridge, alongside the intensive reading he did outside of his studies, were vital not only for his personal life, but also in terms of his education. He and his friends were diligent readers of the authors of the time: Henry James, George Meredith, Tolstoy, Flaubert, Shaw, and others, as well as Jane Austen and the Brontës. Published in 1903, the year after his death, Samuel Butler's *The Way of All Flesh* was particularly influential, as were the novels of Thomas Hardy. He also admits how much he and his friends admired Swinburne, whose poetry they chanted as they walked through the Trinity cloisters. Swinburne had a special resonance for Leonard, who had seen him from time to time when he was growing up in Putney.

There was the Midnight Society, which met at that time on Saturday to read poetry and plays. Formed in 1900, the society met in the rooms of Clive Bell, who regarded it as the true origin of Bloomsbury, perhaps in reaction to his irritation at not being elected a member of the Apostles. It had six members, five of whom, Leonard, Clive, Lytton, Saxon, and Thoby, were crucial in the group's ultimate formation. As Bell recalled, the society

> assembled in my rooms in the New Court, and, having strengthened itself with whisky or punch and one of those gloomy beef-steak pies which it was the fashion to order for Sunday lunch, proceeded to read aloud some such trifles as *Prometheus Unbound*, *The Cenci*, *The Return of the Druses*, *Bartholomew Fair*, or *Comus*. As often or not it was dawn by the time we had done; and sometimes we would issue forth to perambulate the courts and cloisters, halting on Hall steps to spout passages of familiar verse.[4]

There was the Shakespeare Society established to read his plays. There was also the X Society, which replaced the Midnight Society, which met at 8.30 on Saturday to read plays other than those by Shakespeare, although presumably Leonard, Saxon, and Lytton stopped going to it when they became members of the Apostles, since it met at the same time. It was particularly important in its reading of the plays of Ibsen and, to a lesser degree, Shaw. Leonard quoted lines from Ibsen in his autobiography with great enthusiasm as part of the battle against the Victorian age and its "monarchy, aristocracy, upper classes, suburban bourgeoisie, the Church, the Army, the stock exchange" (*Sowing*, 164). There was the Sunday Essay Society, which met to discuss religion, perhaps as an antidote to the compulsory chapel attendance for the Protestant members of college, who constituted the vast majority. (Thoby would wage a campaign against the requirement, much in the spirit of his father. In 1904 he published a short pamphlet addressed to all Cambridge freshmen arguing strongly that, since after 1871 men of all religions could receive degrees, it was against religious liberty to require Protestant undergraduates to attend their college chapels. Although not necessarily strictly enforced, the rule survived until 1913.) For a few days Leonard even considered whether he should become a Christian, as he had become a great admirer of Christ, his fellow Jew. He was also a member of the Magpie and Stump, the college debating society. These societies, the wonderful web of friendships, and the endless talk and reading were the heart of his experience at Cambridge.

The most significant society that he joined, so crucial for the history of Bloomsbury, was the Apostles. It was also central in shaping his ideas. Here the influence of its somewhat older member, already a don, the philosopher G. E. Moore, a Fellow of Trinity, was crucially important. Leonard revered him as an inspiration and a genius, describing him as the most moral person he knew:

> George Moore was a great man, the only great man whom I have ever met or known in the world of ordinary, real life. There was in him an element that can, I think, be accurately called greatness, a combination of mind and character and behaviour, of thought and feeling which made him qualitatively different from anyone else I have ever known. I recognize it in only one or two of the many famous dead men

whom Ecclesiasticus and others enjoin us to praise for one reason or another.... He pursued truth with the tenacity of a bulldog and the integrity of a saint. (*Sowing*, 131–4)

For these young men, he played the role of Socrates.

The Apostles was the unofficial name of the society founded as the Cambridge Conversazione Society in 1820. It became known as the Apostles because of its convention of having a limit of twelve undergraduate members drawn mostly from Trinity and King's colleges. In 1902 there seem to have been only six undergraduate members: Leonard, Lytton, and Saxon from Trinity, plus Keynes, John Sheppard, and Leonard Greenwood from King's. During term it would meet on Saturday evenings to hear a paper given by one of its members. Then all those present would take, as it was called, "a turn on the hearth rug" to comment on the paper. Minute books survive, but they are rarely very informative, since they do not summarize the discussion; the topic may not be accurately described, as the proposition voted on was derived from the paper delivered rather than the topic of the paper itself, and the result of the vote can be unclear. It is officially a secret society and, as far as one knows, still exists. Much has been written about it in biographies and autobiographies of its members over the years and in academic studies. Many of its members had become Victorian worthies, notably churchmen and civil servants. Its most famous early member was Alfred Tennyson, elected in 1829, although he was not particularly active in it; his fellow member was Arthur Hallam, whose early death led to the writing of *In Memoriam*. Generally undergraduate members once they took their degrees officially resigned from the society, took "wings" as it was called, and became "angels." But if they were resident in Cambridge, they would in many cases regularly attend meetings, take part in the discussion, and even present papers. Members who had left the university might return for occasional meetings, and, relevant to Bloomsbury, this was particularly true of E. M. Forster, Roger Fry, and Desmond MacCarthy. The society would also hold an annual dinner in London, and such contacts might well provide an opportunity for older members to help younger brethren in their careers. In the view of the society, these older members who had taken "wings" had left the real world of the university for the phenomenal world outside it.

In England historically, those who might criticize their society in the hope of changing it have nevertheless frequently been trained by its most traditional institutions, the public schools and the ancient universities. They might also in some degree be perceived as outsiders as well, Leonard through being Jewish and perhaps Strachey and Keynes through their homosexuality. Ultimately in the Bloomsbury Group itself, Virginia and Vanessa were insiders by birth, but outsiders as women. There was a dazzling array of dons involved with the society, mostly philosophers who were in Cambridge and would take an active role in its meetings, Bertrand Russell, Alfred North Whitehead, J. T. McTaggart, and, most importantly for Leonard and ultimately Bloomsbury, G. E. Moore. Other dons who would play an influential role were the political thinker Goldsworthy Lowes Dickinson and the historian G. M. Trevelyan. (Years later, another Apostle, Jonathan Miller, would include a skit in *Beyond the Fringe* featuring Russell and Moore discussing how many apples were in a basket.) Here was an intellectual aristocracy, despite the absence of Cambridge scientists, so prominent a part of the Cambridge landscape. The aim of the society was to discuss important issues with the utmost candor but also frequently with some whimsy and wit. The questions posed were often philosophical and designed to challenge received opinion, particularly about religion in the later years of the nineteenth century. The philosopher and earlier Apostle Henry Sidgwick questioned Christianity, but Keynes later mocked his interest in religion on the grounds that Christianity was not worth worrying about. Nevertheless, Leonard, in discussing becoming an Apostle, quotes approvingly Sidgwick's description of the style of the society when he became a member in 1856:

> The pursuit of truth with absolute devotion and unreserve by a group of intimate friends, who were perfectly frank with one another, and indulged in any amount of humorous sarcasm and playful banter, and yet each respect the other, and when he discourses tries to learn from him and see what he sees. Absolute candour was the only duty that the tradition of the society enforced.... It came to seem to me that no part of my life at Cambridge was so real to me as the Saturday evenings on which the apostolic debates were held; and the tie of attachment to the society is much the strongest corporate bond which I have known in life. (Quoted in *Sowing*, 129–30)

Lytton was elected to the society, becoming a "birth" in its language, in February 1901. Saxon and Leonard were both elected in October 1902. Although the original apostles were Jews, Leonard was the first Jew to be selected for the Cambridge version. Presumably Lytton lobbied hard on their behalf, as the other recent "births" were Kingsmen. Although Lytton and Leonard were the closest of friends, it was an unlikely friendship, with Lytton the sardonic, seemingly frivolous, teaser, given to outrageous remarks and judgments, while Leonard was much more serious and earnest. With the election of Strachey and then Keynes in February 1903, the atmosphere of the Apostles became more homosexual, to the distress of some older members such as Russell and Trevelyan. This caused no problem for Leonard, despite his emanating a firm sense of heterosexuality, even though he remained a virgin until the age of 25. Strachey gave his first paper to the society on May 10, 1902, with a characteristically whimsical title "Ought the Father to grow a beard?" It was about the limits of art but also discussed the sexual organs: "I am, in fact, forced to the conclusion that anything is capable of artistic treatment; that the function of Art is to treat of everything whatever its qualities might be." He also raised the question of whether defecation could be considered artistically and at the end paid some slight attention to his title, suggesting that God had been weakened by being depicted without a beard.[5]

With the publication of Moore's *Principia Ethica* in October 1903, ideas crucial to the shaping of Bloomsbury were enunciated. Lytton read it immediately and wrote to Moore:

> I think your book has not only wrecked and shattered all writers on Ethics from Aristotle and Christ to Herbert Spencer and Mr Bradley, it has not only laid the true foundation of Ethics, it has not only left all modern Philosophy befouée—these seem to me small achievements compared to the establishment of that method which shines like a sword between the lines. It is the scientific method deliberately applied, for the first time, to Reasoning.... The truth; there can be no doubt, is really now upon the march. I date from October 1903 the beginning of the Age of Reason.

The same day he wrote to Leonard about the book: "The wreckage! The indeterminate heap of shattered rubbish among which one spies the utterly mangled remains of Aristotle, Jesus, Mr Bradley, Kant, Herbert Spencer, Sidgwick and McTaggart. Plato seems to be the only person who comes out even tolerably well!"[6]

Intriguingly, there is a difference of opinion about the influence of *Principia Ethica* among the members of the Bloomsbury Group, with Keynes emphasizing its importance for aesthetics and personal relations, although in later life he would criticize the limitations of those ideas. Leonard regarded *Principia* as more important for its emphasis on morality and virtue. This crucial difference was discussed years later when Keynes delivered a paper about his early beliefs to the Memoir Club in 1938. Leonard took issue with Keynes's version of what he and his friends believed when they were undergraduates. There can be no doubt, however, that Moore was a crucial influence in shaping Leonard's values. But his Cambridge experience also built on the earlier influence of his Jewish heritage and the Hellenism of his education at St Paul's.

The Memoir Club was an informal group consisting of those at the heart of Bloomsbury, wonderfully depicted in Vanessa Bell's 1943 portrait of the Club. Keynes's talk had come about in reaction to David Garnett's previous presentation to the Club about D. H. Lawrence. Through his father, Edward Garnett, Bunny (as David Garnett was called) had come to know Lawrence well, and he was to be very close to Bloomsbury during the First World War, as Duncan Grant's lover. On a visit to Cambridge in 1915 arranged by Garnett, Lawrence had met Keynes. He took against Garnett's friends, comparing them to beetles skating on the surface of life, and also disliked their homosexuality, urging Garnett to give them up. Instead Garnett reluctantly broke with Lawrence. In any case, Keynes delivered his paper, "My Early Beliefs," in reaction to Lawrence's scorning of Bloomsbury values. But he also conveyed how significant and important Moore's ideas were for him, for Strachey, and for Woolf. "It was exciting, exhilarating, the beginning of a renaissance, the opening of a new heaven on a new earth, we were the forerunners of a new dispensation, we were not afraid of anything." But, in Keynes's view, they discarded Moore's morality. States of mind were the most important thing, to be in communion with love, beauty, and truth. And also he quotes the famous lines, destined to become central to Bloomsbury: "By far the most valuable things, which we know or can imagine, are certain states of consciousness, which can be roughly described as the pleasures of human intercourse and the enjoyment of beautiful objects." But, according to Keynes, this did not seem to result in actual pleasure. He felt Leonard had a particularly gloomy approach to the question, and that, according to him, "all good states of mind were extremely painful and to imply that all painful states of mind were extremely good." Keynes believed that they were led to an excessive belief in rationality, even as there was a rejection of Benthamism, what he characterized as "this thin rationalism skipping on the crust of the lava."[7]

Leonard disagreed and felt that Moore also taught them a sense of morality:

> He and we were fascinated by questions of what was right and wrong, what one *ought* to do. We followed him closely in this as in other parts of his doctrine and argued interminably about the consequences of one's action, both in actual and imaginary situations. Indeed one of the problems which worried us was what part Moore (and we, his disciples) *ought* to play in ordinary life, what, for instance, our attitude *ought* to be towards practical politics. I still possess a paper which I wrote for discussion in 1903 and which is explicitly concerned with these problems. (*Sowing*, 148–9)

Leonard felt that the most salient aspect of Moore's work was the power of common sense, laying the groundwork for the clearing of the obscurities of the past. That was going to be crucial to the future work of the Bloomsbury Group.

> The tremendous influence of Moore and his book upon us came from the fact that they suddenly removed from our eyes an obscuring accumulation of scales, cobwebs, and curtains, revealing for the first time to us, so it seemed, the nature of truth and reality, of good and evil and character and conduct, substituting for the religious and philosophical nightmares, delusions, hallucinations, in which Jehovah, Christ, and St Paul, Plato, Kant, and Hegel had entangled us, the fresh air and pure light of plain common sense. (*Sowing*, 147)

This was also a way to question everything: "I think it to be, not merely my right, but my duty to question the truth of everything and the authority of everyone, to regard nothing as sacred and to hold nothing in religious respect" (*Sowing*, 153). Keynes believed that the gist of Moore's argument was that one should not be involved in the "outside" world. In contrast, Leonard felt that, although Moore was otherwordly himself, ultimately his message was that one should be involved in the world. Although the two men disagreed about the nature of Moore's influence, there can be no question that Moore was a great shaper of what became Bloomsbury's ideas. As Rosenbaum sums it up: "Moore's thought and character shaped Bloomsbury's beliefs about the nature of consciousness, perception and even perhaps mysticism, about the distinctions between right and good, about the importance of personal relations as well as public affairs, about the functions of criticism and the value of art."[8] There is a certain irony in the fact that, while these two Apostles disagreed about what Moore's influence had been upon Bloomsbury, they became the two members of Bloomsbury who were ultimately most involved with the "outside" world.

In his autobiography, Leonard captures what was so wonderful about being an undergraduate; why it was so influential on what one ultimately became; why those days were so important in people's lives:

> My own experience is that I have never again been quite so happy or quite so miserable as I was in the five years at Cambridge from 1899 to 1904. One lived in a state of continual excitement and strong and deep feeling. We were intellectuals, intellectuals with three genuine and, I think, profound passions: a passion for friendship, a passion for literature and music (it is significant that the plastic arts came a good deal later), a passion for what we called the truth. What made everything so exciting was that everything was new, anything might happen, and all life was before us. (*Sowing*, 159)

But, as Woolf indicates, what was vital for him in Moore was that he ultimately led to a concern with politics, although that would be realized in the years after the First World War. In a paper he gave to the Apostles in May 1903 he argued that one must enter Plato's cave and deal with practical politics, combining the philosophy of George Moore with the political radicalism of George Trevelyan. The paper had a typical apostolic title: "George or George or Both." "While philosophers sit outside the cave, their philosophy will never reach politicians or people, so that after all, to put it plainly, I *do* want Moore to draft an Education Bill" (*Sowing*, 149). He was much taken with the promise of the vindication of Captain Dreyfus and felt that it heralded a better world. "We were in the van of the builders of a new society which should be free, rational, civilized, pursuing truth and beauty. It was all tremendously exciting" (*Sowing*, 161).

Naturally these young men, particularly Leonard and Lytton, wanted to be writers, and in fact Leonard did, in a very small way, begin his writing career at Cambridge. He published five poems in the *Cambridge Review*, three of which, "The Song of the Beasts," "Dead Leaves," and "Dreams," were included with other poems in a pamphlet, *Euphrosyne*, (one of the Three Graces), produced by Sydney-Turner and Bell in 1905. Rosenbaum refers to it as "The First Book of Bloomsbury." Half of the poems were by Sydney-Turner, a quarter by Bell, three by Strachey, and a few from authors who were not part of the circle of friends. In the publication itself they were all anonymous, although Leonard's poems had been signed L.S.W. when published in the *Cambridge Review*. The title resurfaced as the name of the ship on which the voyage was taken in Virginia Woolf's first novel, *The Voyage Out*. Poetry was to be an interest in Cambridge, and there are unpublished early poems in Leonard's papers. They tend to have mystical or stoical themes reflecting the pseudo-despair that youth likes to affect. One had as its subject Judas and another a Jewish pawnbroker convicted of manslaughter. Bloomsbury paid little attention to the writing of poetry in later years, even though Lytton and Clive continued to write verse. The only poet of some note of the group was in its second generation, Julian Bell, Clive and Vanessa's son. Leonard's only other publication from his time in Cambridge was a review of a life of Voltaire in the *Independent Review*, edited by fellow Apostles, in February 1904, when he was already in Ceylon. Other than writing a piece in a Ceylon newspaper on a game sanctuary in 1910, he was not to start his publication career until he returned to England.

When the *Euphrosyne* collection was published, Leonard was already in Ceylon. He had thought that he might become a barrister like his father, but while at Cambridge he decided to enter the civil service. As indicated, his academic career was not as distinguished as might have been expected. He decided to spend a fifth year in Cambridge to study for the civil-service exam. In retrospect he felt it was a mistake not to have gone to a crammer in London, but it must have been deeply tempting to spend more time in an ambience that offered such a rich life. Within the home civil service he qualified only for the Post Office or the Inland Revenue, neither of which interested him, and he was already too old for the Home Office. He applied instead to be appointed to the Colonial Service with a request to be sent to Ceylon, and to both his astonishment and dismay he was duly appointed. He was hardly enthusiastic about his future career, but he had to earn a living. He principally wanted to be a writer, but his finances precluded that. Lack of money would also have prevented his becoming a barrister, a possibility he had not entirely forsaken. He declined his sister Bella's offer to help to pay his legal expenses. He might have become a schoolmaster but questioned whether, as a Jew, he would be hired. Instead he backed into the Colonial Service.

Despite his modest examination results, he was profoundly grateful for having been at Trinity.

> It was, I think, a civilized life both intellectually and emotionally. My intellect was kept at full stretch, which is very good for the young, by books and the way I read them and by friends and their incessant and uncompromising conversation. The emotion came from friendship and friends but also from the place, the material and spiritual place, Trinity and Cambridge. (*Sowing*, 194–5)

He goes on to discuss his loyalties to concepts and places, not only Cambridge, but, perhaps rather unexpectedly, England and the British Empire as well as his family, his "race," which he puts in quotation marks and then in parentheses (Jews), and also Kensington, London, Sussex, Ceylon, Greece. He also records taking particular pleasure when St Paul's, Cambridge, or England wins in sports. But, as he says in the case of family, school, and race, his feelings are ambivalent. About St Paul's he wrote:

> I hated its physical ugliness, its philistinism, the slow, low torture of boredom that crept over one as one sat hour after hour listening to the bored voice of the bored master. I still hate it, and yet I have at the same time affection and pride in it.... My loyalty to Trinity and Cambridge is different from all many other loyalties. It is more intimate, profound, unalloyed. It is compounded of the spiritual, intellectual and physical inextricably mixed. (*Sowing*, 196)

He ends this volume of his autobiography with an account of taking the civil-service examination and his departure for Ceylon after a farewell dinner with Thoby and his sisters, Virginia and Vanessa. Following the death of their father, they had just moved to Bloomsbury. Leonard was there when literary history was about to take place. Yet he would not be part of it for the next seven years. Lytton promised to write to him once a week. Indeed in his letter of February 28 he mentioned the first such gathering in Bloomsbury of the group. "I came up on Wednesday—it's now Friday—to go to the Gothic [i.e. Thoby] housewarming party. It wasn't very amusing, but amusing enough. Yesterday I went again as the Goth is 'at home' on Thursday evenings."[9]

In November 1904, Woolf sailed to Ceylon for the month-long voyage, along with seventy volumes of Voltaire in eighteenth-century Baskerville type. His wire-haired fox terrier Charles was traveling out to join him on a different ship. The next chapter of his life was about to begin.

Notes

1. Spotts, 13.
2. S. P. Rosenbaum, *Victorian Bloomsbury* (1987), 119.
3. Ibid. 132.
4. Clive Bell, *Old Friends* (1956), 26.
5. Paul Levy, *Moore* (1979), 230–3.
6. 11 October 1903, *Letters of Lytton Strachey*, ed. Paul Levy (2005), 17, 19.
7. John Maynard Keynes, *Two Memoirs* (1949), 82, 86, 90, 105.
8. Rosenbaum, *Victorian Bloomsbury*, 217.
9. 28 February 1904, *Letters of Lytton Strachey*, 54.

3
Ceylon

The voyage on the *Syria* took a month and a day, so that Leonard arrived in Ceylon on December 16, 1904. He felt it was a birth into a new life as he waved goodbye to his mother and sister Bella at the dock in Tilbury. He found the voyage out more bearable than he had expected. He could get along and have interesting conversations with his fellow passengers. He even formed a friendship with one young woman, but nothing further developed. Ordinarily his fellow passengers would not have been any part of his world of London and Cambridge. Although Ceylon's civil service was less impressive than that of India, it had had a strong reputation ever since the island had been acquired from the Dutch in 1796. They had replaced the Portuguese as the ruling European power in 1658. Once he was there, through frequent letters to Lytton, Leonard kept the Cambridge connection alive, not surprisingly, complaining frequently, with few exceptions, about his fellow British. But he rapidly became very fond of the country itself. At first he was very lonely, although eventually he found he rather enjoyed solitude, particularly at his final posting. As he wrote to Lytton on December 17, the day after his arrival: "I have never felt so lonely in my life as I do at the present moment. . . . If only you were here, everything would be changed, for the place itself is wonderful & superb. I shall die, I hope, very soon."[1]

His first posting was to Jaffna in the far north of the island, where the inhabitants were Tamil—Hindus in contrast to the majority Buddhist Sinhalese population of the island. He was there for three years, holding various titles, modest sounding but in fact quite powerful in terms of ruling the country: Additional Police Magistrate and Assistant Government Agent. He had comfortable accommodation in a bungalow that was part of an early Portuguese fort. He shared it with a fellow civil servant, Wilfrid Southorn, about whom at that point he had reservations. (In 1921 Southorn would marry Leonard's sister Bella, after the death of her first husband, and he would go on to have a distinguished career.) Leonard then occupied a bungalow of his own for a while before moving again to share with another not particularly congenial civil servant. For one reason or another he changed residence fairly often. At the same time he also managed to acquire a group of animals of whom he grew increasingly fond, his wire-haired terrier having died. At one house his housemate had a tame baby leopard, and there was also a deer, five dogs, a monkey, and a mongoose.

Despite being a civil servant, what he most desired was to be a writer, part of the literary world, although what he wanted to write was not clear. It would be his time in Ceylon that would provide him with material for the first of his two novels and four of his published short stories. While in Ceylon he had to postpone that goal in order to be in gainful employment. To begin with, his duties as a civil servant were routine, but he was very efficient and did far more than his share of the work. He felt that he suffered from the social disadvantage of being intelligent, but he hid his true self behind what he came to call his "carapace." Leonard went along with the social conventions of the time, mixing with those who frequented the local British Club. He was talented at tennis and bridge and hence was a social success. Though he felt himself something of an outsider as a Jew and presumably as an intellectual, this did not seem to be a factor in his relations with his fellow countrymen and did not rule him out as a possible husband for the unmarried British ladies present. His first impression was of the great beauty of the place, but he also had a sense of melancholy, reinforced by the brutal way animals were treated and the generally depressed state of his fellow civil servants. As he wrote to Desmond MacCarthy on February 26, 1905: "If you searched the Universe, you could not find 15 more impossible people than the 15 English [in Jaffna].... [But Ceylon] does have an enormous charm for me, the queer tortuous people, the wonderful glaring beauty of the country, & the still oppressive heat which tones it all down to a strange melancholy."[2] He found the fatalism of the Tamils and the Sinhalese attractive and consonant with his own view of the world. His time in Jaffna was devoted to routine and taxing duties. He judged cases, investigated problems, trying to figure out the true stories behind the lies told by both sides in a dispute. He dealt with the multitude of issues presented in the administration of a large area, even though he held the most junior post in the province. He tried to fulfil the ideal of achieving a just British rule despite his lack of respect for most of his colleagues. His aim was to be strict but fair, taking seriously the implementation of regulations. He learned Tamil. He also initiated his sexual life with a "Burgher" woman—that is, a descendant of a Portuguese, Dutch, or British settler in Ceylon, who would visit him once a week. As he wrote rather dispassionately to Lytton:

> I suppose you want to know everything—well, I am worn out or rather merely supine through a night of purely degraded debauch. The pleasure of it is of course grossly exaggerated certainly with a halfcaste whore. The ridiculousness of existence never reaches such heights—the elaborate absurdity made me almost impuissant from amusement. And yet the sheer desperation of life here I really think alone made me go so far.[3]

A month later, when in a house on his own, he described his life to Lytton as living

> with a burgher concubine in a long bare whitewashed bungalow overlooking the lagoon, where time is only divided between reading Voltaire on the immense verandah & copulating in the vast & empty rooms where there is a perpetual smell of bats & damp & the paint & plaster peel off the walls & gather onto the stone floors.[4]

It was not to last long, since shortly thereafter he came down with typhoid from which might well have died. He recovered in large measure thanks to twenty-one days spent in a small American missionary hospital.

In February he embarked on the most dramatic part of his work in the Northern Province. He became one of the four government officials who supervised the seasonal visit of perhaps as many as 30,000 or 40,000 to the pearl fisheries, keeping order and ensuring that the government received its anticipated share of the proceeds from the pearls found in the oysters. Since two of the officials became ill, there were only two civil servants in charge with a few policemen. This was at Mariehchukkaddi, eighty miles west of Jaffna. The two-thirds of the pearls appropriated by the government were auctioned off. The fishing lasted from late February to early April and was done by Arabs and Tamils. Leonard's account in his second volume of autobiography, *Growing*, was seemingly impersonal, but in fact, as he wrote to Lytton, he was very depressed at the time, almost suicidal. "It is due, I suppose, partly to the monotony of perpetual work, the glaring & scorching heat of this place, the want of sleep & the loathsome food."[5] As he summed it up in a letter to Lytton: "I work for 10 to 12 hours a day mostly under a blinding sun walking about through a shouting mob of 10,000 Arabs."[6] He then returned to Jaffna and shared a bungalow with another civil servant and numerous animals. Leonard was always extraordinarily fond of animals and held them in great respect. "If you really understand an animal so that he gets to trust you completely and, within his limits, understands you, there grows up between you affection of a purity and simplicity which seems to me peculiarly satisfactory" (*Growing*, 100). At the same time he was working extremely hard as a civil servant, making himself very unpopular with the indigenous clerks who did so much of the day-to-day work. He demanded efficiency and promptness. Eventually most of those who worked under him realized that he had made things much better. Yet there were protests against his severity, and at one point he thought he might be fired. At least that meant he would go back to London, as he was hankering for leave, but nothing came of the protest. For a month in August he governed one district of 400 square miles all on his own, a considerable responsibility for one who had been in the service so briefly. He much enjoyed, on the whole, the solitude and the authority.

In many senses the most important event in terms of Leonard's life during the time that he was in Ceylon happened in London: the death of Thoby Stephen, the Goth. It might be said that he was the central figure in creating the Bloomsbury Group. Leonard regretted that Thoby had never been elected an Apostle, although at the time there had been no impetus to nominate him. As he later wrote to Lytton: "We shall never be able to answer for not electing the Goth. It is the one thing which I think is unpardonable."[7] Thoby was nevertheless the person at Trinity whom Leonard, Lytton, Clive Bell, and Saxon Sydney-Turner believed to be at the center of their lives. He had also introduced his sisters, Vanessa and Virginia, to them, although they had seen very little of the sisters while they were undergraduates. When Thoby went down to London after taking his degree, it was he who had taken the initiative to invite his Cambridge friends to the house in Gordon Square in Bloomsbury for the "at homes" on Thursday evenings, where he and his sisters as well as their younger brother Adrian had moved on their own, unconventionally, after the death of their father in 1904.

The four siblings had gone on a visit to Greece, Thoby and Adrian traveling there in August 1906; Vanessa and Virginia and their friend Violet Dickinson joined them in September. Vanessa became quite ill there but recovered. But when they returned to London, Thoby and Violet Dickinson came down with typhoid fever, and on November 20 he died. It was a devastating blow. It would appear to be as a reaction that two days later, having refused him ten days before the death, Vanessa agreed to marry Clive. They were married shortly thereafter in February 2007. Their shared grief over the death brought the key figures in the group, Virginia, Vanessa, Lytton, Clive, Saxon, and, even though he was thousands of miles away, Leonard, closer together. He received the news in a letter from Lytton dated November 21. "You will never see the Goth again. He died yesterday.... I don't understand what crowning pleasure there can be for us without him, and our lives seem deadly blank. There is nothing left remarkable beneath the visible moon."[8] On December 12 Leonard replied: "I am overwhelmed, crushed.... He was above everyone in his nobility. God! what an accursed thing life is, great stretches of dull insensibility & then these unbearable bitternesses. If I could only see you & talk to you!"[9]

In August 1907 Leonard was transferred to Kandy, more or less in the middle of Ceylon, second only to Colombo in size, but a far more attractive place with a beautiful lake at its center. It had been the capital of the part of the country that was the last to be conquered, remaining independent until 1815, when it succumbed to the British. His official title was Office Assistant to the Government Agent, but as usual the position was far more powerful than its name implied. He was there for a year, and during half that time his sister Bella came to stay with him. Indeed, she wrote an early guide book to Ceylon as well as two children's books and two collections of essays on the country. The social life in Kandy was quite intense, far more so than in Jaffna, with most evenings spent at the British Club, playing tennis, bridge, or billiards, gossiping and drinking. He even fell in love, with the 19-year-old Gladys Jowitt, the daughter of a tea planter. At this point he was rather dispassionate about falling in love, and the relationship does not appear to have been very serious. The previous May he had written to Lytton that he had fallen in love while in Jaffna with the 19-year-old wife of a planter, but nothing came of it. "Among other things I have been in love lately.... The only thing is that I am mad enough to be able to go on as if I weren't, as if nothing happened or existed.... I am beginning to think it is always degraded being in love: after all 99/100th^s of it is always the desire to copulate."[10] His second romantic interest, Gladys, was single, and this became somewhat more serious. He almost proposed to her, although in his autobiography he was dismissive about having been in love. Yet he had written otherwise to Lytton on November 17, 1907:

> I am really in love with someone who is in love with me. It is not however pleasant because it is pretty degrading, I suppose, to be in love with practically a schoolgirl. Also the complications are appalling when one has, as they say, to 'behave as a gentleman', when one does not intend to marry & when one has to live in a country where everyone knows everything which everyone else does, says or thinks.[11]

Unlike Jaffna, Kandy was full of the British, not only civil servants, but also planters, military officers, and others. He found the Sinhalese of Kandy more congenial than the Tamils of Jaffna. As civil servants were required to learn both languages, they had the opportunity to delve into the life of Ceylon at some depth should they wish, and Leonard was more inclined to do so than most of his compatriots. Much of his work in all his postings was judicial, hearing a variety of cases, including divorces, and supervising prisons. It distressed him to be obligated to witness floggings and hangings, indeed to give the signal for the latter to proceed. And, though irreligious himself, he came to believe that Buddhism was the best possible religion. He was extremely industrious but also socially active. Perhaps the high point of his posting at Kandy was when, as the principal official, because his superior was away, he was called on to entertain the Empress Eugénie, the 81-year-old widow of Napoleon III, during her visit. He also arranged for her to see the most important religious relic in Kandy, the Buddha's tooth. Leonard's successful career greatly impressed his superiors, particularly the acting Governor of Ceylon, Sir Hugh Clifford. He appreciated not only what Leonard had done for the empress but also that he had arranged a grand display of native dancing for a lady friend Clifford wished to please. Clifford also held the post of the Colonial Secretary for Ceylon, the second in command but generally more powerful than the Governor, the ceremonial chief of state.

In August 1908 Leonard was appointed Assistant Government Agent for the Hambantota District, part of the Southern Province. He was the youngest by three years in the Ceylon service to have a position at that level. Despite being called an assistant, he was in fact the senior British official in the district, in effect its ruler. At this point he saw himself, perhaps not without misgivings, spending all of his professional life as a servant of empire. The district, along the southern coast, was among the poorest of the whole island, with an irregular and unreliable agricultural system with salt as the main source of revenue. It was 1,013 square miles in size with a population in 1911 of 110,508. As he wrote, the area was

> entirely rural and agricultural in the west, and a vast stretch of jungle with the game sanctuary in the east. There were no real towns, no railway, hardly any roads. I continually travelled about the district and got to know well almost every yard of it, and to some extent the way of life and attitude to life of its inhabitants.... I was fascinated and deeply moved by the lives of the villagers and their psychology, and also by the perpetual menace of nature, the beautiful and at the same time sinister and savage life of the jungle. (*Diaries in Ceylon*, pp. lxxvii–lxxviii)

He thought highly of the Yala National Game Sanctuary in his district, his only publication in these years being a piece on it in the *Times of Ceylon* in its 1910 Christmas issue. The sanctuary had come into existence not that long before, in 1899, and was about 150 square miles in size. The article attested to Leonard's love of animals, mostly deer, buffalos, and elephants, and his pleasure in observing their behavior. Compared to the large British community in Kandy, in his new posting there were only five other Europeans, a District Judge (Tom Southorn, later his brother-in-law, with whom he had shared a bungalow in Jaffna), two Irrigation Engineers, an Assistant

Superintendent of Police, and a Belgian missionary. Even they were some miles away in various directions; very occasionally they would dine together.

His life in Hambantota from August 1908 to May 1911 was one of intense solitude. There were occasional visits from officials, and he had dealings with European sportsmen who required licenses for big-game shooting. He hunted himself but only for food, while his respect for those who shot for sport rapidly declined. In contrast to Kandy, there was virtually no social life, but he did not feel lonely. He was continually surrounded by and talking to the native people as part of his work. As required, he kept an extensive diary of his official activities; practically every day there can be accounted for, the endless supervision of what was going on, the agricultural problems, the harvesting of salt, the dealing with rinderpest, which was killing the cattle, and the dispensing of justice. During his years in Ceylon he was a willing, if not necessarily an enthusiastic, imperialist, convinced that Britain was doing good things for those it ruled.

That he had first-hand experience of the empire no doubt played a role in his thinking about imperialism. On his return in 1960, there were roads, cars, and buses instead of bicycles, bullock carts, horses, and walking. This constituted a very significant difference and led, he felt, to an increase of prosperity. "These changes are very great and all to the good. And yet beneath the surface there is much, I feel, that has hardly changed at all.... It seemed to me that something of the old village, typically Sinhalese life still goes on there beneath the modern surface" (*Diaries in Ceylon*, p. lxxx). Leonard lived in a bungalow with a view of the sea. It is still the residence of the chief administrator with his office, the so-called *kachcheri*, close by. Leonard's job was to collect revenue, dispense justice, and travel extensively about his district, dealing with all the problems that might arise. At his office, presumably then but certainly now, there is a handsome wooden board listing those who were there as Assistant Government Agents, starting in 1833 with a Captain Dricberg, who may have been Dutch. L. S. Woolf, Esq., with the date 1908, is on the list. Up until 1947 all the names were British, with the exception of two Ceylonese between 1927 and 1932. Since 1948 all the Agents are Sri Lankan, and starting in 1953 their names have been written in Sinhala script.

The building remains much the same as Leonard described it to Lytton in a letter on February 2, 1908:

> The house, really it is worth coming to Ceylon to live in it. It must have originally been built by the Dutch with walls of astonishing thickness & an enormously broad verandah & vast high rooms. It stands on a promontory right away from the town & right over the sea. Day & night you hear the sea thundering away almost at the gates of the compound.[12]

In a way, it was quite extraordinary that this was the life that he was living just a few years after leaving Cambridge. It makes one aware of the paradoxical nature of the British Empire: these young men thrust into positions of immense authority in a world so very different from where they had grown up and been educated. But one of the objectives of their education was to train them to assume such tasks with confidence.

Contrary to what he had once thought, he now no longer saw himself as remaining permanently in the civil service. Looking back in his autobiography, he may be exaggerating the doubts he had about his career at the time: "After two or three years in the Civil Service subconsciously, at the back of my mind, I knew that it was highly improbable that I would make my permanent career in it. I did not want to be a successful imperialist, to become a Colonial Secretary or a Governor. His Excellency Sir Leonard Woolf, K.C.M.G." (*Growing*, 180). He still saw himself as an intellectual, aspiring to become a writer. Nevertheless he was captivated by his district and the people who lived there and wished to understand them. He wanted to make their lives better, diminish poverty, increase cultivation, open schools. In this volume of autobiography he writes movingly about his time in Ceylon, most evocatively about nature, such as a night spent watching animals at a water hole during a full moon. It was also in Ceylon that he honed his skill of being extremely efficient, determined to dispatch business promptly. (He established a pattern as far as possible of answering all correspondence on the day that it was received.) But he was also conscious that in his ruthless pursuit of efficiency he could be abrupt and offend others by his ways. As he wrote to Lytton on October 2, 1908: "I work God, how I work. I have reduced it to a method & exalted it to a mania."[13]

Again, in many ways the most significant event for Leonard's future took place in London. Within her circle there was a feeling that it was time for Virginia Stephen to be married, and there were several men who were interested in her. She was 27 and wished to be married. Rather casually, Lytton had written to Leonard on October 29, 1908: "Don't be surprised whatever might happen, or if you hear one day—I don't know if you ever will—that I've married Virginia."[14] Then, dramatically on February 17, 1909, Lytton proposed to her and was accepted. Almost immediately they both decided that it was a mistake, perhaps Virginia more reluctantly than Lytton. On February 19 he wrote to Leonard:

> The day before yesterday I proposed to Virginia. As I did it, I saw that it would be death if she accepted me, and I managed, of course, to get out of it before the end of the conversation.... I think there is no doubt whatever that you ought to marry her. You *would* be great enough, and you'ld have too the immense advantage of physical desire. I was in terror lest she should kiss me. If you came and proposed she'ld accept. She really would. As it is, she's almost certainly in love with me, though she thinks she's not.

He added a postscript the next day: "I've had an éclairissement with Virginia. She declared she was not in love with me, and I observed finally that I would not marry her.... I told Vanessa to hand on your proposal."[15]

Before this exceedingly brief engagement, Lytton had written to Leonard some time before, on Christmas Day 1908, suggesting that Leonard should marry Virginia, although they had seen one another only a few times.[16] Leonard's reaction, perhaps not entirely serious, indicated interest; he felt that Lytton might indeed marry her. He wrote in a letter to Lytton on February 1 before the abortive engagement had taken place that Lytton did not receive until February 19:

> The most wonderful of all would have been to marry Virginia. She is I imagine supreme & then the final solution would have been there, not a rise perhaps above all horrors but certainly not a fall, not a shirking of facts. Of course I suppose it is really impossible for the reason (if for no other) that I cannot place you in it.... Do you think Virginia would have me? Wire to me if she accepts. I'll take the next boat home; & then when I arrived I should probably come straight to talk to you.... I wonder if after all Virginia marries Turner.[17]

There followed a lapse in their correspondence. Lytton responded on May 27 that he had heard nothing from Leonard for quite a while and hoped that perhaps he was coming home.

> If you came, as I think I've mentioned, you could marry Virginia, which would settle nearly every difficulty in the best possible way. Do try it. She's an astounding woman, and I'm the only man in the universe who would have refused her; even I sometimes have my doubts. You might, of course, propose by telegram, and she'ld probably accept.[18]

Marriage was very much in the air, his sister Bella writing to him on July 27: "You'd better marry as soon as you have got into a class where the Govt. doesn't faint at matrimonial intentions. But I can't think of any girl that would suit you in Ceylon. You need a very special sort of girl–& if you don't find her you'd better steer clear of matrimony."[19] She herself had married her first husband, Robert Heath Lock, the Assistant Director of the Royal Botanical Gardens, in Ceylon in September 1910. Lytton wrote to Leonard on August 21:

> Your destiny is clearly marked out for you, but will you allow it to work? You must marry Virginia. She's sitting waiting for you, is there any objection? She's the only woman in the world with sufficient brains; it's a miracle that she should exist; but if you are not careful you'll lose the opportunity. At any moment she might go off with heaven know who—Duncan? Quite possible. She's young, wild, imaginative, discontented and longing to be in love. If I were you, I should telegraph.[20]

It is hard to tell how deeply this prospect affected Leonard. He wrote to Lytton on September 14:

> Of course I know that the one thing to do would be to marry Virginia. I am only frightened that when I come back in Dec 1910 I may. For though one had & everything was completed & consummated, life would probably at last be supreme; the horrible preliminary complications, the ghastly complications too of virginity & marriage altogether appall me. Really if it weren't for that & for the question of money I would actually telegraph. But I wont &, as you say, she will probably marry a German baron & I, when I'm forty, will marry either a widow (I hope she will be one then) or an exprostitute.[21]

But he was to be in Ceylon for two more years devoting himself to managing his district. He worked so hard and thoroughly on that job that in his last year and a half correspondence with his Bloomsbury friends practically ceased.

His official diaries, published in 1963 by the Hogarth Press in London, the press that he and Virginia founded in 1917, included a preface by him. The Ceylon Historical Society had previously published the book in 1962. The diaries record what he did every day of his administration, although some days have only the notation "Routine." They begin on August 28, 1908, and conclude on May 20, 1911, with the notation "Handed over to the Government Agent preparatory to proceeding on a year's leave" (*Diaries in Ceylon*, 244). (He had hoped to go on leave the previous December but needed to stay some time longer to oversee a scheduled census.) This painstakingly detailed document also includes two explanatory introductions outlining the context of the Ceylon civil service as well as the three stories that he had written based on his experiences there. But it mainly consists of his official account recording his multiple duties as Assistant Government Agent. Rigorous as an administrator, he did what he thought was for the best for the inhabitants of his district. His close monitoring of the salt trade greatly irritated its participants by eliminating the various corrupt ways by which they had increased their profits. He dealt with the wide range of problems, a daunting task for one so young. Leonard possessed a natural air of authority, reinforced by his being the agent of the British Empire, whose dominance he did not question. Most of the entries in the official diaries concern local issues, the agricultural life of the district, which presumably had been much the same for many years. The system of cultivation, the so-called *chenas*, worked by moving from plot to plot of land, exhausted the land's fertility in the process. At the same time, more superficially, Britain itself was an influence, as in the entry for October 2, 1909: "Hambantota beat Tangalla at cricket for the first time amidst enormous excitement" (*Diaries in Ceylon*, 104).[22] The following April he noted the plans for the celebration of Empire Day and on May 20 a day of mourning for the death of Edward VII, at which an address was read in English, Sinhala, and Tamil to an assembly of a thousand. It is quite impressive how extensive so many of his entries are and the detail he provides of the multiple issues he had to deal with in administering the district. At the end of each month he would record the number of miles he had traveled, and it generally ran from about 150 to 250. He went around his district for innumerable inspections, making decisions about multiple problems involving agriculture, water, the harvesting of salt (a government monopoly), revenue from the opium trade, education, crime, and anything else that might occur. He had to preside at murder trials at which it was extremely difficult to determine what had happened. The state profits from opium he used to finance schools. In June 1910 he even had to supervise a pilgrimage of thousands to Kataragama in his district, a shrine holy to Buddhists, Muslims, and Hindus. He continually moved about on foot, bullock cart, horse, and bicycle. Thus he came to know his district extremely well, particularly its villages and their inhabitants, which provided so much of the material for his novel *The Village in the Jungle*. He worked incessantly, between twelve and sixteen hours a day, every day of the week, taking days off only when he was ill.

A summary of his experience in Hambantota appears in *Growing*:

> In the main my obsession with work was stimulated by two things, both of which were immensely developed and encouraged as soon as I found myself in charge of the District of Hambantota. I fell in love with the country, the people, and the way of life which were entirely different from everything in London and Cambridge to which I had been born and bred. To understand the people and the way they lived in the villages of West Giruwa Pattu and the jungles of Magamparttu became a passion with me. In the $2^3/_4$ years in Hambantota, it is almost true to say, I worked all day from the moment I got up in the morning until the moment I went to bed at night, for I rarely thought of anything else except the District and the people, to increase their prosperity, diminish the poverty and disease, start irrigation works, open schools. There was no sentimentality about this; I did not idealize or romanticize the people or the country; I just liked them aesthetically and humanly and socially. (*Growing*, 180)

He acquired a deserved reputation as a severe administrator, sparking complaints about him to his immediate superior, Charles Lushington: "Your Asst Sir is a jew brought up by an unconverted jewess, he does not know the love of God, he has not been brought up to live the life that enobles man."[23] When Sir Hugh Clifford visited in March, at one point while accompanied by Leonard, he was greeted with a demonstration against the Assistant Government Agent.

Leonard subsequently wrote about his experiences after his 1960 visit in the *New Statesman*.

> Though not fully aware of the fact, I entered as an imperialist, one of the white rulers of our Asiatic Empire. I remained there seven years, becoming a highly efficient ruler and bureaucrat. . . . Fifty years ago the Sinhalese and Tamils had no say at all in the government of their country. . . . The government was wonderfully paternal. Nearly all of us meant well; we liked the country and the people, genuinely desired their good, and had a high sense of duty and responsibility. . . . Fifty years ago I was in intimate contact with the ordinary people—the villagers—in my district; I really knew to a large extent what they thought and how they lived. This was because I was continually riding through their villages, sitting down under a tree to hold an enquiry, listening to their difficulties, their complaints, their feuds.[24]

Leonard was an exceptional civil servant, extraordinarily dedicated and conscientious, and, had he remained in the service, he would undoubtedly have risen in the ranks. One of his major claims to distinction was connected with the earliest part of his career—as a commentator on imperialism. But, if he had done what he most wanted, he would have devoted himself to being a creative writer. Leonard's main interest as a writer on his return from Ceylon was fiction. Of the five short stories and the two novels he did publish, four of the stories and one of the novels were based on his experiences in the empire. Although they were written after he returned to England, it is appropriate to consider his "imperial" texts in the context of his time in Ceylon.

Three of the short stories were published some years later in 1921. "A Tale Told by Midnight," written just after he had finished writing *The Village in the Jungle*, and "Pearls and Swine" are in the tradition of writing about the interaction between the British in the empire with the world they found themselves in. Both are told in a Conradian style by a narrator speaking to some others. The "Tale" takes place in Colombo and tells the story of a visiting English novelist who is taken to a brothel by his narrator host. There he becomes infatuated with a beautiful prostitute, buys her out, and lives with her but later leaves her. She has become devoted to him and kills herself on being abandoned. The brief story is beautifully written and perhaps reflects Leonard's relations with a prostitute in Jaffna. "Pearls and Swine" also dwells on the differences between the imperialists and those they rule. It draws on his experience in the pearl fisheries and tells the story of two Englishmen, one young and callow, the other old and drunken, who dies of the DTs. Neither of the Englishmen had the dignity of the Arab divers in their handling of the death of a compatriot. The crassness of the British is contrasted with the serenity of those they rule.

It is intriguing that Leonard should have appropriated the celebrated phrase from Matthew 7:6, "pearls before swine," as the title for the story. It is somewhat unclear who are the swine—perhaps the British—as the pearl fishers themselves, particularly the Arabs, are depicted rather favorably. Some years later Leonard would seek another biblical allusion for the title of his second novel, *The Wise Virgins*, the parable of the wise and foolish virgins. Here too there are ambiguities. Are the suburban virgins or the intellectual virgins with whom the main character has become involved foolish or wise? Certainly, most readers of the time would have caught the biblical echoes of both these titles. Leonard's familiarity with the New Testament doubtlessly derived more from his schooling at St Paul's than from his upbringing.

The third story, "The Two Brahmans," has no one British in it but rather tells the story of two Brahmans and how they lost caste status by, in one case, fishing for the pleasure of doing so and, in the other, digging a well in order to save money. The story is striking in that it deals only with indigenous figures, but, as in the other two, it emphasizes the nature of the society upon which the British had imposed themselves. A fourth story, "Memoirs of an Elderly Man: Seddon and Miss Thomas," was published years later in 1945 in the periodical *Orion*, although there is no indication of when it was written. It takes place in India in a somewhat earlier timeframe than Leonard's tenure in Ceylon, but otherwise the narrator's colonial experiences are virtually the same as his own. The story itself is about a totally unsuccessful marriage, but, unlike the other tales, it does not tell its readers much about the empire or Leonard's feelings about it. His time back in London after Ceylon would appear to have been a period of great creative activity, and his papers contain an assortment of poems, drafts of possible short stories, and the beginning of a third novel, "The British Empire." It was started but never finished after writing his second novel, *The Wise Virgins*.

Leonard started to write *The Village in the Jungle* in October 1911, shortly after his return, and it was published in February 1913. Despite claims that it has been neglected, perhaps because he ceased to write fiction and was overshadowed by the far greater literary accomplishments of his wife, it nevertheless has received considerable attention over the years, being published in the United States in 1926, reissued as a paperback by the Oxford University Press in 1981 and by another publisher in 2005. It was made into a movie in Sri Lanka in 1980 with Arthur C. Clarke, the science-fiction writer, perhaps Sri Lanka's most famous English resident, playing the cameo role of the Woolf figure in the book. Translated, it has been a set book in Sri Lankan schools. Admittedly less well known than the novels of Kipling and Conrad or E. M. Forster's *A Passage to India* or George Orwell's *Burmese Days*, it ranks with them as a significant novel written about the British Empire. But, dramatically unlike them, and almost all other novels written by the British that take place in the empire, it is much more a work about those whom the British ruled than about the relationship between the rulers and the ruled. It is a story of the Sinhalese themselves. The jungle itself is a character. Through his years in his district, and his endless traveling within it at a slow pace, Leonard was able to come to know it extremely well and enter more profoundly than almost any other writer into the arduous life of the villagers.

The title is extremely accurate. The jungle is evil to an extent, but deeply embedded in the life of the main figure in the novel, Silindu, a hunter who knows it well. Leonard's sensitivity to animals contributes to the power of the novel, and he brilliantly evokes their presence in the jungle. The other powerful force in the novel is the desire of men to possess certain women. Silindu is a very poor man in a tiny village of ten dwellings, Beddagama. He has twin daughters, their mother having died shortly after their birth. One, Punchi Minika, is desired by Babun and returns his passion. In his determination to live with her, Babun alienates his brother-in-law, the headman of the village, who wishes him to make a better match. Her sister, Hinnihami, is coveted by the local medicine man, but, when her father refuses to let her go, he casts a spell on Silindu, which makes him deathly ill. In order to seek a cure, the family sets out on a pilgrimage to a shrine that Leonard knew well from having supervised such a pilgrimage. But the only solution is that the daughter must be given to the medicine man in order that her father may recover. Without condescension, Leonard is able to write about the power of belief in spells and religious actions to determine what might happen. Having given herself to him and seeing her father cured, Hinnihami has the courage to leave the man who bewitched her father. The book relentlessly captures the grimness of the life of the village, the death of children, the failure of crops. The next turn of the plot concerns Fernando, a moneylender coming to the village and coveting Punchi Minika. As she is not willing and Babun refuses to cooperate, he is accused of stealing, and the allegedly stolen goods are planted in his hut by the moneylender with the collusion of the headman. At his trial, the English judge, modeled on Leonard himself, is dissatisfied with the story and senses that he has failed to discern the truth of the matter. But, because of the lack of refutation, he feels he has no choice but to sentence Babun to six months of imprisonment. In effect the two cultures cannot really meet; there are two different worlds, two different conceptions of justice.

Leonard might have felt uneasy about the incompatibility of the two cultures, but he had not yet reached the conclusion that imperial rulers should not have the right to impose their ideas of how a society should be run. He did not necessarily believe that indigenous populations were equally adept at running a state, particularly in Africa, about which he would write extensively in later years. Nevertheless, from his experience in Ceylon, he came to believe passionately that one nation had no right to rule another. This was a moral decision. When he revisited Sri Lanka in 1960, he was confronted by a man who complained about a decision he had made fifty years before, imposing two ten rupees fines on him, the first for owning a diseased cow that would spread the dreaded rinderpest among others, and the second, on the same man, as headman, for not taking action against himself as the owner of the animal. The man called out to him, fifty years later, "Was it just? Was it just?" Leonard felt he had still acted justly in British terms, but he conceded the point that it could be seen as unjust in terms of another culture, one that had as much right to exist, indeed as the culture of the country, even more so than the seemingly legitimate regulations of those who ruled. When he wrote his novel, he was not yet a convinced anti-imperialist, but the idea of the incompatibility of the cultures is already present in his thinking. By what right should the workings of British justice determine what happened in Ceylon?

The extraordinary accomplishment of this grim novel, written in powerful prose, is effectively to enter the lives of the people of Ceylon. In its spare style it reproduces their language and their ways of thinking. Leonard certainly does not idealize them but depicts their world with understanding and sympathy and without any sentimentality. In fact, quite the contrary. There is not a whiff of patronizing their way of life, although fully recognizing how primitive it is and how it is, particularly in the jungle, so full of evil spirits. In the spirit of the Apostles, he gets to the essence of the life that was lived in the area that he came to know so well. His prose, like the life it depicts, is rendered very directly as he reproduces the language of the poor Ceylonese, the most unsophisticated of village dwellers.

The novel takes a dramatic turn as, after Babun's trial, Silindu shoots both the headman and the moneylender who had framed his son-in-law. He then turns himself into the authorities. He is tried and condemned to be hanged, but then his sentence is commuted to twenty years' imprisonment. He understands little of what is going on. His daughter has remained in the village, which goes into decay, the jungle taking it over. Babun has not returned, even though the six months of his sentence have passed. Punchi Menika travels to the prison to discover that he has died there. She goes back to the village; ten years pass and her hut is the only one remaining. She lives alone as both her aunt and her sister have died. "The jungle surged forward over and blotted out the village up to the very walls of her hut. She no longer cleared the compound or mended the fence, the jungle closed over them."[25] One is not told, but presumably Silindu died in prison. The weakened Punchi Meniki is dying of starvation as a boar comes into the hut to kill her. The novel is hard to read, since it is so relentlessly grim, but it is also an extraordinary accomplishment, a rare feat in depicting the life of the residents of the district that Leonard ruled. It also demonstrated how important was his time in Ceylon for his development as the writer he wished to be. And it helped shape so many of his interests and writings when he ceased to write fiction.

Sir Hugh Clifford, who had appointed Leonard to the post, wrote an essay on the book shortly after its publication, in the June 1913 issue of *Blackwood's Magazine*. It is mostly about the power of the jungle, but in conclusion he remarked that the novel was

> the most faithful, the most true, and most *understanding* presentation of the Oriental peasant life that has ever been placed before Western readers by a European. Written with first-hand knowledge of the people and their surroundings, with real psychological insight and sympathy, this book not only gives a picture of village life in the less favoured portions of Ceylon which is true in every detail, but it affords to the reader a convincing explanation of why it is as it is.[26]

In a sense, the novel contained what would be Leonard's fatalistic credo that ultimately, as he would write, "nothing matters." Yet at the same time one had to devote oneself, vain as it might be, to make the world a better place. Silindu killed two evil men. The Leonard-like figure in the novel attempted as best he could to be just. Leonard himself as a colonial civil servant tried to improve the lot of those who were in his charge, even though he ultimately came to believe that those such as he had no business playing that role in the empire. Similarly, upon his return to England, he would devote himself to creating a better world, on the individual level in nurturing the talent of his wife-to-be, Virginia Woolf, and, though he despaired at how effective he might be, in his political activity as a writer and doer.

Notes

1. Spotts, 68.
2. Ibid. 80.
3. Ibid., 1 October 1905, 102.
4. Ibid., 12 November 1905, 107.
5. Ibid., 21 March 1906, 115.
6. 25 February 1906, LW Papers, University of Sussex Library (courtesy of Ian Britain).
7. Spotts, 23 October 1908, 140.
8. *Letters of Lytton Strachey*, 113–14.
9. Spotts, 122.

10. Ibid., 19 May 1907, 128.
11. Ibid. 134.
12. Spotts, 138.
13. Ibid. 137.
14. *Letters of Lytton Strachey*, 164.
15. Ibid. 173–4.
16. Spotts, 144 n.
17. Ibid. 145–6.
18. *Letters of Lytton Strachey*, 180.
19. Spotts, 148.
20. *Letters of Lytton Strachey*, 185.
21. Spotts, 149–50.
22. Ibid. 104.
23. Quoted in Glendinning, 110 (no source given).
24. LW, "After Fifty Years," *New Statesman*, 23 April 1960.
25. LW, *The Village in the Jungle* (Oxford edn, 1981), 177.
26. Sir Hugh Clifford, *Blackwood's Magazine* (June 1913), 859.

4
Virginia and After

Leonard arrived back in England in June 1911 for a year's leave, traveling home with his sister Bella. Two of his brothers, Herbert and Edgar, met them at the dock, and he went directly to Putney to be with his family. Almost immediately he visited Cambridge to stay with Lytton for some days and to plunge back into the life of the Apostles. At the end of June he attended the annual Apostles dinner in London, sitting between Strachey and Keynes. He went to see old friends in Cambridge and elsewhere, visited relatives in Denmark and Sweden, and enjoyed the cultural excitement of London, most notably the Russian ballet. On July 3 he dined with Vanessa and Clive Bell and would become a regular in their company, which included Virginia. But he felt uncertain about his future. He had no doubt that he had been and could continue to be a very successful civil servant and would rise in the ranks. He had had particular satisfaction from his last posting and would prefer, if he remained in the service, to be engaged in work that brought him into direct contact with the indigenous population rather than seeking a higher administrative post. But he realized it was unlikely that he could avoid advancement to more prominent positions. Yet he was now captivated by Virginia Stephen, whom he barely knew. While they had met only three times before he went to Ceylon, they were very soon on familiar terms. He was invited to the house she had rented in Firle in Sussex. He would also see the Bells and Virginia in Gordon Square and come to the gatherings there. In his diary he referred to Virginia as Aspasia, the lover of Pericles, no doubt casting himself as his hero Pericles. And within a few months, in December 1911, he had taken two rooms with some meals at the rent of 35 shillings a week in the house in Brunswick Square that she shared with her brother Adrian, Keynes, and Duncan Grant. At this point Virginia was in charge, running it as a boarding house with rules and regulations. More significantly, almost at once he fell seriously in love with her.

The idea that Virginia should get married was certainly in the air, and she did not lack for suitors. Born in 1882, she was now approaching 30. One problem was that the men in her immediate circle, Strachey, Keynes, and Grant, were not that way inclined, although she and Lytton had been engaged for moments, an overnight excitement. She was certainly a beautiful woman, but she was also a formidable lady. It was rumored that Hilton Young, a Cambridge figure, had proposed to her. Walter Lamb was also interested. Another possibility was Sydney Waterlow, who also proposed to her. In a sense her most romantic and entirely unsuitable involvement before Leonard was with Clive Bell, her brother-in-law. Vanessa and Clive had had an extremely happy marriage in its early years. But after their first child, Julian, was born in 1908, they began to drift apart; Clive resented the time and devotion Vanessa lavished on Julian, as Virginia did as well. (It could be said that in many ways Julian was the greatest love of Vanessa's life as she was to him, a further reason that his death in the Spanish Civil War proved such a devastating blow.) The relationship between Virginia and Vanessa was extremely close. It was the very core of the Bloomsbury Group, but its period of greatest strain and even a degree of estrangement between the sisters was the mischievous flirtation of Virginia and Clive, who might not have been reluctant to have it go further. The flirtation probably lasted for two years. There is no doubt that the relationship caused Vanessa much pain. Afterwards she and Clive continued to drift apart, he taking mistresses and she having an intense affair with Roger Fry and then settling into a long-term relationship with the homosexual Duncan Grant, living together almost completely non-sexually (although they did have a daughter, Angelica). There was the paradox of Vanessa and Virginia, committed to sexual freedom in theory and conversation but eventually leading comparatively chaste lives. Vanessa was the more passionate of the two, with Virginia apparently not much interested in making love, perhaps the effect of her sexual molestation by her Duckworth half-brothers.

Undoubtedly Leonard's most important activities in the first two years that he was back in England were his courtship of and marriage to Virginia and the writing of his two novels. Other than

E. M. Forster, who was older and had a somewhat tangential relationship with the Group, Leonard was perhaps unexpectedly its first novelist. Virginia had not yet published *The Voyage Out*, on which she had been working for some time. Leonard's deepest desire was to be a creative writer, but he would abandon that pursuit after the publication of his slim *Stories of the East* in 1921. And it seems likely that he had written those stories some years earlier. It may be that the last work of fiction he actually wrote was the story "Three Jews," published in 1917. *The Village in the Jungle* had been a critical success and had sold well. His second novel, *The Wise Virgins*, appearing at the outbreak of the First World War, had earned him a grand total of £20. Perhaps he also came to feel that he should not rival his wife as a fiction writer. He was hardly present, except as the English magistrate, in *The Village in the Jungle*, but his second novel, *The Wise Virgins*, was decidedly autobiographical. Although it ends with the marriage of the central character to someone other than Virginia, he started writing it in Spain while actually on his honeymoon. There is a nice irony there, as the novel tells the story of the unsuccessful courtship by the Leonard character of the Virginia character, when of course he had actually married her. At the same time he was also embarking upon what would come to dominate his writing and professional life: national and international political questions.

The very first paragraph of *The Wise Virgins* suggests a transition from *The Village in the Jungle*. It points out that human beings lived first in caves, then in primitive villages, and then in houses in cities, where his second novel takes place. Yet the individuals who live there may not be all that different. But certainly it is a world of England rather than Ceylon, based on the immediate experiences he had on his return to London. It is a dramatic contrast to his first novel and is written very much from the inside. The central character, Harry Davis, who is studying to be an artist, is a quite negative version of himself. He lives in the suburban world of Putney but is also becoming involved with Leonard's Cambridge world, notably with two sisters who are versions of Virginia and Vanessa. Harry, depicted as active and aggressive, sees this as part of his Jewish character. In the novel he portrays his own family in an unflattering way. There are virgins in the novel but who are the wise ones and who the foolish? Next door in the suburb where Harry is living with his family there are the four Garland sisters, including Gwen, the one who will interest him. In dramatic contrast are the artist Camilla Lawrence and her sister Katharine. They are clearly modeled on Vanessa and Virginia, the only difference being that Harry falls in love with Camilla, the artist sister. There is the power of Harry's sexual drive, inhibited by social conventions, in contrast to life in the Ceylon village. In fact, the novel has its denouement in an act of sexual aggression not by Harry, but by Gwen. In many ways the novel is about Leonard falling in love, yet he presents himself with characteristic and unsympathetic severity. When he was writing it, Clive Bell was Vanessa's husband, as Leonard had become Virginia's. There was tension between them, as Leonard was deeply concerned that Clive's attentions would unsettle Virginia, as he told him in no uncertain terms. Clive was jealous of Leonard's devotion to Virginia, going so far some years later as to refer to him in a letter to Lytton as a "pestilent Jew."[1] Virginia was uneasy about Leonard being Jewish, and he was concerned with that aspect of their relationship as well. This is reflected in words he puts into the mouth of Arthur Woodhouse, the Clive character in *The Wise Virgins*: "It's a characteristic of your race—they're intellect and not emotion; they don't feel things.... You were all right when you lived in Palestine before the dispersal. You were farmers and agriculturists; you produced Job and Ecclesiastes. Since then you've been wandering from city to city, and you've produced Mendelssohn and Barney Barnato."[2] Yet in the novel the remark does not cause an estrangement between the two. To a degree, Harry even agrees with Arthur. Indeed, Arthur is depicted as being sympathetic to Harry, unlike the rather Lytton-like character, Lion Wilton, who says that no Jew could be a good painter. Harry becomes increasingly involved with Gwen, particularly after an excursion the two families take on the Thames, vividly described, to Maidenhead. (It is intriguing that in fact it was with Virginia that Leonard made an expedition on the river to Maidenhead.) Harry becomes increasingly fond of Camilla, particularly after he visits her and her family at their country cottage in Kent. But it is a failed courtship, despite its similarity to Leonard's ultimately successful courtship of Virginia. In the novel, Harry declares his love to Camilla, who responds that she does not reciprocate his love. Harry enunciates the credo that Leonard adhered to until the end of his life, that "nothing matters." At this point Leonard was not yet committed to political action, although he was beginning to move in that direction. From the beginning he lived his life as if it mattered despite his nihilistic statement. The novel ends with Harry marrying the suburban Gwen after she has seduced him, and he feels obliged to do the right thing.

His friends had mixed feelings about the novel when they read it in manuscript; his mother was very upset and hurt about how she was depicted. His sister Bella advised against publication, sending him nine pages of criticism. But *The Wise Virgins* is well written and worth reading and is ultimately more sympathetic to most of those in it than one might have expected. Harry being a Jew is a dominant factor in the book, but it does not preclude him and his family from being part of the suburban scene. Even though he is married in a church, he and his mother think of it as having synagogue-like associations. Harry clings to his creed that nothing matters, yet the world that he has chosen does not seem to be a tragic one. Perhaps Gwen and Camilla are the wise virgins who have made the right choices. It might be said that Leonard had a spiritual life that appeared to be empty yet was somehow full of possibilities for the many years that lay before him. The failure of the novel was one reason he turned to journalism and political activism rather than what he really wanted, to write fiction. Nevertheless he would be deeply involved in the literary world through the Hogarth Press, his numerous reviews and articles on literary themes, and his editorial work, and by becoming crucially such a supportive and facilitating force for Virginia's writing.

When Leonard returned to England, he now felt, as he recalled in *Beginning Again*, that at the age of 31 his youth had ended. In August he started to write *The Village in the Jungle*. And by the end of 1911 he had fallen in love with Virginia. This raised the question of his future with the civil service. He requested an extension of leave but declined to state the reason. In January he had proposed to Virginia, who was not yet prepared to commit herself. Since the Colonial Office was unwilling to grant an extension officially, he took the bold step of resigning without knowing whether Virginia would accept him. (The Under-Secretary had offered on his own authority to grant the extension, but Leonard decided to stand by his decision to resign, which he did on April 25.) In any case he was having growing doubts about whether he wanted to continue in the Colonial Service. But he was taking a great economic risk; he would be without income after May 1912. He did have a nest egg of £600, derived from a horse-racing sweepstake he had won in 1908, enough to sustain him for two years. Virginia had an unearned income of £400 a year. Although their first novels were critical successes, they did not in fact earn them very much money.

Leonard's devotion to Virginia is perhaps very well summed up in the dedication to her of *The Village in the Jungle*, published the following February.

> I've given you all the little, that I've to give;
> You've given me all, that for me is all there is;
> So now I just give back what you have given—
> If there is anything to give in this.

He was a paradoxical figure. He would appear on the surface to be cold and austere. Yet his letters to Virginia, full of passion, make clear how much in love he was with her. As he wrote to her on January 11, 1912, after he had proposed to her that very day. "I never realised how much I loved you until we talked about my going back to Ceylon. After that I could think about nothing else but you."[3] Virginia was clearly uneasy about Leonard. She was not convinced that she wanted to marry at all, even though the possibility had been on her mind for some time. Yet at the same time, now 29, she felt it was time to be married. His proposal had unsettled her. And truth to tell, she was somewhat disconcerted by his being Jewish, so clearly somewhat "other" no matter how much he was part of her brothers' and closest friends' Cambridge world and even how many interests they shared. She wrote to him coolly on January 13 that she would like to go on as before and that she thought his proposal should be kept entirely secret, except from Vanessa. (Vanessa wrote him an encouraging letter on January 13 "to say how glad I shall be if you can have what you want."[4]) For some months, by her wish, they had little contact. But then in the spring they began to see each other constantly. In the letters she wrote to friends about the engagement, once it became public, Virginia identified him as a "penniless Jew."

This raises the persistent question about whether or not Virginia was anti-Semitic and to what degree. Certainly over the years both before and after her marriage she would make very nasty remarks about Jews and her wish to avoid them. Mean as her remarks might be, it is still quite difficult to determine how deeply ingrained they were and to what extent they reflected the superficial anti-Semitism of her time and her class. In a way she was no more negative about Jewish characteristics than Leonard himself was about his fellow Jews. Yet being a Jew himself somewhat legitimized his critical remarks. He had described the character based on his mother in *The Wise Virgins* in rather anti-Semitic terms, as he did the characteristics of the anti-hero based on himself. Virginia would put up with her mother-in-law ungraciously and described her in unflattering ways. Anti-Semitism in England was certainly pervasive at the time, and derogatory remarks were very common. Nasty as they were, they rarely translated into actions, and Jews figured prominently in the English world. There was no problem for Leonard to attend St Paul's and Cambridge. Nor is there any indication that being Jewish created obstacles in his career or his personal life. Yet certainly he and others were very conscious that he was Jewish. His Jewish heritage, despite his being totally irreligious, was important in shaping his ideas and his rather austere style. It certainly could be a disadvantage to be Jewish in certain areas of English life. For instance, Leonard's brother Philip, despite superior qualifications, was rejected by the Foreign Service, which ranked higher on the social scale than the colonial service, no doubt because he was Jewish. His being a Jew by birth and tradition was more important to Leonard than it was to Virginia. Was it as Jews or as anti-Fascist writers or both that they were on the Nazi list to be rounded up after the invasion of Britain? They felt sufficiently threatened that they planned to commit suicide should the Germans land.

Virginia and Leonard had lived in the same house, although at this point it was more a boarding house than a shared residence. They went frequently to Asheham, the country house in Sussex that Virginia and Vanessa had leased after the semi-detached one Virginia had occupied in Firle. They went about together a lot in London to the opera and the ballet, although he did not share her and Saxon's devotion to Wagner. Vanessa was very much in favor of the match, no matter what Clive might think. On May 1 Virginia wrote to Leonard dispassionately about the possibility of marrying:

> The obvious advantages of marriage stand in my way, I say to myself. Anyhow, you'll be quite happy with him; and he will give you

companionship, children, and a busy life—and then I say By God, I will
not look on marriage as a profession.... I feel angry sometimes at the
strength of your desire. Possibly, your being a Jew comes in also at this
point. You seem so foreign.... I want everything—love, children,
adventure, intimacy, work.... As I told you brutally the other day,
I feel no physical attraction in you.[5]

Yet on May 29 she told him that she loved him. By June, Virginia consented, and quite soon thereafter, on August 10, 1912, they were married at the St Pancras Registry Office. It was a quiet, small wedding; Leonard deeply offended his family, particularly his mother, by not inviting any of them to the ceremony. She wrote him a rather touching letter on August 7 expressing her regret at not having been asked.

To be quite frank, yes, it has hurt me extremely that you did not make it
a point of having me to your marriage.... You are the first of my sons
who marries, it is *one* of *the* if not *the* most important day of your life.
It would have compensated me for the very great hardships I have
endured in bringing you all up by myself, if you had expressed the
desire that you wished me before anyone else, to be witness to your
happiness.[6]

The only guests at the event were Vanessa, the sisters' half-brothers George and Gerald Duckworth, Duncan Grant, Roger Fry, Saxon Sydney-Turner, her aunt Mary Fisher, and the painter Frederick Etchells, a rather improbable guest who was not a close friend, although he was part of the Omega Workshops. Perhaps Fry had brought him along. Virginia had mixed feelings about her Duckworth half-brothers, yet they were her adored mother's sons. The next year she would spend two months in George's country house (although the Duckworths were not there at the same time) after her suicide attempt. Gerald's firm, Duckworth, would publish Virginia's first two novels. Vanessa and George acted as the official witnesses. Oddly, Clive appears to have been absent. In May he had written a rather ambivalent letter about the match to Molly MacCarthy:

It is really very satisfactory, I suppose, but it would be rather horrible to
think that, most probably, people would feel for one's children what none
of us can help feeling for Jews—"Oh, he's quite a good fellow—he's a Jew,
you know—." Don't you think it would be rather painful to get oneself
into that plight? And Woolf's family are chosen beyond anything.[7]

Yet he wrote to Virginia immediately after her marriage: "You must believe that, in spite of all my craziness, I love you very much, and that I love your lover too."[8]

On their honeymoon they went first to Asheham, then to an inn in Somerset, and then spent several months travelling in France, Italy, and Spain. Although apparently consummated, the marriage would never be sexually fulfilling. On return, they took rooms in Clifford's Inn, spent time in the country, and devoted themselves to writing, she her first novel, and he his second, as well as his story "The Three Jews," published in 1917. He also began his prolific output on policy, politics, and literature. There were difficulties as Virginia had serious breakdowns. Leonard's crucial role as a caregiver began to emerge, becoming almost a calling, a commitment to a genius. As a married couple, these crises began with her suicide attempt in September 1913, followed by temporary recovery, and then an attack of madness in February 1915. There were recurrent bouts of depression and madness, especially after she completed books, until her suicide in 1941. Although Leonard knew that she had problems, he did not realize how deep they were until after their marriage. A major concern was whether they should have children. Virginia had expected that marriage would bring children, and some of her doctors thought maternity would help her. Leonard came to the conclusion that she would be unable to cope, a conviction that Vanessa shared. This was not a decision that he had come to easily, knowing how much Virginia wished to have a child. There is no question that over the years she expressed regrets that she was childless, and her happy relations with Vanessa's children demonstrated that she was good with them. But it seems probable that full-time responsibility for children would have been too much for her. There was a great deal of physical affection in their relationship, so their marriage was not necessarily without erotic satisfactions. As she wrote to him, when they were apart briefly some years later: "There's no doubt I'm terribly in love with you. I keep thinking what you're doing, and have to stop—it makes me want to kiss you so."[9] Leonard's decision about children has been the subject of much controversy since, and he has been attacked for taking it. Despite his detractors, it seems improbable that Virginia would have accomplished as much if it had not been for the constant care that Leonard provided.

Certainly the need for his care was most intensely felt in the months after her suicide attempt in September 1913. Presumably to celebrate a year of marriage, they had gone to the Somerset inn where they had spent their second married night, but Virginia was in a deteriorating mental state, having great difficulty eating and sleeping. It is impossible to determine the extent to which her mental fragility was affected by her marriage, as Leonard took such good care of her, choosing what he considered the best course of action. There is a minority view, strongly held by some critics, that his decisions were wrong and made her situation worse. Leonard was so concerned while they were at the inn that he had asked her friend Ka Cox to join them to help him look after her. They had then returned to London for a medical consultation. Left alone for a while, she deliberately overdosed on sleeping pills found in Leonard's case, inadvertently left unlocked. Of course he deeply regretted this, but, as he pointed out in his autobiography, he lacked a sense of sin and therefore did not brood about mistakes that were made and could not be undone. There was some consideration of placing her in an asylum, which would have been legally possible after a suicide attempt, since she could have been certified. Leonard went so far as to visit some asylums but found them quite unacceptable. He was under terrible strain and had hardly any time to launch his career as a political commentator and activist. Yet they were as deeply in love with one another as ever, Virginia in her own way. She would continue to have nursing care to some degree until February 1914. And even after that, should Leonard need to be away from her, he would ensure that there was someone to look after her. In March 1915 she had a relapse. By then they were living in Richmond, as Leonard felt it would be much better for her mental health not to be in the center of London. It was at this time that they began to think casually about acquiring a printing press. He informed Lytton, on February 10, 1915, of their intention to move into Hogarth House in Richmond: "We think of setting up a printing press in the cellarage. Now Ray [Lytton's sister-in-law] tells us you know all about printing presses. Is this true & can you tell how & where one gets them & what they cost?"[10]

The years 1914–18 were dominated by the counterpoint of the First World War itself and Virginia's illness, as well as moving to Hogarth House in March 1915 and the founding of the Hogarth Press. Moving into the house coincided with Virginia's second serious breakdown and the renewed need for nursing care at home. They still had the country cottage in Sussex. When they were apart they wrote to each other frequently, short letters full of affection, his signed M. standing for his pet name, Mongoose; she in return used her pet name, Mandrill.

Leonard and Virginia had been thinking about the possibility of becoming printers for some time, but her health prevented them from moving forward until 1917. There were personal reasons for wanting to become publishers. They loved books and wished to produce them. They came to three decisions at a birthday tea Virginia and Leonard had on January 25, 1915, at Buzzard's on Oxford Street in the center of London. They would lease Hogarth House, an eighteenth-century building close to where they were then living in Richmond. Hogarth was buried comparatively nearby in Chiswick, but there does not seem to be a particular connection with Richmond. The building did not acquire the name until 1876, when the original house was divided into two, Suffield House and Hogarth House. It was, rather nicely, on Paradise Road, although the area, close to the high street, was by this time already built up and somewhat noisy. They would live there for nine years. In 1920 the owner refused to renew the lease but offered the total house for sale, which they bought for £2,000. Then, in 1924, they moved back to central London, to 52 Tavistock Square in Bloomsbury. Leonard actually felt that this was a mistake, fearing that being in central London would lead to Virginia undertaking too much social activity and overstraining herself. Eventually Virginia wore down Leonard's opposition, and they returned to Bloomsbury. (There is a wonderful scene in the movie *The Hours*, presumably invented, in which Virginia says that, if she had to choose between Richmond and death, she would prefer death.)

They also decided at their 1915 tea that they would purchase a printing press. The third decision was to buy a bull dog, probably to be called John. That did not happen, although Leonard had been devoted to the dog Charles that he had in Ceylon. In any case, they did have a dog called Max and in 1926 they were given a cocker spaniel, Pinka, by Vita Sackville-West; Pinka adorns the dust jacket of the Hogarth Press first edition of *Flush* (1935), the autobiography of Elizabeth Barrett Browning's dog. Hogarth House was acquired on lease in 1915, but because of Virginia's mental health the press itself had to wait two more years.

A major precursor and influence upon the creation of the Hogarth Press were the Omega Workshops, founded by Roger Fry in 1913. They mostly made decorative objects, ceramics, some furniture, although they did publish a few books. The look of their work was distinctly modern. Although it tended to down play this aspect, Omega was in the tradition of William Morris and the Arts and Crafts movement. It shared with Morris the feeling that anyone could do anything if they just put their mind to it. Both enterprises had that particularly English combination of professionalism and amateurism, implying that they were appropriated by members of the "gentle" classes. They were not averse to making money, yet at the same time wished to avoid the stigma of "trade."

When they applied for instruction in printing at the St Bride Foundation near Fleet Street, they were not admitted, as they were unwilling to join the union, despite Leonard's radical leanings. And the printing trade was notoriously misogynistic. In any case, the Woolfs had no choice but to learn by doing. Each of them regarded the printing enterprise as therapy for the other. As Virginia gradually recovered from her breakdown, the work of printing might be of great assistance. Writing her novels was a great strain upon her; she was particularly vulnerable when she had just finished one. Leonard felt it would be very useful for her to have a manual occupation that would be totally different from the effort of writing and worrying about what she had written. The plan was that they would both write in the morning and print in the afternoon. On Virginia's part, she felt that the press, as very time consuming, would distract Leonard from being too politically active and being exploited, so she thought, by that other powerful couple, Beatrice and Sidney Webb. She felt that they claimed too much of Leonard's time in their projects to improve the world. But, since Virginia had had a serious mental relapse, needed much attention and nursing, the project of having a press had to be put on hold.

Finally, on March 12, 1917, they acquired a small hand press for £20 from the Excelsior Printing Company in London as well as some Caslon Old Face type and a sixteen-page booklet to teach them how to begin printing. They had seen various printing tools in the company's window, staring "through the window at them rather like two hungry children gazing at buns and cakes in a baker shop window" (*Beginning*, 234). Inspired by William Morris's Kelmscott Press in the last decade of the nineteenth century, there had been a considerable private press movement in Britain for some years. Staffed by designers and craftsmen, those presses began at a far higher level of professionalism than the Woolfs possessed. They were rank beginners, although Virginia had an interest and some experience in book binding. They seemed to be able to master the techniques on the basis of the booklet, as they were assured by the man who had sold the equipment to them. "By following the directions in the pamphlet we found that we could pretty soon set the type, lock it up in the chase, ink the rollers, and machine a fairly legible printed page" (*Beginning*, 234). The Hogarth Press was in the modernist style in the tradition and look of Omega and carried on in its spirit after Omega went bankrupt in 1919. The press was even a simpler operation, requiring very little capital. It was situated in their house, and in its early years they did all the work themselves in the afternoons. Virginia did most of the typesetting because Leonard's hand tremor limited his dexterity; he did most of the machine work. Their first press was very simple and could fit on their kitchen table. The Woolfs also loved being in absolute control; they could print whomever and whatever they wished.

Two months after starting work in May, they produced their first book, *Two Stories*, one by her, "The Mark on the Wall," significant in marking her move to more experimental ways of writing, the other Leonard's "Three Jews." Together the stories marked a striking contrast in terms of style and content. It was issued in an edition of 150, of which they sold 134. It had four woodcuts by Dora Carrington, the most charming being of the snail that had caused the mark on the wall. His story dealt with Jewishness, its heritage being so much a part of shaping his personality, as the character of Harry in *The Wise Virgins* revealed. Its narrator visits Kew Gardens, comparatively close to where the Woolfs were then living. There at a café a fellow non-believing Jew sits down at his table, and they begin to talk about not really belonging to the English world but rather being still part of Palestine. He tells the narrator a story about visiting his wife's grave. The third Jew is the cemetery's keeper, with whom he has a further conversation when he visits again with his new wife. Then there is a third visit on the next anniversary of the first wife's death in which the cemetery keeper tells him that he has disowned one of the two sons for marrying their Christian serving girl. He found the class difference even more unacceptable than the religious one. What is one to make of the story? Leonard had married a Christian, but hardly a servant, as did all of his married siblings. Leonard would always feel something of an outsider in English society, despite his "establishment" education, being a colonial civil servant, and part of an elite English circle. Though the narrators of the story are unbelieving Jews, an atavistic feeling of being part of a separate group persisted.

This first publication was also deeply significant in terms of Leonard's and Virginia's writing careers. It probably marked Leonard's last venture in pursuit of his ambition to become a writer of fiction. In his remaining years, although he would write a prodigious amount in a wide variety of forms—books, articles, reviews, journalism—he did not return to fiction. But more significantly it also marked the beginning of the transformation of Virginia from the writer of conventional novels into one of the greatest novelists of the twentieth century. This was the Hogarth Press's only book in 1917. The next year they published only two. As they did all the work in producing their books themselves, it was very slow going. Leonard also decided to sell the books through subscription rather than offering each on its own or through the usual channels of bookstores and advertising. The A list would receive all the publications and the B list would have the option to purchase. This scheme continued until 1923, when the press began to act more like a regular commercial publisher.

Although these were hand-crafted, short books, they were not really in the Kelmscott tradition. Since the Woolfs were so new to printing, their main object was not to produce works of art. Unlike most private presses, they were exclusively interested in publishing new texts. Leonard, strong-minded, felt that private presses were too preoccupied with display rather than content. The Hogarth Press was in a way a hybrid. In its early years it was a private press issuing limited edition, hand-printed books that they typeset themselves and that reflected the choice of the proprietors. But, unlike the owners of many private presses, the Woolfs had comparatively little interest in the aesthetics of printing in the sense of producing the book beautiful. They did wish, however, that their books should have some artistic content in their jackets and illustrations. They were learning on the job, and most of their books were not aesthetic triumphs, although they were pioneers in introducing a modernist look, particularly in their cover designs. Leonard condemned what he regarded as the style of private presses. He wrote that most private press books

> are meant not to be read, but to be looked at. We were interested primarily in the immaterial inside of a book, what the author had to say and how he said it; we had drifted into the business with the idea of publishing things which the commercial publisher could not or would not publish. We wanted our books to "look nice" and we had our own views of what nice looks in a book would be, but neither of us was interested in fine printing and fine binding. We also disliked the refinement and preciosity which are too often a kind of fungoid growth which culture breeds upon art and literature. (*Downhill*, 80)

Although he admired some private presses more than this statement might imply, he definitely did not want the Hogarth Press to follow that tradition.

It was only a real private press in its early years. By 1932 they had entirely stopped typesetting and printing themselves, probably because of other demands upon their time, including running the business of the press, and their interest in actually doing the machine work was waning. But both of them, Leonard more than Virginia, continued to be closely involved with the press, sharing its premises with their home, first in Richmond and later in London. Of the 315 titles that Hogarth had published up until 1932, only 34 were physically produced by the Woolfs themselves. In a letter of May 2, 1917, when they were setting up the notice for subscriptions to their first book, Virginia wrote:

> After 2 hours work at the press, Leonard heaved a terrific sigh and said "I wish to God we'd never bought the cursed thing!" To my relief, though not surprise, he added "Because I shall never do anything else!" You can't think how exciting, soothing, ennobling and satisfying it is. And so far we've only done the dullest and most difficult part—setting up a notice, which you will recieve [*sic*] one day.[11]

At the end of the month she was at work on her story "The Mark on the Wall." "I haven't produced mine yet, but there's nothing in writing compared with printing."[12] They were also looking for subscribers: "We find we have only 50 friends in the world—and most of them stingy."[13] The first book was finished in July, taking a month to complete. Their next, Katherine Mansfield's *Prelude*, twice as long at 68 pages and 300 copies, took nine months. One reason it took so long was that its preparation was interrupted by the death of Leonard's brother Cecil, killed at the battle of Cambrai. Assisted by his brother Philip, Leonard and Virginia printed a very short memorial volume of poems by Cecil. This is the rarest of Hogarth titles, with only four surviving copies now known. After printing eighteen pages of Katherine Mansfield's *Prelude*, they decided that the job was too much for them to complete on their press at home. They continued to set the type and then printed it themselves at a nearby commercial printer, the Prompt Press, using a press that could do four pages at a time rather than just two.

Virginia had a rather love/hate relationship with Katherine Mansfield, who was in her early thirties and did not yet have much of a reputation, having published only one book previously. *Prelude* was a short story about a family moving, in which not very much happened. It too, like Cecil's poems, was a memorial dedicated to her brother, who was killed in the war, as well as to her lover and later husband, John Middleton Murry. Virginia commented on the book: "The title page was finally done on Sunday. Now I'm in the fury of folding & stapling, so as to have all ready for gluing & sending out tomorrow & Thursday. By rights these processes should be dull; but its always possible to devise some little skill or economy, & the pleasure of profiting by them keeps one content."[14] Leonard later remarked: "When I look at my copy of *Prelude* today, I am astonished at our courage and energy in attempting it and producing it only a year after we had started to teach ourselves to print" (*Beginning*, 237).

The other significant press choice that year was a negative one: Harriet Weaver had published James Joyce's work in the journal, the *Egoist*. She showed the Woolfs the first four chapters of his unfinished novel, *Ulysses*, with the idea that they should publish the entire work, but they turned it down. It is too easily assumed that Virginia did not like Joyce's work. Although recognizing his literary genius, she was, however, less than a total admirer. In any event, it was much too long for them to print themselves, and they knew they would not be able to find a printer who would take it on, as undoubtedly the state would have prosecuted for obscenity any publisher and printer who produced the work. In the end they told Harriet Weaver that it was much too large a job for the press. The entire work was published in Paris in 1922.

It might be appropriate here to venture a bit further into the history of the press, so much a joint enterprise by Leonard and Virginia. They published five books in 1919, three of which they printed themselves, including a short book of poems by T. S. Eliot and their first notable success, Virginia's story *Kew Gardens*, which, thanks to a favorable review in the *Times Literary Supplement*, sold very well. Its initial printing of 150 was supplemented by 500 more by a commercial press. It had a cover and illustrations by Vanessa Bell. Its success meant the press was transforming itself into a growing business venture. There were three publications in 1920, and that year they also bought a bigger press, which was installed in their basement. They were thinking of expanding, hiring an assistant, and opening a bookshop in the house. As Virginia wrote to Roger Fry on August 13, 1920: "We are in rather a turmoil about the press—The bookshop idea seems to be too difficult, and we now think of setting up a proper printing plant and doing all the production ourselves—that is with a manager." Later in the letter she remarked that "Eliot is coming here, a little to our alarm, and wants us to publish something of his, so what with you, Clive, and him we should start well."[15] Roger's proposed translations of Mallarmé in fact were not issued until 1936, after his death. But in 1921 they did publish twelve of his woodcuts. In that year they produced six books—quite short ones, four of which they printed themselves. That same year they bought their third press, a Minerva platen press, worked by a treadle.

The year 1921 was also notable for the publication of Leonard's *Stories of the East*, although it is likely that they were written earlier. They received a favorable review from Hamilton Fyfe in the *Daily Mail*, which provoked a moment of jealousy on Virginia's part, suggesting another reason why Leonard abandoned fiction. He might well have thought that there should be only one creative writer in the marriage. Fyfe had written: "Among the famous short stories of the world I think 'Pearls and Swine' will certainly find a place." In reaction, Virginia commented: "Am I jealous? Only momentarily.

But the odd thing is—the idiotic thing—is that I immediately think myself a failure—imagine myself peculiarly lacking in the qualities L. has."[16]

In 1922 they published nine books, just two printed by them. This year also marked the publication of three books by Russians: Ivan Bunin, Dostoevsky, and Countess Tolstoy. They had already published works by Gorky in 1920 and 1921. Their Russian books over the years (eleven in total) were translated by S. S. Koteliansky, who did a literal translation that was then gone over, as a co-translator, by either Virginia or Leonard, both of whom also learned some Russian themselves. They had a great success with Maxim Gorky's *Reminiscences of Leo Nicolayevitch Tolstoi*, and, of the nine short books they published in the first four years of the press, it was very much the one that sold the best. Leonard came to consider his commitment to the work of the press half of his professional life. Given his extensive political involvement and writing and the obligation to look after Virginia's health, he was fully occupied. In 1924 they took over the publication of the works of Sigmund Freud in English, for which the principal translator was Lytton Strachey's brother James. They became good friends with Eliot and also his initial publisher, most famously of the first English edition in book form of *The Waste Land*. Considering how comparatively few books they issued, their importance and variety were outstanding. That same year they published *Jacob's Room*, Virginia's third novel and the first written in her new manner, which became an essential part of her contribution to literature. Her first two novels *The Voyage Out* and *Night and Day* had been written in a conventional style, but *Jacob's Room* was written from within the characters, who viewed Jacob in a stream-of-consciousness way. This was also not only the first full-length book emanating from the press, but also the first produced by R. & R. Clark, printers in Edinburgh, who subsequently did much of their work. There were 1,200 copies published, and it has remained in print ever since. In his autobiography Leonard proudly points out that over the years Virginia's books made much more money than now-forgotten bestsellers. For the press's first three years it was almost more a hobby than a more serious pursuit, but by 1920 it was launched as an increasingly active, though still small, trade publisher. When Koteliansky had brought them the proposal that they publish a translation of Maxim

Gorky's *Reminiscences of Tolstoy*, they decided to print 1,000 copies, which obviously they could not do themselves.

> It was our first commercial venture.... The success of Gorky's book was really the turning point for the future of the Press and for our future. Neither of us wanted to be professional, full-time publishers; what we wanted to do primarily was to write books, not print and publish them. On the other hand, our three years' experience of printing and publishing had given us great pleasure and whetted our appetite for more. (*Downhill*, 67)

Virginia, hypersensitive to criticism, was also very pleased that it would not be up to the judgment of others, even her supportive half-brother, to decide whether or not her material was worthy of being published. No doubt it was Leonard's managerial skills and financial shrewdness that made the press a successful enterprise.

Together, but more Leonard than Virginia, they made the Hogarth Press an important publishing house. It was a very unusual venture, as there must be few commercial publishers that began as a private press and with thirty-four of its books physically produced by two of the most distinguished writers of twentieth-century Britain. As from 1920, it is true that they acquired their first part-time assistant, Ralph Partridge. Over the next years there would be others employed at the press, most notably George "Dadie" Rylands, and John Lehmann, who, after withdrawing for some years because of the difficulty of working with Leonard, returned to become a partner in the firm. These relations were rarely placid, and Leonard recognized that he was not an easy person to work with, being punctilious and obsessed by detail. (This is evident in his frequently noting, in his autobiographies, to the penny, how much various books, especially those by Virginia, earned.) Lehmann underscored the difficulty by entitling his memoir of the time *Thrown to the Woolfs*. Leonard, always very argumentative, had that deeply irritating quality of generally being right. Day-to-day managing of every aspect of a publishing enterprise, while doing so much else besides, could prove daunting. Yet it would be difficult to overestimate how important the Hogarth Press was as a contribution to cultural life in Britain. Characteristically, Leonard was a stern taskmaster to those few who worked with him. One suspects that he enjoyed the variety that it provided in his life and the

Virginia and After 69

satisfaction of keeping meticulous records. Through the initiative of Lehmann, who had come to them as a friend of Julian Bell, they became the publishers of the most iconic writings of the 1930s, not only of Christopher Isherwood and Edward Upward, but notably in their poetry series. *New Signatures* in 1932 was instrumental in introducing the public to the poetry of William Empson, W. H. Auden, Stephen Spender, and Cecil Day Lewis. The Hogarth Press became a major publisher of Bloomsbury writings, including works by Virginia and Leonard themselves, but also of the next dominant literary wave, the Auden generation. In 1938 Lehmann became a partner, replacing Virginia, although she still played a role in deciding what should be published up until the last week of her life. Through 1937 the 423 books and shorter works issued by the press were, it was noted, produced by Leonard and Virginia Woolf at the Hogarth Press. From 1938 on, the publisher was simply the Hogarth Press. In 1946 Chatto & Windus bought Lehmann's share, and the press became a joint venture of that firm and Leonard. The Hogarth Press continues to function, like Chatto & Windus, as part of the Random House group. While Leonard was still alive, he was the most important figure in deciding what the press should publish.

One of their most successful authors was Vita Sackville-West in her novels and other writings. She and her husband, Harold Nicolson, the diplomat and later prolific writer, lived not far from the Woolfs' house in Sussex, first at Long Barn and then at Sissinghurst, where Vita created one of the most famous of English gardens. Although the Nicolsons had two sons, they were both homosexual and had numerous lovers. Her affair with Virginia lasted for about three years in the 1920s, a result of which was Virginia's wonderful *Orlando*, a love letter to Vita, published in 1928. In the course of her life Virginia would become emotionally attached to several women, both before and after her marriage, but this was probably the only relationship that was physical as well. Even in this case it is not clear how intense it was on Virginia's part. Or, to put it another way, it was probably emotionally intense and briefly physically as well. Vita and Virginia did take a trip on their own to France, and Virginia spent time with her alone at Sissinghurst. At the same time she retained her sense of judgment about Vita's writings, admiring them only up to a point, while appreciating how well they did commercially as Hogarth Press publications.

Leonard seemed to take the affair in his stride; as far as one knows, it was the only one that Virginia had. He was more concerned that with her fragile psyche it might overly excite her and cause mental problems, rather than fearing that it would damage their long-lasting and solid relationship.

The press was a mixture of literature and business, and it might be said that this sort of combination dominated the rest of Leonard's life. From now on, except for the translations from the Russian and his 1939 political play, *The Hotel*, virtually all of his writing was nonfiction, mostly political, on both specific topics and broader questions until the great achievement of the five volumes of autobiography in the 1960s, the last decade of his life. According to one of his bibliographies, he made 1,566 contributions to periodicals, beginning with a poem in the *Cambridge Review* in 1901 and ending with an obituary of Kingsley Martin, the former editor of the *New Statesman*, for the *Political Quarterly* in 1969. In fact the number is probably higher, as this does not include all the unsigned pieces he wrote. Quite a few of his signed and unsigned writings would be reviews of a wide range of books, particularly as literary editor of the *Nation*. He also reviewed many recordings of classical music, which no doubt provided much of what Virginia and he frequently listened to after dinner.

A central part of his life until her suicide in 1941 was the support of Virginia's literary activity (and he continued to support her literary works in the years after her death). At the same time, they led an active social life in London, but also at Monks House, the country cottage they acquired in Rodmell in Sussex after having to give up Asheham.[17] There was the constant back and forth between that house and nearby Charleston, where Vanessa, Duncan, and her three children spent much of their time. The members of the Bloomsbury Group saw each other both in London and in the country, although they were sadly diminished by the early deaths of Lytton in 1932 and of Roger in 1934. The group had mixed feelings about Keynes's marriage to the Russian ballerina, Lydia Lopokova, in 1925, yet he remained a close friend, a friendship reinforced by his generosity and his neighboring country house, Tilton. The coherence of the group was also helped by the establishment in 1920 of the Memoir Club. At its meetings the Bloomsbury figures read to one another pieces about their shared past, quite a few of which were subsequently published. Many of Leonard's contributions were incorporated into his autobiography.

In many ways the 1920s and 1930s were the time of greatest accomplishment for the Bloomsbury Group, when some of them became very well known, although they had actually met together more frequently before the war. Forster was recognized as a major English novelist. With his *Economic Consequences of the Peace* of 1918 and his later theoretical work, Keynes became the most influential economist in England. Strachey, despite his early death, was perhaps its most famous biographer. And Virginia's writings of those two decades established her as a significant writer. Leonard did not achieve at quite the same level, but he was having a very successful career. No longer a creative writer, he was making a considerable mark as a publisher, the literary editor of the *Nation*, and the author of a considerable number of columns and reviews, of books on domestic, international, and imperial questions, as well as being politically active on many committees. Virginia was more interested in society than he was, enjoying such gatherings as those at Lady Ottoline Morrell's house in nearby Bedford Square or at her country house at Garsington, outside Oxford. She also attended Lady Cunard's lunches for literary lions and others. They loved their country cottage, where Leonard in particular developed into an avid gardener. When in the country they would write in their separate rooms in the morning, and then in the afternoon Leonard would generally garden and Virginia go for walks, thinking all the while about her work. They competed fiercely with one another at bowls, Leonard, to Virginia's irritation, usually winning. At Monks House they entertained frequently and also spent much time at nearby Charleston. As a result of the success of Virginia's novels, they were much better off financially and could now afford to install various improvements to modernize their property. He carefully monitored her mental state, tried to prevent her from doing too much and becoming overexcited, and reassured her about her writings, thereby performing a major service to English literature. After finishing the manuscript of one of her novels, she was particularly vulnerable to severe depression, and Leonard needed to keep a close watch on her state of mind. Yet, despite the travails of these two decades, the Depression starting in 1929, and the rise of Fascism and

Nazism, these years were a time of success and fulfillment for Leonard as well as for Virginia. Though they never were extravagant, their income was such that they could easily afford to make Monks House much more comfortable. Even when less well-off, they were never without servants. From 1928 on they owned a car and regularly went to the Continent. Virginia in particular much enjoyed the exhilaration of travel, especially going to Cassis on the French coast, where Vanessa, Duncan, and family had rented a house.

The years between the wars were highly productive ones for both Virginia and Leonard, but by the late 1930s they had to face the prospect of another world war. The war became very immediate when German bombers flew over Rodmell on their way to and from London, and there was always the possibility that they would drop unused bombs in the vicinity on the return trip or deliberately target the area. When the planes flew overhead, they laid themselves prone on the grass. German planes were shot down nearby, occasionally flying sufficiently low over the house that they could see their swastika markings. Their London house in Mecklenburgh Square was partially destroyed in the bombing. In any case, they were primarily living in Monks House, going up to London only about once a week. Their former house in Tavistock Square was also bombed, creating a surrealistic view of decorations by Duncan visible from the street. The Hogarth Press continued, moving to a printing office in Letchworth Garden City, where many of its books had been produced. In anticipation of a German invasion in the fall of 1940 and their probable arrest if in German captured territory, they secured from Adrian a prescription for morphine to kill themselves, and acquired enough gasoline so that, as an alternative, they could do so through carbon monoxide. Though they went up to London on very slow trains from time to time, they now had become primarily country dwellers. They were seemingly content, even though the possibility of death from bombing or invasion was ever present in their minds. The war itself was not a major factor in causing Virginia's depression. The idea of death had always been present in her mind, as the two previous suicide attempts revealed.

Leonard became increasingly concerned about Virginia's mental health in early 1941, and there were consultations in nearby Brighton with Dr. Octavia Wilberforce, a descendant of William Wilberforce of

Virginia and After 73

the Evangelical Clapham Sect and Virginia's third cousin. She had finished her draft of *Between the Acts*, which she had enjoyed writing. It was difficult for Leonard to decide how to cope and whether increased supervision might only heighten Virginia's anxiety. He did feel that she had not been as badly off since her suicide attempt in August 1913. On March 28, 1941, she drowned herself in the river Ouse, which flowed past the house, putting a large stone into her coat and walking into the river. Her body was not found until April 18.

The letters she wrote in the last days of her life were quite extraordinary. Under great mental strain, she wrote several matter-of-fact letters to Lady Cecil, Lady Tweedsmuir, Vita Sackville-West, and John Lehmann on March 21, 22, and 23, although she had written her first undelivered suicide note to Leonard probably on March 18. It is a powerful statement of their relationship and deserves quotation here:

> Dearest, I feel certain that I am going mad again: I feel we cant go through another of these terrible times. And I shant recover this time. I begin to hear voices, and cant concentrate. So I am doing what seems the best thing to do. You have given me the greatest possible happiness. You have been in every way all that anyone could be. I dont think two people could have been happier till this terrible disease came. I cant fight it any longer. I know that I am spoiling your life, that without me you could work. And you will I know. You see I cant even write this properly. I cant read. What I want to say is that I owe all the happiness of my life to you. You have been entirely patient with me and incredibly good. I want to say that—everyone knows it. If anybody could have saved me it would have been you. Everything has gone from me but the certainty of your goodness. I cant go on spoiling your life any longer. I dont think two people could have been happier than we have been. V.[18]

Probably on March 23 she wrote to Vanessa in response to her sister's letter urging her to be sensible. But she didn't send it; had she done so, Vanessa would undoubtedly have made sure that she was never alone, since it was also a suicide note. As she wrote in it: "All I want to say is that Leonard has been so astonishingly good, every day, always; I cant imagine that anyone could have done more for me than he has. Will you assure him of this? I feel he has so much to do that he will go on, better without me, and you will help him."[19]

And then on March 28 she wrote a further letter that Leonard found in her study along with the earlier one. It sent him frantically looking for her. In conclusion she wrote: "All I want to say is that until this disease came on we were perfectly happy. It was all due to you. No one could have been so good as you have been, from the very first day till now. Everyone knows that."[20] Unable to find her, he surmised that she had drowned herself.

Now his life was dominated by grief and the complications of death, letters he received about her death, the inquest after her body was found, and her cremation on April 21. In many ways it had been a very happy and fulfilling marriage, and he had done so much in enabling her to write. As he had before, for the rest of his life he would be her literary custodian, editing or supervising posthumous publications of her work, such as a selection from her diary as well as essays and short stories, appointing her nephew Quentin as her biographer, giving some and selling others of her papers, despite her request that her papers be destroyed. Increasingly, both in correspondence and in person, he was very helpful to the growing number of scholars and others writing about Virginia. Despite his belief that one should not feel guilty about what could not be changed, he still felt intensely that if he had acted otherwise she might well have recovered, as she had before. Outwardly most of the time he remained calm and business-like (though he did break down in tears as well) and kept various appointments in London. He believed that his fatalism as a Jew, a people who experienced centuries of oppression, helped sustain him during his grief. His addiction to work, which he also felt was a Jewish trait, also helped him. But underneath that carapace, there was a passionate man. As he wrote on a scrap of paper:

> They said "Come to tea and let us comfort you." But it's no good. One must be crucified on one's own private cross.
>
> It is a strange fact that a terrible pain in the heart can be interrupted by a little pain in the fourth toe of the right foot.
>
> I know that V. will not come across the garden from the Lodge, and yet I look in that direction for her. I know that she is drowned and yet I listen for her to come in at the door. I know that it is the last page and yet I turn it over. There is no limit to one's stupidity and selfishness.[21]

Shortly after Virginia's death, in April, Alice Ritchie, who had published two novels with the Hogarth Press, was dying of cancer, and

Leonard visited her and lent her some money. In the past, she had worked for the Hogarth Press, selling its publications to bookstores. He also slightly knew her sister Marjorie, known as Trekkie, who had done art work for the press, designing a pair of book jackets in 1930, one of them for her sister's book, one for Vita Sackville-West's *All Passion Spent* in 1931, another in 1932, and then three jackets for Hogarth books in the 1940s. (Somewhat ironically, she would, ten years after Leonard's death, design a book jacket for the English reissue of *The Wise Virgins*, the novel whose major theme was Leonard's fictionalized courtship of Virginia.) She had an extensive career illustrating various books and other publications. Trekkie was also known to him as the wife of Ian Parsons, the editor who would become most involved with the Hogarth Press when it was absorbed by Chatto & Windus in 1946. But he had not actually seen her for ten years until they renewed contact because of his involvement in her sister's illness. Despite being twenty-two years younger than he, she would become his closest friend for the rest of his life, and indeed he fell deeply in love with her. The relationship undoubtedly greatly enriched his remaining years. As he wrote to her on September 3, 1943: "I think you do know that it is because you & your work—which means too your happiness—are to me now infinitely the most important things in life." Or on April 13, 1944: "I've never known a human being so perfect as a work of art.... You've never said anything or made a movement which did not seem to me beautiful & give me the feeling of ecstasy or satisfaction mental & physical which one gets from a work of art."[22] His letters were much more passionate than hers to him. Hers, although affectionate, were mostly devoted to what she had been doing. In many of his letters there was a touching focus on his love for her. It is not clear whether they physically became lovers, probably not, but psychologically they certainly were. Leonard probably wished that they were sexually intimate, but Trekkie, although apparently no longer sleeping with Ian, resisted the idea. Leonard's love letters were interspersed with news of daily events, their mutual passion for gardening, and reports on his pets. She never left her husband Ian (who had a long affair, much resented by Trekkie, with Norah Smallwood, an editor at Chatto & Windus).

The Parsons acquired a country cottage in the village next to Rodmell and also eventually a flat on Victoria Square in London next door to Leonard. Later they occupied rooms in his housse, although the three were generally only there together one day a week. But Monks House, particularly given Leonard's passion for gardening and his love for his numerous pets, became the physical center of his life. He continued the pattern he had had there with Virginia: reading Greek and Latin texts before breakfast, writing and dealing with correspondence in the morning, gardening in the afternoon, frequently ending, if he had visitors, with a game of bowls, listening to classical music in the evening and reading books, mostly those he needed to consult for his writing or those he might be reviewing. With weekly visits to London, quite a bit of travel abroad with Trekkie, this became the pattern for the rest of his life, almost thirty years after Virginia's death. He would often invite people in for a meal and continued to have the help of his housekeeper, Louie Everest. The Parsons would generally spend the weekend at their cottage; they would all go up to London on Monday, Tuesdays Leonard would spend in the office of Chatto & Windus, and then he and Trekkie would return to Monks House for the rest of the week. Trekkie seemed adept in balancing the two relationships and would write Leonard letters about her fairly frequent travels abroad with her husband. On at least one of her trips Ian's mistress accompanied them! She would also take trips with Leonard, short ones around Britain and to the Continent, but also longer ones to Israel and Sri Lanka. They also traveled to the United States, which he enjoyed but felt was not a place where he would wish to live. Leonard did not seem troubled in sharing the relationship with Trekkie with Ian or, to put it another way, he was so in love with Trekkie that he was willing to accept the situation. There are, however, some indications that her marriage caused her some distress, as an enigmatic entry in her diary in 1958 reveals: "I cry when I think of Ian and but for the tears feel like a dry river bed.... I wish I could force myself not to think and think of what I hate to think of."[23] But there is no indication that there was a problem having Ian as a fellow occupant of his London house or as his publishing colleague. She would eventually become Leonard's heir and executor.

His literary career had begun with fiction, two novels and several short stories. Much of his writing over the years was distinguished, but it might be argued that his finest writing was in the last decade of his life in his five short volumes, cited frequently in this text, of memoir/autobiography, the first, *Sowing* in 1960, written when he was 80, the last *The Journey not the Arrival Matters* in 1969, shortly before his death at nearly 89. Some found the volumes quite discursive, but that is intrinsic to their charm and power. They do tell us what he accomplished, but they are primarily a meditative and wise commentary on his own life. In many ways they were his last testament, his statement of his beliefs. He was a relentless empiricist with little interest in philosophy and theories. But he would never have supported taking steps against whatever people happened to choose to believe unless it caused harm. He firmly believed in toleration and liberty, yet that did not prevent him from being judgmental. Each volume reveals his characteristic charm and the power of his prose and personality, a rigorous discursiveness that gives the work its special quality of free association, or better yet, of free conversation, combined with an extraordinary tough-mindedness. But the "wandering effect" is deceptive, for almost every word, every incident, is made to count. The last volume, *The Journey not the Arrival Matters*, is in many ways a Stoic's ruminations about death. In 1967 he published a commonplace book, a collection of aphorisms for each day of the year, entitled *A Calendar of Consolation: A Comforting Thought for Every Day in the Year*. The title is deeply ironic, as most of the quotations are extremely bleak, the first being E. M. Forster's "Life never gives us what we want at the moment that we consider appropriate" and the second from Jonathan Swift: "A nice man is a man of nasty ideas." The last day of the year is represented by a stanza of Shelley's "written in dejection near Naples."

Yet there were many pleasures in life, which he enumerated in his last volume: "Eating and drinking, reading, walking and riding, cultivating a garden, games of every kind, animals of every kind, conversation, pictures, music, friendship, love, people" (*Journey*, 182–3). The pleasures are contrasted with his having spent so many hours trying to improve the world with so little positive result. Yet he had a strong commitment to life, to which he alludes in the sentimental recollection of having to drown a puppy when he was a child and its desperate attempt to stay alive. Though tough-minded himself, he had an intense sympathy and concern for all creatures, human and animal. Haunted as he undoubtedly was by Virginia's suicide, he managed to spend the remaining decades productively and happily. Much of it was involved with dealing with the ever-growing interest in Virginia, her burgeoning popularity and influence after her death, but also continuing his own life of considerable accomplishment, enriched by his relationship with Trekkie.

Notes

1. Clive Bell to Lytton Strachey, 29 April 1914 (private collection).
2. LW, *The Wise Virgins* (1979 edn), 93.
3. Spotts, 168.
4. Ibid. 170.
5. VW, *Letters*, i. 496.
6. Spotts, 178.
7. 14 May 1912, quoted Lee, *Virginia Woolf*, 321.
8. VW, *Letters*, ii. 1n.
9. 17 April 1916, VW, *Letters*, ii. 90.
10. Spotts, 210.
11. VW to Margaret Llewelyn Davies, VW, *Letters*, ii. 151.
12. VW to Vanessa Bell, 22 May 1917, VW, *Letters*, ii. 155–6.
13. VW to Lady Ottoline Morrell, May 1917, VW, *Letters*, ii. 154.
14. *Diary of Virginia Woolf* (1977–84), i. 164.
15. VW, *Letters*, ii. 439–40.
16. VW, *Diary*, 3 May 1921, ii. 116. Fyfe quoted in footnote.
17. Monks House is alternately spelled Monk's House. We have followed the spelling that Leonard employs in his autobiography. According to Glendinning, who also spells it without an apostrophe, the name was given by the previous owner, Jacob Verrall. It does not appear ever to have been occupied by monks.
18. VW, *Letters*, vi. 481.
19. Ibid. vi. 485.
20. Ibid. vi. 487.
21. Quoted in Glendinning, 332 (no source given).
22. *Love Letters: Leonard Woolf and Trekkie Ritchie Parsons (1941–1968)* (2001)), 69, 124.
23. Ibid. 233.

Figure 1. Leonard Woolf by Barbara Strachey, 1938 (National Portrait Gallery)

Figure 2. Leonard and Virginia, 1939 (Photo Gisèle Freund/IMEC/Fonds MCC)

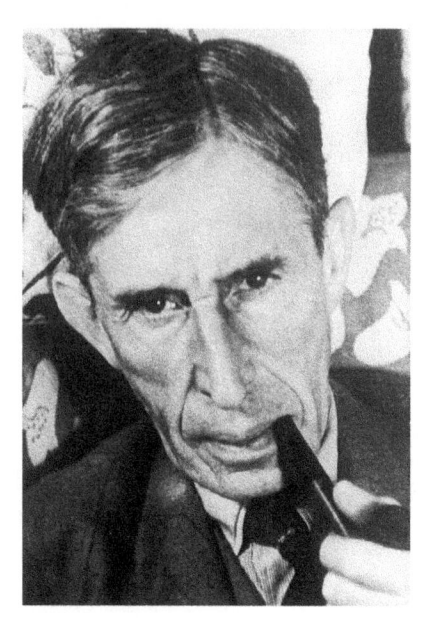

Figure 3. Leonard Woolf with pipe, *c*.1945 (Mary Evans Picture Library/ SIGMUND FREUD COPYRIGHTS)

Figure 4. Leonard with dogs, *c*.1965 (*Jewish Chronicle*/Heritage Image/age footstock)

PART II
The Political Journey

5
International Government

When Leonard returned to London from Ceylon in June 1911, there was every expectation that he would resume his duties in Hambantota at the end of his year's leave. While his misgivings about imperialism were increasing, he was acknowledged as an unusually competent and rigorous administrator who had been promoted rapidly, becoming the youngest Assistant Government Agent in the colony. He fantasized about returning to make Hambantota the most efficiently run district in Asia, capping his career with a governorship and a knighthood. At the same time, the isolation and monotony of his life as a colonial servant had taken their toll, and he recognized that marriage to Virginia would be incompatible with his overseas career. Having assumed his cadetship in the colonial service in 1904, shortly after leaving Cambridge, he had neither professional qualifications nor family resources to fall back upon. Until he resigned from the Ceylon civil service, Leonard drew a salary of £22 a month and had also amassed savings of £600, which he thought might suffice for two years. Virginia's additional inherited income ensured that initially they could live in relative comfort while pursuing literary careers, but her mental instability, apparent within a year of their wedding, curtailed her earnings amid increasing medical expenses. *The Village in the Jungle*, written between August 1911 and the following summer, was published to critical acclaim in February 1913 but generated little income. By 1929, over 2,000 copies having been sold, his earnings from the book amounted to only £63. Despite their frugality and disregard for money, they had no obvious means of earning the £400–£500 a year that Leonard calculated as necessary. Journalism seemed a plausible option, and Virginia had already begun to review for the *Times Literary Supplement*, but what was he to write about, and how was he to establish links to periodicals? His Cambridge contemporary R. C. Trevelyan introduced him to the editor of the *TLS*; Leonard asked to review books on industrial questions but was instead sent ones on French poetry. Cambridge had turned him from a budding classical scholar into an aesthete and a decidedly apolitical intellectual. In a paper presented to the Apostles in 1903, he noted that "it would be no unfair charge if anyone summed me up as ignoring politics."[1] The Dreyfus trial appears to have been the only international incident that aroused his indignation. Like others of his generation, and perhaps more pointedly as a Jew, he regarded the victimization of the Jewish French army officer as of cosmic significance for civilized values, comparable to the trial of Socrates or Jesus.[2]

During 1912 and 1913, politics remained peripheral to Leonard's literary ambitions. It was in a Spanish hotel on their honeymoon, in September 1912, that he began his second novel, *The Wise Virgins*, completed in August 1913 but not published until December 1914. Virginia described their work habits in a letter to Violet Dickinson: "All the morning we write in two separate rooms. Leonard is in the middle of a new novel; but as the clock strikes twelve, he begins an article upon Labour for some pale sheet, or a review of French literature for the *Times*, or a history of Co-operation."[3] Later, in 1913, as the manuscript of *The Wise Virgins* was making the rounds of friends, family, and his publisher, Edward Arnold, he toyed with a third novel, provisionally titled "The Empire Builder." It began, he later recalled, "with a boy of 16 kicking a stone along a towpath at Richmond, imagining how the stone, which had lain for years in one spot, suddenly found itself uprooted to a completely new world 50 yards away. Symbolical? Autobiographical? I think it may have been a good beginning, but it never got any further."[4]

All of Leonard's fiction, his short stories as well as his novels, real and projected, dealt with alienation from one's own culture and offered a way to come to terms with his sense of himself as an outsider, caught between two worlds, never quite belonging to either. He felt the need to assert his own identity apart from his Jewish background or as an imperialist who questioned the validity of British domination of a native population. While the content of *The Village in the Jungle* and his *Stories of the East* (1921) derived from his experience in Ceylon, *The Wise Virgins* and "The Three Jews" explored Jewish distinctiveness within the dominant Anglo-Christian culture. It was the hostility of his family, no less than its commercial failure, that undermined his confidence as a novelist and as an interpreter of Anglo-Jewry. Leonard claimed defensively that the onset of war killed the book commercially, but he later refused to reprint it, perhaps out of deference to the misgivings of his mother and siblings. Some years later, however, he did contemplate writing "a revised version of the Wandering Jew," according to Virginia, who found it "very original & solid," but nothing ever materialized.[5] By the time that he finished *The Wise Virgins*, Virginia was in the throes of a serious mental breakdown, during which she attempted suicide. Their joint careers as creative writers had to be put on hold, at least until she recovered her sanity. Her illness, especially during its most acute phase in 1913–14, dominated his life to the point that his own health suffered, as he spent more of his time providing care. As her earnings dwindled and the financial burdens of medical and nursing care mounted, it was incumbent upon him to discover new, more lucrative sources of income than the writing of fiction.

While his years in Ceylon had shaped his views of imperialism, Leonard had returned with a meager understanding of domestic social conditions and even less of a perspective on how to respond to them. His empathy for those under his authority in Ceylon was not readily translated to the disadvantaged at home. During the summer of 1912, before he departed on a two-month continental honeymoon, Virginia's cousin Margaret (Marny) Vaughan inveigled him into working for the Shoreditch Care Committee, an affiliate of the Charity Organisation Society, dispensing relief to the East End poor. It took only two home interviews to convince him that he was unsuited to the role of benevolent philanthropist in Hoxton, whereupon he promptly resigned from the Care Committee and the COS. Imogen Booth, daughter of the great social investigator Charles Booth, had invited Leonard to become secretary of the Hoxton branch, but, as he told, Molly MacCarthy, "I don't much believe in that work after what I saw of it."[6] Shocked by the depths of misery of the inhabitants, he later observed that he "would rather have lived in a hut in a Ceylon village in the jungle than in the poverty stricken, sordid, dilapidated, god-forsaken hovels of Hoxton" (*Beginning*, 100). Later in the year he accepted an invitation from Roger Fry to act as secretary for the second Post-Impressionist Exhibition at the Grafton Galleries, a temporary job that involved dealing with inquiries from prospective buyers and fending off philistine critics. However brief, it seemed preferable to enlisting as a rent collector in the London slums.

What Leonard had witnessed in the East End transformed him from a conventional liberal into a socialist without providing a focus for his burgeoning political convictions. Through the Apostles he had come to know two Llewelyn Davies brothers, friends of the Stephen family. Virginia was also acquainted with their formidable sister, Margaret, the secretary of the Women's Co-operative Guild, who became a mentor and lifelong confidante to Leonard and exposed him to the lives of working-class women in northern England. Starting in August 1912, under Margaret's influence, he wrote a number of unpaid articles for the *Co-operative News* and the *Daily Citizen*, visited industrial towns to learn about cooperative factories and businesses, staying with families, lecturing to local branches, and attending a three-day Women's Co-operative Congress in Newcastle in June 1913. His reports on its deliberations, which appeared in both the *Nation* and the *New Statesman*, attracted the attention of Sidney and Beatrice Webb, who were eager to discover bright young men to enlist in Fabian research projects. In later years he would write numerous pamphlets and several books on the cooperative movement, whose guiding principles remained at the core of his socialist convictions. Having published six articles on scientific management in 1912, mostly in the *Co-operative News*, he broadened his topical scope and periodical audience with twenty-two articles and reviews in 1913 and thirty-two in 1914, while Virginia became a semi-invalid, his work appearing in the *Nation*, the *New Statesman*, *The Times*, the *TLS*, the *Labour Leader*, the *New Weekly*, *War and Peace*, and the *Manchester Guardian*.

In the autumn of 1914, seemingly undaunted by the outbreak of war, Beatrice Webb approached Leonard, who had joined the Fabian Society the previous year, about taking part in the Fabian Research Department's investigation of professional organizations, which would complement the Webbs' earlier books on trade unionism and the cooperative movement. His task would be to gather information about the legal profession in England, America, "and as many of the continental countries as you can get hold of."[7] This material would then be incorporated in their proposed survey, although Beatrice later intimated that Leonard's report might be published as a companion volume. It was never entirely clear whether his role was primarily that of a research assistant or of an independent writer. Remuneration, not mentioned, was no doubt assumed by Leonard, who agreed to the proposal, despite his lack of qualifications, aside from being the son of a barrister and QC. The Fabians seemed to regard any willing neophyte as a potential expert, if given the opportunity to undertake serious research. Plans were, however, overtaken by international events, and Bernard Shaw, still prominent in Fabian circles, persuaded philanthropist Joseph Rowntree to contribute £100 to underwrite a limited inquiry into international mechanisms for the prevention of war. On December 16, less than a month after her first overture to Leonard about the legal profession, Beatrice invited Leonard to undertake the executive role in the inquiry, serving as a secretary to the International Agreements Committee of the Fabian Research Department. This time a fee of £50 (half of the Rowntree grant) was offered as "a small remuneration for the drudgery entailed." As a further enticement, she indicated that the ensuing report would be published by the Fabian Research Department with Leonard identified as author, provisions to which he agreed. He stipulated that nothing should appear over his name of which he was not the author.[8] Somewhat unrealistically, she added a postscript hoping that he might complete his study on the legal profession before tackling international peace.[9] Such was not to be: Leonard scrapped that research in favor of the international project. Initially overwhelmed by the enormity of the task (and the meagerness of the fee), he resolved to resign his commission and substitute a pamphlet on international arbitration.[10] Soon overcoming his trepidations, he moved ahead with dispatch. Virginia noted in her diary on January 26, 1915: "He has already grasped his Arbitration—such is the male mind—& will, I see, go through with it straight off."[11] Within weeks of accepting the offer, he delivered an outline of proposed topics to the committee, largely ignoring Sidney Webb's injunction to avoid proposing alternatives or treating the subject historically. He advised Leonard to confine himself to what could be included in the peace treaty and to exclude what could be done in the future to diminish the frequency of wars.[12] At first he was engaged to prepare a report embodying the results of the committee's work, but this quickly evolved into autonomous research on his part, with the committee offering merely perfunctory oversight. Despite wide disparity of views about the war among members of the International Agreements Committee, they confirmed that the report would be published over Leonard's name, that he would have a free hand as to its scope, and that he would be paid a fee of £100. It was a crucial milestone in his political career and launched what would become his most influential publication.

Although Virginia suffered a relapse in February 1915 that continued through the spring, Leonard forged ahead with his investigation into the causes of war, international treaties, and the history of European conferences and congresses since 1815. As he wrote to Lytton:

> I have been absolutely submerged in Internationalism. The result will I imagine be the lowest pit of dullness. It would make it easier if I knew something about history. I met my "Committee" last week—14 wretched creatures led by the Webbs, Eagle [J. C. Squire], & Shaw. The only thing they did was to pass a resolution that they would not even ask me what I was going to do.[13]

This jocular, self-mocking tone may have more closely reflected his epistolary style to his closest friend than his actual mood. He completed the first part of the project in time for Webb to explicate it to a joint conference of the Fabians and the so-called Bryce Committee, including Leonard's Cambridge friend Goldsworthy Lowes Dickinson, which was also interested in international organization, at Barrow House, near Keswick, in May 1915, and it was published in July as a *New Statesman* special supplement. Years later, reflecting on this period in his autobiography, Leonard noted that "in 1915 I worked like a fanatical or dedicated mole on the sources of my subject, international relations, foreign affairs, the history of war and peace. By 1916 I had a profound knowledge of my subject; I was an authority" (*Beginning*, 185). The difficulty lay in the scarcity of books on the subject. This required original research in Blue Books, White Papers, and annual reports of an array of international organizations from the Universal Postal Union to the International Institute of Agriculture, and interviews with civil servants, representatives of non-governmental bodies, as well as participants in international congresses. His aim was not to prod the government toward peace negotiations, but rather to enlighten officials about the types of institutional machinery available to alleviate the risk of war in the future. This was Fabian research par excellence, involving much of the "drudgery" about which Beatrice had warned, yet, somewhat surprisingly, given his background and ongoing marital travail, he demonstrated extraordinary aptitude for the undertaking.

Once the first report had been published with the title "Suggestions for the Prevention of War," Leonard readily accepted Webb's advice to expand his report into a book by investigating all nongovernmental international associations. They collaborated on the formulation of a treaty to establish a supranational authority to prevent future war and published their proposal a week later in a second *New Statesman* supplement called "Articles Suggested for Adoption by an International Conference at the Termination of the War." Given the alacrity with which he had completed his task, the Fabians urged him to extend his research, offering an additional £100. Challenging the common view that international government neither existed at present, nor could be viable in the future, he elucidated wide areas of human activity that demonstrated cooperation among nations. This inquiry, longer than either of the *New Statesman* supplements and occupying him for much of 1915–16, constituted the most original portion of his book *International Government*, published in July 1916 by the Fabian Society and George Allen & Unwin, incorporating all three parts of the Fabian project. Leonard was listed as sole author, although "a Fabian committee" claimed responsibility for the concluding chapter, essentially the draft treaty devised by Leonard and Sidney Webb. The original plan was for Shaw, as chairman of the Fabian Research Department, to contribute a foreword. He had, after all, been instrumental in promoting the original project by securing the Rowntree subvention. Leonard insisted that the British edition be published without Shaw's contribution "on the ground that, as a young man and writer, I wanted my book to be judged on its merits and defects; it should stand solely on its own legs" (*Beginning*, 123). A year later Allen & Unwin published *The Framework of a Lasting Peace*, with an introduction by Leonard, the Fabian draft treaty written with Webb, and seven alternative schemes put forward by other interest groups for a League of Nations. These differed on such issues as compulsory arbitration and whether a league should comprise all independent nations or only the victorious powers.

In retrospect, Leonard's book was prophetic, anticipating a host of publications by British and American writers that proliferated in the later years of the war. Whatever he hoped would emerge from the conflagration, he proposed only what seemed practicable, leaving aside aspirations toward world government or attempts to undermine the sovereignty of nations. "We must build not a Utopia upon the air or clouds of our own imagination, but a duller and heavier structure placed logically upon the foundations of the existing system" (*International Government*, 8). Nor did he advocate—at least initially—outlawing war, suggesting instead mechanisms for resolving conflicts short of armed struggle. It would be foolhardy to attempt to make war impossible, but it might be rendered less likely: "If war is ever to become an impossibility or even an improbability in the society of nations, there must be in that society a regular, easily working, recognised system of obtaining in *some* kinds of international disputes a judicial decision" (*International Government*, 18). Above all, he tried to persuade readers that his proposals either emulated past settlements or followed current practice in social and professional organizations. International government did not require rigid, centralized structures: it could be flexible and pragmatic, as circumstances warranted.

After tracing the various causes of war—legal, political, territorial, questions of honor—Leonard underscored the importance of international law, contending that the violation of its rules did not constitute proof that they did not exist. Furthermore, "unless there are certain general rules regulating the conduct of nations, a peaceful solution of international differences will always be doubtful" (*International Government*, 12). Although he was writing in wartime, he wanted to show that a rudimentary system of international relations had evolved during the previous century. Its key feature was concerted action to resolve political disputes, which he illustrated by reference to European congresses from Vienna in 1815 to Berlin in 1878 to Algeciras in 1906. Legal disputes should be resolved by tribunals, but, where conflicts stemmed from political disagreements, a special congress would be more appropriate. His underlying assumption was that international conflicts could be settled only by the collective decision of the powers. The reference of political disputes to conferences or arbitration tribunals should be made compulsory, so long as they did not infringe the independence or sovereignty of nations. Within the sphere of its independence, every state "must remain absolute master of its own destiny" (*International Government*, 80). While arbitration might resolve certain disputes, he was skeptical as to whether making it obligatory was feasible. Using Irish Home Rule as an example, he doubted whether the contending parties would be willing to comply with the decision of a court of arbitration. It followed that treaties that bound nations to refer all disputes where negotiation failed to arbitration were "useless and dangerous" (*International Government*, 48). While arbitration had a role in the pacific regulation of conflict, it was not a panacea. If a judicial tribunal were unable to settle a dispute that posed a threat to European peace, reference to an international conference should be made compulsory. This was an alternative to the traditional way of settling disputes: negotiation or war. It also reduced the risk of secret diplomacy, perceived by British radicals as fomenting wars. Little progress could be made "unless the rights of an international majority to bind a minority...are admitted" (*International Government*, 43). Had such a conference taken place in 1914, war among the powers might have been averted. In that crisis, warmongers played upon popular fears, ignorance, and patriotic sentiment. An international authority, however perfunctory, might have proven instrumental in preserving the peace:

> It would allay unreasoning excitement; it would let in the light; it would strengthen the hands of those persons who were working for peace. But perhaps its most potent influence would come from another side. The holding of Conferences whose decisions would be binding...would involve the formal recognition of that principle upon which the future stability of international society depends—the principle that the nations have the right collectively to settle questions which imperil the peace of the world. (*International Government*, 87)

To be sure, much of this was wishful thinking. His notion that lack of machinery to resolve conflicts was a principal cause of war underestimated the role of ideology, propaganda, and power politics. In his mind, international government, rationally organized, could transcend aggressive instincts. He was eventually to modify his faith in reason during the 1930s, as the threat of Fascism loomed over Europe.

The substantial middle section of *International Government* began with the presupposition that international hostility stemmed from popular misconceptions that the interests of one country were inimical to the interests of others. A growing recognition that national interests were also international was the "great social discovery of the last 100 years" (*International Government*, 96). During the course of the nineteenth century, cosmopolitan institutions had begun to proliferate. Participation in international bodies did not imply any sacrifice of national interests, but it might almost imperceptibly restrict sovereignty. Leonard cited not only the emergence of intergovernmental organs, like the Universal Postal Union or the International Telegraphic Union, but also hundreds of voluntary bodies set up to meet specific needs. He enumerated the spontaneous growth of at least 500 international associations to promote social causes, to maintain uniform standards, or to serve the interests of professions. Such bodies might combat the slave trade or prostitution, control maritime safety, improve labor conditions, promote temperance, regulate public health, or focus attention on grievances. Advances in communications, transcending national frontiers, facilitated the organization of international commissions or periodic conferences. He cited science as the most obvious area in which voluntary international societies broke down national barriers that impeded the progress of knowledge. There was, he concluded, "hardly a sphere of life in which a consciousness of international interests had not penetrated, and led to men of every tongue and race joining together to promote those interests" (*International Government*, 106). Integral to the book's theme was the idea that associations of citizens from different countries constituted embryonic forms of international government. Upholding the chimera of sovereignty would impede the intercourse between peoples. To insist upon national legislative autonomy was incompatible with the evolving modern state, which was in "perpetual and intimate and intricate relationship with other states;" there was no "department of life in which their most vital interests and relations [were] not international" (*International Government*, 217). To establish even limited international authority would be a major step toward the elimination of war. These arguments served as a kind of preamble to the more elaborate plans for international organization, constituting the third part of the book and based on the joint initiative by Leonard and Webb that appeared in the *New Statesman* in July 1915.

In order to make their draft treaty appear less objectionable, they limited its goals to what might prove palatable to existing governments. There would be no merging of independent states into a world federation or imposing national disarmament. If nations could not resolve disputes through the projected machinery, they would retain the right to go to war, even at the risk of perpetuating international anarchy. The alternative to war was adherence to law, reinforced through institutions, but they were for the most part voluntary. The key component was an International High Court, to which nations would be obliged to submit legal or justiciable disputes. If a nation refused to accept its judgment, they would be subject to social and economic sanctions. Leonard deliberately ignored the implications of military sanctions in the event that economic ones failed to constrain a recalcitrant state. In principle, the international community might be compelled to enforce its authority by resorting to war, so abhorrent a prospect that he largely discounted it in his formulations. The difficulty of enforcement remained an unresolved dilemma in his work.

Parallel to the court, but not subordinate to it, he advocated an International Council with representatives from some forty or more independent nations that might voluntarily choose to join. An immediate difficulty was that roughly half of these states were in the Western hemisphere, so separate regional councils were proposed for matters touching Europe or America. A further complication was the inequality of nations in power, wealth, and population. The eight Great Powers—Austria–Hungary, the British Empire (perceived as a unit), France, Germany, Italy, Japan, Russia, and the United States—would be permitted to nominate five representatives to the council, while smaller states would be limited to two. Any of the Great Powers had to right to refer a question either to the entire council or the council of the eight. In the International Council, voting power would be weighted so as to ensure preponderant influence to the powers, whereas in the regional and partial bodies states would be treated equally. This cumbersome machinery, envisaging separate proceedings by a Council of the Great Powers or a Council for Europe or for America, as well as by the full International Council, was probably unworkable, since so neat a division of interests rarely occurred. Flexibility was intended to make operations more efficient, to prevent the council from being swamped with problems pertinent only to a specific region. Its primary function was to provide an arena for the amicable settlement of disputes that involved national honor or a vital local interest rather than questions of law, which were the province of the International Court. This scheme presupposed the inclusion of all states, not merely the victorious powers, a goal that did not survive the deliberations over the founding of the League of Nations. Constituent states were, however, bound to avoid committing aggression or violating the territory of other nations for a year after disputes were submitted to the International High Court or the International Council. Coordinating these units was an International Secretariat, whose function would be to organize inquiries, manage funds, and communicate decisions of the court or council to states. What the scheme involved was the establishment of an international civil service both as a counterweight to the machinations of statesmen and to provide stability in the face of shifting political leadership. It was to prove crucial to the operations of a League of Nations.

International Government was not only a visionary tract: it was, like all of Leonard's political writings, polemical and propagandist. He tried to apply Fabian beliefs in regulation to the field of international relations, blaming nationalism and capitalism for the persistence of international anarchy. Arguments against international government had long been couched in terms of allegedly vital national interests, but these turned out to be either the concerns of a small class in one nation pitted against those in another, or those of the capitalist predators against dispossessed working people. Purely national government made it easy for powerful economic forces to delude the populace through specious appeals to patriotism. International government would strengthen the ability of the masses to combat capitalist exploitation, so that the interests of the majority would be advanced, not hindered, with the growth of international institutions. "The world is full of communities which have lost their souls, and they have lost them through war or by conquest. For so long as there is nothing between absolute independence and absolute dependence, the world must be divided between communities which oppress and communities which are oppressed" (*International Government* 230).

Late in 1917, Leonard published a brief study, *The Future of Constantinople*, an offshoot of his larger work. Its radical recommendation for international administration attracted little attention. Coupled with international control of the Straits, internationalization would serve as a guarantee against Russian aggression and a barrier to German military expansion. Instead of perpetuating the system of aggression and imperialism after the war, an International Commission, including the United States, could provide a reasonable probability of security for Russia. A test case of the success of Allied aims, it would avoid exclusive control and offer a practical solution to the conflicting interests of Russia and Turkey after the collapse of the Ottoman Empire. As long as Constantinople and the Straits remained neutralized, under the control of an international authority, the risk of future war in the region would be diminished: "If it can be, and is given to any one State, it means the rule of the world by war; if in the hands of an International Commission it be administered by all for all, Constantinople means the rule of the world by peace."[14]

Published under the aegis of the Fabian Society, *International Government* attracted a limited, but influential, audience and respectful reviews. H. N. Brailsford, journalist and early proponent of a League of Nations, lauded it as "a brilliant book,"[15] and scholars on both sides of the Atlantic cited it throughout the interwar years as a pioneering work. In a lengthy review of several of his publications, the *Athenæum* referred to Leonard as "the ablest of a small group of thinkers and writers who have devoted themselves to the study of International Reconstruction and the League of Nations." In an analysis containing anti-Semitic overtones, the reviewer noted "his shrewd analytical Jewish brain," which had "dissipated many of the mists with which sentimentalists have been allowed to envelop the subject." Even though he performed "the immense service of bringing the whole subject down from the clouds," his conclusions were nonetheless flawed. While he recognized that enemy combatants were unlikely to be reborn as international patriots, his intellectual approach failed to come to terms with national selfishness. A mechanism for preventing war might prove effective in normal times, but it ignored the "deeper moral forces" and provided no security in a crisis.[16]

If *International Government* failed to attract a popular readership, it had considerable influence on policymakers at home and abroad.

Translations of the book appeared in Paris, Stockholm, and Zurich during the peace negotiations, and President Wilson's agent, Edward M. House, supervising the draft American proposals, was known to possess a copy. Sydney Waterlow, Cambridge acquaintance and former suitor of Virginia, now a Foreign Office official employed in the League section under Alfred Zimmern, "lifted almost verbatim" Leonard's arguments in a brief prepared for Lord Robert Cecil, who was formulating the position of the British delegation to the January 1919 peace conference. Cecil incorporated "virtually the whole of Woolf's ideas" into the British draft covenant submitted to Wilson in Paris. According to Philip Noel-Baker, Leonard played a key role "in giving concrete form to the general ideas about a League" and "in launching the conception of the League's technical, social, economic and financial work."[17] Zimmern's Foreign Office memorandum of November 1918 also foregrounded Leonard's views for British negotiators, readily acknowledging "the masterly analysis of Mr Woolf," which "drew attention to the existing international administrative agencies and offices and to the possibility thus opened up for co-ordination and development."[18]

When Leonard first accepted the Webbs' invitation in 1915 to undertake the study, he was scarcely known in radical political circles, with only two novels and a handful of articles on cooperation to his credit. By the time *International Government* appeared, he had become recognized as a leading authority, whose participation in internationalist groups, Fabian research, and Labour Party activities was eagerly sought. He was no longer merely the Webbs' young protégé, a reliable Fabian workhorse who could in a few months acquire expertise, as he had done so adroitly in his investigation of international government. The Fabian Society was a convenient sponsor of his work, but he was never fully committed to its collectivist views on domestic reform. Sidney and Beatrice classified him as "the ex-colonial civil servant," someone to turn to when foreign questions, in which they were not greatly interested, arose. Much to Virginia's relief, he slowly disengaged himself from their clutches while continuing to acknowledge his debt to them. The Women's Co-operative Guild had introduced him to the world of labor, setting the course of his evolution as a socialist, but he ultimately found it too parochial. Indeed, having spent seven years in Ceylon, his preoccupation was always with foreign and imperial affairs in both his journalism and his public activities. In his personal life his friendships were chiefly among Cambridge and Bloomsbury intellectuals, whose interests were mainly artistic and literary.

One exception was Dickinson, a Fellow of King's and an Apostle, who served as his intermediary to pro-League activism. Goldie, as he was known to friends, originally coined the term "League of Nations" and was the dominant figure in the Bryce Group, named for Lord Bryce, Oxford professor and former British Ambassador to the United States. Common goals reignited Leonard's ties to Dickinson through discussions to coordinate plans for an international authority. That collaboration resulted in 1915 in the founding of the League of Nations Society, whose executive committee included Leonard and Goldie. Its objective was to propagandize for a league that would be incorporated into the eventual peace treaty. In 1917 the society arranged a roster of five speakers, among them Leonard, Goldie, and Brailsford, who would follow each other at weekly intervals, delivering lectures in various towns on the idea of the league just as it was beginning to arouse interest. The movement gained momentum from President Wilson's pledge to join a league and to employ American economic and military might against any power making war. Late in 1917, the League of Free Nations Association, an establishment group with greater financial resources, promoting a league based on the Allied War Council but excluding Germany, emerged on the scene. This flew in the face of the society's contention that Germany should join the league from the outset to prevent it from becoming a club of victors. In a letter to the *Nation*, Leonard had protested the insufficient attention paid in the British press to Chancellor Bethmann-Hollweg's pronouncement that Germany, as part of a negotiated peace, was ready to join a union of peoples, an apparent willingness on the part of the enemy to accept "the principles for which we are fighting."[19] In the summer of 1918, as war was winding down, Leonard negotiated terms of amalgamation, which merged the two groups into the League of Nations Union. A compromise formula declared that Germany must eventually enter the league but not until it had fully democratized. Leonard was elected to the Executive Council of the Union and later to its research committee, but *International Government* remained his most substantive contribution to the league movement in Britain.

Goldie also linked him to the radical founders of the Union of Democratic Control, men of the left, such as Brailsford, Hobson, E. D. Morel, and Norman Angell, who had never succumbed to the Fabian embrace. He persuaded Leonard to enlist in the effort to secure parliamentary control over British foreign policy by becoming a member of the Union of Democratic Control (UDC) in November 1915. In the spring of 1917, celebrating the hopeful early phase of the Russian Revolution, Leonard joined a handful of other activists to establish the left-wing 1917 Club, financed by Maynard Keynes, in a building in Gerrard Street, Soho. Among the founders were prominent UDC and Independent Labour Party figures, including Ramsay MacDonald. In due course its radical orientation was superseded by a more bohemian element, including Virginia and Strachey, actors and artists, dissipating the political tone. Leonard, of course, easily straddled both groups, and, while generally refusing to join clubs, he enjoyed the ambience of the 1917.

For British radicals, the overthrow of the Czarist regime offered a moment of optimism amid the horrors of the First World War. Leonard's own exhilaration recalled his sentiments when Dreyfus was exonerated earlier in the century. He served as a delegate of his local branch of the Independent Labour Party to the Leeds conference in June 1917, convened by party and trade-union leaders to extol the Russian Revolution as an example for socialism in Britain. It was a high point of pro-revolutionary agitation in Labour circles, much of which evaporated rapidly after the Bolshevik takeover. Although he refused to sanction British intervention in the Russian civil war, Leonard developed an antipathy toward the policies adopted by Lenin. His ambivalence in the 1920s yielded to outspoken hostility once Stalin came to power. As he commented to Margaret Llewelyn Davies: "I hope you don't think I'm anti-Bolshevik. I'm not. I think they're the only people who've made an honest and serious attempt to practice what I believe in. But I cant help seeing their faults & mistakes which, if persisted in, will undo the good they've done."[20]

As well as reviewing books on foreign affairs regularly for the *New Statesman*, he joined the editorial committee of Angell's monthly magazine *War and Peace* in 1916, temporarily replacing its editor in December 1917. In addition, for a brief time, he served as lobby correspondent for the Independent Labour Party's *Labour Leader* until MacDonald complained of Leonard's failure to devote enough coverage to party leaders. When *War and Peace* became a supplement of the *Nation*, he attempted to transform it into an international socialist review with European, as well as British, contributors. He sought endorsements from Belgian socialist Camille Huysmans and British leaders, such as MacDonald, Arthur Henderson, the Webbs, and Robert Smillie, head of the Miners' Union. All concurred, except the devious MacDonald, who may have viewed it as a potential competitor to his *Socialist Review*. Arnold Rowntree agreed to finance a less ambitious publication, with Leonard as editor but without the abortive international editorial board. "Rowntree had been greatly bitten by my scheme for a *Review*," he told Lytton, "& will certainly finance it unless the expense proves too terrific."[21] In December 1918 the *International Review* began to circulate but survived only thirteen months. In addition to editing, Leonard contributed an "International Diary," treating crucial topics of the day, and a documentary section. Regrettably, the *International Review* incurred mounting financial losses, which Rowntree was unwilling to sustain. He did, however, offer Leonard the editorship of a new international section of the established monthly *Contemporary Review*, to continue the kind of documentary journalism that he had pioneered earlier. He needed to find material inadequately covered in newspapers but soon became frustrated with the constraints and space limitations. In 1922 he resigned from the *Contemporary Review* to become political editor of the *Nation*, replacing Brailsford, recently appointed editor of the *New Leader*. This seemed a promotion on the journalistic ladder, a testament to his growing reputation. Within a few months, however, the situation had changed: H. W. Massingham, longtime *Nation* editor, had fallen out of favor with the Rowntrees, mainly because his allegiance was shifting from Liberals to Labour in the 1920s. They decided to sell the paper, and, when Massingham failed to raise sufficient funds to buy it himself, a consortium headed by Keynes took over, with economist Hubert Henderson assuming the editorship. When Keynes offered him a choice of roles, Leonard opted for the position of literary editor (after T. S. Eliot had declined it) from April 1923, indicating that he would relinquish the foreign affairs leader, despite Keynes's plea to continue. His assignment was to write a weekly 1,200-word review article ("the World of Books") and to oversee the literary pages, spending two and a half days in the *Nation* office every week at a salary of £500 per annum. It was a curious decision for him to take, since international relations had become his forte, the area in which his expertise was acknowledged, but he may have feared that his socialist proclivities would not sit easily with Keynes's avowed Liberalism. Still, he had never abandoned his literary interests, now given scope in the Hogarth Press and in his cultivation of reviewers among young *literati*. As he confided to Strachey:

> I expect you have heard that, having failed as (a) a civil servant, (b) a novelist, (c) an editor, (d) a publicist, I have now sunk to the last rung... —literary journalism. I am now Literary Editor of *The Nation and Athenæum*, and I would not even have sunk to that, if I had not been told that you had agreed to write for it...[22]

After Webb and Henderson had drafted a new constitution for the Labour Party in 1918, reflecting its national ambitions, they proposed several advisory committees to provide expert advice to the bulk of working-class MPs, whose knowledge of foreign and domestic issues was often deficient. Leonard may even have suggested the idea to Webb, who promptly invited him to become secretary of an Advisory Committee on International Questions. (ACIntQ). Although soon replaced by Charles Roden Buxton, Webb was initially designated as chairman. The two had collaborated in the past, but it was obvious that Leonard was destined to become the facilitator and dominant figure, since Webb was untutored in foreign relations. Confirming Leonard's appointment, Henderson charged the committee with advising the Labour Executive "through me" about current international developments.[23] He may have been trying to provide a back channel for the committee, whereas it saw its function as helping to formulate a democratic foreign policy, a substantial innovation in the way that parliamentary government operated. It was to find that influencing foreign policy was less straightforward than anticipated, even during the very few interwar years when Labour was in power. Leonard served as secretary from 1918 to 1939 and again after it was reconstituted late in the Second World War, retiring only in 1946. He was predictably industrious, drafting minutes, producing memoranda, and coordinating the committee's various inquiries. The ACIntQ, which met weekly in a committee room of the House of Commons, comprised a number of experts drawn from retired civil servants, journalists, and regional specialists, many of whom had been active in the Bryce Group or the UDC. The countless memoranda and reports produced were impressive for the information gathered, but their impact did not live up to expectations. Some Labour MPs attended its meetings, gaining new insight into foreign or imperial problems, valuable training for eventual office. It would not be incorrect to conclude that the ACIntQ was more effective in its advisory and propaganda role than in policy formulation. While the Labour Executive rarely interfered, the committee jealously guarded its autonomy, especially when MacDonald, who perceived it as an irritant, sought to circumvent the proffered advice. Henderson, on the other hand, was far more supportive, welcoming its counsel, even when unable to implement its proposals.

At the outset the ACIntQ was preoccupied with the peace settlement and the establishment of the League of Nations. Its fear was that the League, dominated by Britain and France and without a balancing American presence, would simply perpetuate traditional diplomacy rather than embody a new order. Leonard had warned that, for the League to prove an effective agent of peace, it could not be merely a forum for the victorious allies. The chances for economic recovery, fundamental to a restored European comity, had been compromised by the harsh conditions imposed on Germany. The ACIntQ conceded that Germany should make some restitution to Belgium, but Leonard proposed that an international commission should settle claims with any additional reparations payments coming from an international fund.[24] His denunciation of the peace terms anticipated Keynes's incendiary *Economic Consequences of the Peace*. In a blatantly anti-French leader in the *International Review* in June 1919, he fulminated that "it is not a peace but a truce in the armed struggle between Latin and German." At its core were "vindictive punishment, subjection and economic discrimination."[25] He was less critical of the League's structure than some on the British left, because, at least functionally, the council, court, and secretariat closely approximated his earlier guidelines. Softening his tone in an anonymous article a month later, he observed that "the League is not quite so bad a League as the peace is a bad peace." Since the covenant incorporated Wilsonian principles, the League marked "an enormous advance in international relations."[26] An ACIntQ memorandum in July, probably drafted by Leonard, recommended extending equality of opportunity to all colonies, with Germany included as a mandatory power, and the establishment of a World Economic Council to manage the distribution of food and raw materials and prevent international profiteering.[27]

These themes recur consistently in his articles and memoranda through the early 1920s. A 1922 draft resolution condemned a treaty of alliance with France or even a limited guarantee against German aggression as inimical to an inclusive League of Nations.[28] Before shifting his focus entirely to the literary side of the *Nation*, Leonard wrote a series of vituperative leaders in response to the French occupation of the Ruhr in January 1923. The British should "wash our hands of Reparations and resign all claims under the Treaty."[29] The government should not only refer French actions to the League Council for consideration, but should "make it perfectly clear to France that, short of arms, we shall use every instrument available to oppose her present policy."[30] Inaction by the Council confirmed his fears that the League was proving ineffective in the face of Great Power provocation. This did not, however, foreshadow a diminution of the pro-League policy within the ACIntQ. Leonard never hesitated to suggest reforms of the covenant, while reiterating that the League must remain the cornerstone of Labour's foreign policy. Although *International Government* had alluded to the limits of arbitration, Leonard and Will Arnold-Forster sketched out a plan in 1927 for a system of arbitration in non-legal disputes, moving beyond the League formula for conciliation. The cumbersome procedure was never adopted and, in any event, depended on a willingness of the parties to renounce war.[31] When *Labour and the Nation*, the party's campaign manifesto, masterminded by Henderson, appeared in 1928, its international policy section was largely written by Leonard and Noel-Baker. Doubtlessly the result of compromise, it called for disarmament and arbitration without mentioning economic or military sanctions. Instead, it reflected an increasingly tenuous reliance on the League: "the whole structure of peace and of a foreign policy of cooperation must be built on the foundation of the League of Nations."[32]

His years as literary editor of the *Nation* were never free of tension that ultimately led to his resignation in 1930. Leonard wanted autonomy in choosing his reviewers, but Hubert Henderson, irritated by the flippant style of younger critics, such as George ("Dadie") Rylands and Raymond Mortimer, tried unsuccessfully to veto their employment. In addition, Leonard complained that Keynes was "materially deteriorating the literary side" of the weekly in 1924 by focusing more on politics to serve the interests of the faltering Liberal Party, while its competitor, the *New Statesman*, was enhancing its literary section at the expense of the political.[33] The literary pages of the *Nation* benefited from his dual role as editor and publisher, with his retinue of Hogarth authors. Conversely, the magazine's reviews uncovered potential authors for the press. But the grind of a weekly column on books, sometimes on performances or recordings, took its toll, and the job became increasingly tedious. These columns revealed the breadth of Leonard's reading and his admirable skill as a reviewer. Increasingly restive, he informed Keynes in 1927 that he intended to relinquish the editorship, but a compromise was devised: he would spend less time in the office and accept a pay reduction to £250. Finally, at the end of 1930, he quit as literary editor, vowing "never again to take a full time journalistic job" (*Beginning*, 132). His work as literary editor confirmed "the corroding and eroding effect of journalism upon the human mind" (*Downhill*, 128). Financially, the decision was facilitated by Virginia's commercial success with *To the Lighthouse* (1927) and *Orlando* (1928). The Woolfs—especially during this period of mental stability for Virginia—could now more easily afford to rely on income from the Hogarth Press, their books (mainly Virginia's), and occasional articles or reviews.

In 1927, William Robson, a young member of the LSE teaching staff, conceived the idea of a progressive political quarterly and approached his colleague, Kingsley Martin, on the verge of becoming a *Manchester Guardian* leader writer, as a potential collaborator. Shaw contributed £1,000 to launch the journal, and a small organizing committee, which included Leonard, Keynes, and Harold Laski, was set up. The social historian and journalist J. L. Hammond was approached to become editor, but he declined, even when offered a joint editorship with Leonard, who had been sounded out as to his availability. Leonard was willing to serve as joint editor, but, in the event, Robson and Martin were appointed, despite the fact that the latter was then living in Manchester, and the *Political Quarterly* began publication in January 1930. When Martin wrote to express discomfort about displacing him, Leonard responded courteously:

> There is no need for you to feel bad. I always tell the truth unless there is a very good reason for telling a lie, and in this case there was no reason for me to do so. The *Quarterly* interests me, and I like having a finger in interesting pies, but as I said (truthfully) I have not really the time for it and was glad to get out of it for that reason.[34]

This was not completely accurate: Leonard had not withdrawn his name from consideration, in case the committee had second thoughts about Martin, who had a reputation for impetuosity. In the autumn of 1930, Martin, fired by the *Manchester Guardian*, returned to London and was almost immediately offered the editorship of the *New Statesman*, about to be amalgamated with the *Nation*. Since it would have been impossible to edit a weekly review and a quarterly periodical simultaneously, Martin withdrew from the *Political Quarterly* after only one year and was succeeded by Leonard, who served as joint editor with Robson until 1958 and continued on the editorial board until his death.[35] The two worked harmoniously, with Leonard acting as sole editor from 1940 to 1945, while Robson was involved in war work. Willie (as he was known) became one of his closest friends during the years they shared editorial duties, as well as one of his few Jewish associates. Virginia regarded him as pedantic, but Leonard cherished their relationship. He discovered that co-editing a quarterly review was far less onerous than filling the literary pages of a weekly magazine. It also provided a vehicle for his own commentaries on international affairs: between 1930 and 1945 he published fourteen substantial essays on a range of topics, thoughtful analyses of the world scene that provided greater scope than allowed in brief articles for the *New Statesman*, to which he continued to contribute throughout Martin's editorship.

Leonard had little to add in the 1920s to his earlier work on international government, aside from the strongly pro-League foreign-policy section of *Labour and the Nation*. His first contribution to the *Political Quarterly* in 1930 was an assessment of the League and foreign affairs since the end of the First World War. He contrasted the old spirit of national rivalry, symbolized by Sarajevo, with the new internationalist spirit embodied in Geneva, the headquarters of the

League. The war had undermined the appeal of nationalism, although it had dictated much of the peace settlement. The framework of a new Europe was reconstructed as though the new international psychology had not penetrated the minds of statesmen. Even so, French troops had evacuated the Rhineland and a reparations agreement was in the works. The remarkable fact was "the unexpected strength and position developed by the League in the short time of its existence." It had become "a visible rallying point and focus of internationalism." In his 1916 tract he had tried to demonstrate how national interests had become internationalized through the proliferation of organizations. Now, as he surveyed the activities of the League, he could conclude that "in the every-day internationalism of European society Geneva and the League are already playing a dominant part." In shouldering many of the burdens of post-war Europe, the League had achieved a level of stability "which it could not possibly have won in ten years if it had merely remained an instrument to be used in emergencies for preventing war and for the pacific settlement of international disputes." It was becoming what he had not dared to imagine—or to express—in 1916: a "Super-State in embryo." All that was lacking was the growth of international psychology, which was "still weak, vacillating, and uninstructed."[36] Nationalist passions survived as a perpetual menace to the emergence of a civilized system of international relationships. An ominous portent was the refusal of the Conservative government in Britain to sign the so-called Optional Clause requiring that justiciable disputes be submitted to arbitration. This implied that Tory politicians were still wedded to traditional diplomacy, leaving each nation the judge of its own self-interest, impervious to the needs of the world community. He underscored the absurdity of imagining that nationalist psychology was compatible with a League system.

By the beginning of 1933, Leonard's prognosis was far gloomier. He noted a recrudescence of virulent nationalism and militarism, especially in Germany. The League had failed to deal with Japanese aggression in Manchuria, and the persistence of unregulated armaments provided neither peace nor security. The choice for the Great Powers was clear: as long as they obstructed efforts at general disarmament, it was futile to expect an international system based on the League to develop. What was needed was for every state to commit itself to aid victims of aggression. Nor was Britain's refusal to surrender its naval dominance entirely the fault of the National Government. Public opinion was also culpable: pacifists on the left refused to face up to the dilemma posed by collective security. They might endorse a League-oriented foreign policy, but not at the price of resisting aggressors. "If we want to know where to place the blame for the League's failure, we must look to the governments of the Great Powers and to the people who send nationalist governments to Geneva."[37] Even Leonard had not fully resolved the dilemma for himself: was pooled security compatible with general disarmament? Nations should meet their obligations to resist aggression, but how were they to do so if stripped of their weapons? A move toward a League military force under international command was nowhere on the horizon. The ACIntQ was hardly more resolute, concluding that alternatives to supporting the League were even less plausible once Hitler came to power. Distrust of national armaments blocked any move towards providing the League with adequate resources to combat aggression. While the League's record since 1930 was abysmal, unless there was some kind of system, like the League, "another large-scale war in Europe is sooner or later inevitable."[38] Robson described this article, ostensibly about Henderson's tract *Labour's Foreign Policy*, as "profoundly disturbing, utterly realistic and merciless in its analysis of the inevitable consequence of the failure of the League."[39] Still clinging to the League and the goal of collective security, Leonard was not yet ready to resort to sanctions and risk armed conflict. Even after the Nazis had come to power, he advocated revision of Article 231 of the Versailles Treaty to assuage German sentiment over the war guilt clause and sought ways, perhaps through the mandate system, to respond to Germany's colonial grievances. Within a few years, however, his attitude began to shift, as League impotence and the menace of Hitler became indubitable. He was frustrated by the weakness of the party and the trade-union movement in facing up to growing international threats, yet his commitment to the movement never wavered. However divided its views and inconsistent its policies, Labour's values were ones he fostered in his writings and organizational activities. In addition to the ACIntQ, he was appointed to the Executive Committee of the New Fabian Research Bureau and became head of its International Section. He had acquired a reputation for sound judgment and political integrity, a man to be trusted in perilous times.

Notes

1. Quoted in Spotts, 12.
2. Lord Annan remarked that the Armenian massacres and the Dreyfus affair "gave Woolf his vision of what justice and mercy meant in this world" (Noel Annan, "Leonard Woolf's Autobiography," *Political Quarterly* (January–March 1970), 36).
3. 11 April 1913, VW, *Letters*, ii. 23.
4. LW to William Plomer, 12 August 1968, Spotts, 568.
5. VW, *Diary*, 17 April 1921, ii. 111.
6. LW to Molly MacCarthy, 28 September 1912, VW, *Letters*, ii. 8.
7. Beatrice Webb to LW, 23 November 1914, *Letters of Sidney and Beatrice Webb*, iii. 44.
8. LW to Beatrice Webb, 21 December 1914, Spotts, 384.
9. Beatrice Webb to LW, 16 December 1914, *Letters of Sidney and Beatrice Webb*, iii. 45–6.
10. VW, *Diary*, 18 January 1915, i. 22.
11. VW, *Diary*, i. 28.
12. Sidney Webb to LW, 21 January 1915, *Letters of Sidney and Beatrice Webb*, iii. 46–7.
13. LW to Lytton Strachey, 8 February 1915, Spotts, 385.
14. *The Future of Constantinople* (1916), 107.
15. H. N. Brailsford, *A League of Nations* (London: Headley Bros., 1917), 317.
16. *Athenæum* (November 1917).
17. Obituary by Philip Noel-Baker, *The Times*, 21 August 1969.
18. Alfred Zimmern, *The League of Nations and the Rule of Law, 1918–1935* (London: Macmillan, 1936), 171.
19. *Nation*, 2 December 1916.
20. LW to Margaret Llewelyn Davies, 5 April 1920, Monks House Papers, University of Sussex.
21. LW to Lytton Strachey, 6 May 1918, Spotts, 278.
22. LW to Lytton Strachey, 4 May 1923, Spotts, 283.
23. Arthur Henderson to LW, 26 March 1918, LW Papers.
24. ACIntQ, Memorandum No. 37, November 1918.
25. *International Review* (June 1919).
26. *International Review* (July 1919).
27. ACIntQ, Memorandum No. 69, July 1919.
28. ACIntQ, Memorandum No. 223, 1922.

29. *Nation & Athenæum*, 13 January 1923.
30. *Nation & Athenæum*, 3 February 1923.
31. ACIntQ, Memorandum No. 355a, 1927.
32. *Labour and the Nation* (London: Labour Party, 1928), 41.
33. LW to J. M. Keynes, 13 December 1924, Spotts, 290–1.
34. LW to Kingsley Martin, 26 July 1929, Spotts, 300–1.
35. This account is based on William Robson, "The Founding of *The Political Quarterly*," in Andrew Gamble and Tony Wright (eds), *The Progressive Tradition: Eighty Years of The Political Quarterly* (2011), 2–15.
36. "From Serajevo [sic] to Geneva," *Political Quarterly* (April–June 1930), 191–2, 195, 197.
37. "From Geneva to the Next War," *Political Quarterly* (January–March 1933), 42.
38. "Labour's Foreign Policy," *Political Quarterly* (October–December 1933), 508.
39. William A. Robson (ed.), *The Political Quarterly in the Thirties* (1971), 21.

6
Anti-Imperialist

In *Growing*, published in 1961, Leonard reflected on his experience as a colonial official and his ultimate disenchantment with the imperial project. Starting as a 24-year old cadet, he describes himself as a "very innocent, unconscious imperialist" (*Growing*, 25) who came to enjoy his position of authority and "the flattery of being the great man and father of his people" (*Growing*, 158). His extraordinary diligence earned both praise from his superiors and occasional communal hostility. He tried to be both strict and fair, an enforcer of regulations, perhaps in the manner of a public-school prefect, a model familiar to the St Paul's graduate in dealings with subordinates. Ambitious for success, he prided himself on his efficiency and relentless work ethic. While tolerating the formulaic sociability of the tiny British community—tennis, bridge, and gin—Leonard was contemptuous of his feckless compatriots in this colonial backwater. To alleviate his loneliness, he immersed himself in the duties of his job, riding on horseback to distant parts to hear complaints and resolve disputes. In time he "fell in love with the country, the people, and the way of life" (*Growing*, 180), so alien to the elite British culture that he had forsaken in 1904. His fascination with Ceylon increased along with his administrative responsibilities, especially after he became Assistant Government Agent in Hambantota, exerting authority over 100,000 people: "the more remote that life was from my own, the more absorbed I became in it and the more I enjoyed it" (*Growing*, 225). An exemplar of empire, he was genuinely dedicated to the welfare of those he governed, his eagerness for professional advancement notwithstanding.

To believe that by 1911 Leonard had become convinced that the people of Ceylon ought to be allowed to govern themselves strains credulity,[1] although he conceded that "the Europeanizing of non-Europeans is a mistake" (*Growing*, 157). He had come to realize that villagers regarded him as "part of a white man's machine which they did not understand,"[2] but never doubted that his rule was benevolent and that the Sinhalese and Tamils still required the expertise that colonial administrators could furnish. Local headmen were notoriously corrupt, and representative institutions were non-existent. While somewhat disillusioned with the imperial mission, he clung to the paternalist values of British progressives: advanced European nations had a moral duty to monitor the development of inferior races through sound governance. When asserting that he "disapproved of imperialism and felt sure its days were already numbered" (*Growing*, 248), he was writing with the hindsight of half a century of anti-imperial propaganda, including his own contributions. Leonard's altered perspective developed gradually in London, not in Ceylon, stemming more from research into exploitation in Africa than from first-hand knowledge. As Peter Wilson has observed: "It was not the raw experience that led to his radicalization, but rather the radicalization that led him to reconstruct his experience of the previous decade."[3] Aside from occasional outpourings of frustration to Strachey, there is scant evidence of dissatisfaction with imperial hegemony while he was in Ceylon. What motivated his request for leave and eventual resignation from the colonial service was a disheartening isolation and homesickness, aftereffects of bouts of malaria,[4] typhoid fever, and eczema, and the hope, at the age of 31, of married life.

Ceylon intruded on his life in London unexpectedly in 1915, after riots broke out in Kandy and Colombo. Denouncing the outbreak as seditious, British officials imposed martial law, condemning scores of participants to death. In contrast, Leonard saw it as another manifestation of internecine conflict endemic in Ceylon. When the Sinhalese sent a deputation to England to oppose government measures and demand an impartial inquiry, they appealed to him to mobilize activity on their behalf. His attempts to initiate parliamentary action through Philip Morrell and Ramsay MacDonald in 1917 proved futile. The Anti-Slavery and Aborigines Protection Society sent a delegation to the Colonial Office in January 1918, including Leonard, who interceded on behalf of the Sinhalese, but its plea was rejected. In November he submitted a note to the Advisory Committee on International Questions (ACIntQ), urging the government "to give the same measure of responsible government to Ceylon as it gives to India." The Sinhalese were the equals of the peoples of India in education and political capacity. To concede measures of self-government to India but not to Ceylon would be "grotesque and impossible."[5] The denial of these claims helped to foster his anti-imperial inclinations, which grew apace during the years in which he wrote about empire.

In 1916 Leonard was enjoying the notoriety achieved after the publication of *International Government*, acclaimed on both sides of the Atlantic. Sidney Webb approached him about undertaking a parallel study, this time on the movements of international trade, about which Leonard's knowledge was meager. After imposing several stipulations, he signed a contract with the Fabian Society in February 1917 but soon found the subject overwhelming. In October, with Webb's encouragement, he shifted the scope to imperial trade and exploitation with a focus on Africa. Here again he had leapt into a project with insufficient preparation. It required intensive research, facilitated by the assistance of Virginia and Alix Sargant-Florence, who copied out statistics and consular reports borrowed from the London School of Economics library. Little had been written on the subject, aside from the polemical critiques of Hobson and Brailsford,[6] and published material was not always easy to come by. When he appealed to his Fabian sponsors for advice, Webb told him: "We have none of us practical knowledge. As to methods and scope we must leave it to you."[7] Leonard had to educate himself, delving into company balance sheets, trade figures, and annual reports, with few signposts to guide him. How to evaluate disparate sources from several imperial powers proved a monumental undertaking that occupied him for almost a year and a half, but he managed to complete the manuscript by February 1919, writing his daily complement of 500 words. Virginia noted in March that Webb "finds his book a most remarkable piece of work" and expected it to be published in June.[8] *Empire and Commerce in Africa* ultimately appeared in January 1920, George Allen & Unwin again serving as his publisher in association with the newly formed Labour Research Department.

If *International Government* established Leonard's reputation as a proponent of the League of Nations, the voluminous *Empire and Commerce in Africa* transformed him into Labour's pre-eminent critic of empire. As Hobson had done, he contended that the motive behind imperialism was primarily economic: both authors regarded imperialism as a conspiracy of international financiers seeking profit in Africa and elsewhere and pressuring governments into acquiring territory. However, unlike Hobson, Leonard supplied a mass of empirical data to underpin his argument, making his book an essential source for the incipient anti-colonial movement in Britain. Hobson had visited Africa before writing his seminal *Imperialism: A Study* (1902) as a journalist for the *Manchester Guardian*, covering the South African war. Leonard never went to Africa, but his credentials as an analyst of empire were burnished by his years as a colonial official. No other figure in the interwar Labour Party, aside from Sydney Olivier, sometime Governor of Jamaica, had as much first-hand experience of a British colony. From his vantage point as secretary of the ACIntQ, he was instrumental in formulating policy, his position enhanced further when a separate Advisory Committee on Imperial Questions (ACImpQ) was established in 1924 with Leonard serving as its secretary as well. He had suggested to Webb as early as 1918 that a separate committee to address colonial questions might be appropriate, but it was not until Labour gained office for the first time that the need for expertise on imperial affairs became apparent. Thereafter most of his political activity centered on efforts to institute reforms and guide subject peoples to self-government. He was ahead of most of the party leaders, as well as the trade-union movement, in advocating independence for India, Ceylon, Egypt, and Ireland after the First World War. Virtually every party document on the empire issued from the 1920s to the 1940s bore his imprint. If he did not actually draft them, as he did with several key manifestos, he was responsible for piloting them through the committee and ensuring that they reached the party executive. The composition of the ACImpQ shifted over time, but for more than two decades his commitment was unflagging, and he endured the bi-weekly meetings without complaint.

Leonard's treatment of Africa was selective, most likely determined by available material. As he had done in *International Government*, he provided a laborious historical narrative of the partition of Africa by competing European powers after 1880. Germany, France, and Britain had taken what they wanted, incorporating territories within their empires. It was, he claimed, "the policy of grab." This might be rationalized by imperialists on the grounds that "for the good of the world the 'uncivilized' must be placed openly and completely in the power and under the government of the 'civilized'" (*Empire*, 54–5). He concentrated particularly on the European encroachment in Abyssinia and the British annexation of Uganda. Analyzing the conquest of Algeria, Tripoli, and the Congo enabled him also to include the expansion of France, Italy, and Belgium, but his examples stressed similarity rather than national differences. In his general indictment he found Britain less culpable: "as regards murder, robbery, savagery, and dishonesty in Africa, our record is better than that of any other State of Europe" (*Empire*, 256). His assessment of tropical Africa discounted strategic or idealistic motives and exaggerated official reluctance to annex more territory. He did concede that in Egypt, Tunis, Tripoli, and Morocco economic motives merged with considerations of strategy and balance of power. Misled by propaganda generated by company directors and colonial secretaries, European governments imagined that acquiring undeveloped land in Africa would provide economic advantage over their rivals. By 1900 almost all of Africa, much of it virtually inaccessible, had been incorporated into European empires. For Leonard, a consistent advocate of better conditions for subject peoples, the scramble for Africa was nothing less than a crime against humanity:

> European civilization, through the machinery of State and trade, has carried some considerable benefits into Africa; but the autocratic dominion of European over African has been accompanied by such horrible cruelty, exploitation, and injustice, that it is difficult not to believe that the balance of good in the world would have been and would be infinitely greater, if the European and his State had never entered Africa. (*Empire*, 259)

Even so, while he decried the impact of European conquest, he did not believe that jettisoning ill-gotten territorial gains was the answer. Since Africa was inhabited mainly by "non-adult races," the native population needed protection from "the cruel exploitation of irresponsible white men." Oversight by European governments was preferable to the excesses of landowners and financiers, except perhaps in the Belgian Congo. "No change for the better would be brought about by the European State withdrawing its control. Economic imperialism has itself created conditions in which that control must inevitably continue" (*Empire*, 357–8). Imperial powers should make amends in the twentieth century for reprehensible conduct in the nineteenth. The case studies of annexed African territories, laden with historical detail about colonial adventurers and statesmen, were less compelling than Leonard's efforts to prove that the economic benefits of imperialism were largely illusory. He doubted whether the possession of an African empire had added either to the power or to the wealth of any European nation. Further, the use of military force in Africa in support of economic interests had hampered international relations, the consequences of which became apparent in 1914. The lesson to be drawn was that, "so long as policy is dominated by this hostility and competition of economic imperialism, and the power of the State is controlled and directed by the profit-making desires, there can be internationally no stability or security, no real harmony or co-operation" (*Empire*, 321).

He employed statistical evidence to show that British East Africa was of negligible value to British industry, either as a source of raw materials or as a market for manufactures. Some Englishmen—financiers or planters—had made or lost fortunes, but trade and industry reaped little profit. The poverty of African natives curtailed their demand for British manufactures, while the infrastructure required to extract minerals was lacking. The totality of its East Africa holdings supplied a mere 1 percent of British imports and consumed only 1 percent of British exports (*Empire*, 331–4). French North African colonies were scarcely more lucrative: Algeria and Tunis together took 11 percent of French exports (*Empire*, 329). Germany and the United Kingdom were far more important for French commerce than the whole of its African empire. "Nothing could show more clearly," he declared, "that the economic beliefs behind economic imperialism are dreams and delusions" (*Empire*, 330). Nor was it possible for any imperial state to reserve colonial products for its own industries: capitalists sold wherever they found buyers. European powers exported more to and imported more from each other than from their colonies, negating the justification for seizing African lands in order to supply raw materials and markets for manufactured goods.

As for the general effects of imperial policy in Africa, these, in Leonard's judgment, "have been almost wholly evil." In bitter competition before 1914, European states ruthlessly appropriated lands to which they had no justifiable claim. "By fraud or by force the native chiefs and rulers were swindled or robbed of their dominions" (*Empire*, 352–3). Unless the principles of the League Covenant were applied to Africa, especially the concept of trusteeship, the "black non-adult races will remain subject to the autocratic government of alien white men" (*Empire*, 356). In a first intimation of ideas he was to develop in later writings, Leonard envisaged imperial government of African colonies yielding to international control, perhaps by means of a mandate system, making imperial powers accountable to the league for their administration of colonies. For Europe to become a force for good, a social revolution was necessary to replace "the ideal of profit-making and buying cheap and selling dear" (*Empire*, 361) with a goal of serving the Africans, reserving land for the natives, and providing education to enable them ultimately to govern themselves. Although Leonard continued to reiterate stereotypes about racial inferiority in Africa—using terms such as backward, primitive, and non-adult—he could embrace anti-imperialism while still promoting enlightened administration by colonial officials. In describing the varieties of subject peoples, he compared "highly civilized Chinese or Indians" with "African savages who have never risen above a primitive tribal organization of society."[9] Racial inferiority was not innate among African natives; rather it was the social consequence of economic exploitation and ignorance. His targets were the white oppressors, not the disinterested experts who sought to address their needs. The ultimate aim was the welfare of colonial subjects, but for the foreseeable future this required imperial administrators to control the process, gradually introducing as much self-government as each territory was prepared to receive. In truth, this was a forward-looking colonial policy rather than an anti-imperialist one. Injecting a moral purpose justified continued imperial control, and if European powers declined to assume the burden, then international authorities must supplant them. Since the league was not yet capable of internationalizing Africa, transferring trusteeship over the non-adult races to mandatory states might prove a feasible alternative. The trouble was that "the Western world has no belief in or desire for trusteeship. Europe will continue to pursue its own economic interests, and not the interests of the natives in Africa" (*Empire*, 366). Even though subsequent critics refuted his perspective, *Empire and Commerce* was hailed as a landmark in the historiography of imperialism.

Later in 1920 Leonard managed to condense his findings in a brief volume in a series of international handbooks, edited by Dickinson, under the title *Economic Imperialism*. It allowed him to extend his analysis to Asia but also to modify his mono-causal explanation for imperialism. Economic beliefs and desires "supplied the original motive power which set in motion the power of the State" (*Economic Imperialism*, 34). If the initial impulse came from financiers and joint-stock companies, he now conceded that moral, sentimental, and strategic factors, while not fundamental, helped to generate popular support for retaining empire. Here we find the first hints of his later preoccupation with "communal psychology." In the competition for commercial advantage, China too was subjected to exploitation, but mainly through railway or mining concessions. In contrast to Africa, China resisted Western encroachment in a desperate clash of civilizations that produced economic chaos and political anarchy. Looking to the future, he warned that neither Africans nor Asians would submit indefinitely to European despotism, their hostility destined to increase with the passing years (*Economic Imperialism*, 103). Once again, he hoped the League might help subject peoples adapt to the modern world. China and other Asian countries were already capable of governing themselves, provided they received guidance and technical assistance from the West.

In principle, the idea of consigning former German and Ottoman colonies to the trusteeship of the victorious powers seemed like a propitious change, as long as they were not simply subjected to British or French tyranny. Leonard's view of mandates oscillated between suspicion that they were a sham, concealing exploitation by the mandatory nations, and hope for their potential to dismantle European empires. The subject recurred often in his books and articles, most notably, in a pamphlet, *Mandates and Empire*, issued by the League of Nations Union in the autumn of 1920. In it he seized upon the prospect of Article 22 of the covenant transforming the relations between European states and those parts of Asia and Africa subject to colonial rule by requiring these territories be administered solely for the well-being and development of the native population. After years when African subjects were sacrificed to the greed of white settlers and exploiting companies, here was an opportunity to ensure that the mandatory power govern in a way that would protect native interests. He urged the League to emulate British policy in West Africa by guaranteeing native rights in land and prohibiting its alienation to Europeans. In addition, forced labor should be prohibited, along with any tax that compelled natives to work for Europeans. To enable these people to "stand alone as free people," it was essential to widen gradually the sphere of responsible and democratic government. The provisions of the article denied the mandatory power sovereignty over the land, but this could be ensured only if the League exercised supervision and held the mandatory accountable. "The League cannot shuffle off responsibility on to the Mandatory, for it is the League which has accepted the sacred trust of civilization" (*Mandates*, 14). His prescription for native education stressed primary and technical schools, so that native communities could make the most effective use of their land, but he did not foresee industrial development. Although the mandate system was applied only to holdings of defeated powers, Leonard looked beyond these limitations. If the system fulfilled its intended purpose, then it was "essential that it should be extended to all subject peoples" (*Mandates*, 17).

His views about the relative political maturity of mandated African and Asian territories differed sharply: in Palestine, Syria, and Mesopotamia national independence should be conceded at once, not vitiated by artificial boundaries devised to satiate the greed of Britain and France. The peoples of the Middle East must administer their own territory, looking to Europe merely for guidance. Should pre-war methods of despotic control persist, he anticipated "perpetual trouble," ending "in a blaze which will tax all our military resources to extinguish." It was essential for the League to revoke the mandates if the powers violated their terms. Without strict adherence to Article 22, "the whole mandatory system is nothing but a worthless scrap of paper."[10]

In *Downhill All the Way* Leonard tends to conflate both advisory committees, even though the ACImpQ emerged six years later than the international one. Its significance was that "it enabled me, as secretary, to try to get the party and its leaders to understand the complications and urgency of what was happening in remote places and among strange peoples about whom they were profoundly and complacently ignorant" (*Downhill*, 223).

As the author of a pioneering study on Africa with extensive colonial experience, he was regarded as an expert but equally as an invaluable facilitator of policy discussions and reports. The two committees gathered information that was then disseminated in as many as 200 memoranda per year. The title of secretary belied his dominance on the ACImpQ, and in his collaborations with others, such as C. R. Buxton or Norman Leys, he generally assumed the dominant role. In a *New Statesman* letter, written months before his death, he discounted the impact of such writers as Hobson and Morel on interwar African policy. Instead it was "worked out in detail" by the Labour Party ACImpQ. From the outset its approach was "politically anti-imperialist," insisting that "the gross neglect of African colonies must be ended."[11] Leonard's reputation within the movement was based not only on his scholarly and polemical writings but on his involvement in party deliberations. His continuous activity turned him into one of the principal architects of Labour's foreign and imperial policies. In contrast, not only to Fabian imperialists, but also to prevailing popular attitudes, he sought to dismantle the empire, although only at a pace dictated by the readiness of the colonial peoples. Little wonder that Beatrice Webb, who admired Leonard, described him as "an anti-imperialist fanatic but otherwise a moderate in Labour politics."[12]

The first detailed Labour manifesto on Africa, drafted by Leonard and Buxton, was approved by the ACImpQ, adopted by the executive and party conference, and published as *The Empire in Africa: Labour's Policy* in 1920. A slightly revised version by Leonard and Leys was issued in 1926 as *Labour and the Empire: Africa*, portions of which reappeared in the *Reports and Proceedings* of the Labour and Socialist International Congress in 1928. After surveying the extent of the African crown colonies, whose administration was "absolutely autocratic," the pamphlet compared British East Africa, where land and people were exploited for the benefit of the white capitalist, with West Africa, where native land rights were preserved and native economic interests fostered. These contrary models of colonial rule indicated the way forward: "Labour's policy, if based on Labour principles, must be the abolition of economic exploitation and the education of the native so that he may take his place as a free man both in the economic and political system imposed upon Africa" (*Empire in Africa*, 3). Much of what followed echoed Leonard's conclusions in *Empire and Commerce in Africa*.

Confining natives to reserves and subjecting them to forced labor and exorbitant taxes, increasingly prevalent in the East African colonies, such as Kenya and Uganda, "does not aim at the creation of a self-respecting race of African producers secure in their possession of the land, but at the evolution of a race of servile labourers in European employ divorced from their land" (*Empire in Africa*, 4). It was creating a discontented, landless proletariat, threatening British occupation with eventual insurrection. He was no less outspoken in criticizing government policy, which, under pressure from the settlers, was complicit in exploiting indigenous people. If left in possession of their own land, natives were capable of working it more effectively than the European landowner, as cultivation of cash crops in West Africa confirmed. Labour's policy stipulated that land must be treated as the property of the native community, rejecting European expropriation. Slavery and all forms of compulsory labor must be prohibited. British authorities should also enforce the elimination of any color bar, opening all occupations without regard to race. In addition, native local government should be encouraged, but, until a genuinely representative system developed, tribal self-government must suffice. The goal was native participation in legislative councils and the gradual transfer of authority to these bodies. In line with Leonard's expressed views, the principle of trusteeship under the League of Nations should be extended to all tropical Africa. Finally, the colonial government had a duty to make primary education accessible to all school-age children, supplemented by technical colleges and teacher training schemes. The plan also provided for an African university with a curriculum substantive enough to be recognized by professional authorities in Europe and America. The aim should be to train not more African lawyers but rather scientific agriculturalists, doctors, and health officers.

When Leonard, as spokesman for the ACImpQ, responded to a questionnaire on subject peoples in January 1926, he called for immediate self-government in Iraq, Ceylon, and also in Palestine, although only in accord with the provisions of the mandate and the Balfour Declaration. Turning to African colonies, he contended that African natives were not yet capable of governing themselves: "The immediate grant of self-government would be disastrous.... No measure of 'responsible government' can at present be granted and it should never be granted unless and until it is certain that the Government will be responsible to and controlled by the African inhabitants."[13] Meanwhile legislative and executive power must remain in the hands of the Colonial Office. Such pronouncements were not so much "politically anti-imperialist," as Leonard argued in his 1969 *New Statesman* letter, but rather expressions of benevolent paternalism, keeping Africans under British tutelage until imperial authorities deemed them ready to take control of their own affairs. It also implied that the consent of the subjects was less vital than the opinions of well-intentioned experts, who knew what was best for the natives. The ACImpQ was slow to abandon the idea that self-government was something best doled out in gradual stages rather than conceded all at once. Nor was it merely self-government that would be dictated from London: economic and social programs should also continue to be managed by British officials. This attitude toward Africa began to alter only when emerging nationalism awakened critics of imperialism to new realities.

The policy statements contained pledges that could be implemented if a Labour government came to power, a dubious prospect in 1920. The ACImpQ continued to press for a commitment to future self-government in the colonial empire, but even when the executive adopted recommendations, they had few opportunities to carry them out before 1945. Nor did Labour pursue a forward policy when in office in 1924 or 1929–31. As prime minister, MacDonald had bigger fish to fry, and when, in 1929, Leonard and Buxton approached Sidney Webb (Lord Passfield), the Colonial Secretary, to complain that in Kenya expenditure on education and roads discriminated against Africans, taxed disproportionately for minimal returns, Webb, progressive on social policy but a conservative defender of the empire, denied their appeal for budgetary revision. Leonard followed up with a letter to his erstwhile patron, stressing the need for a Labour government to demonstrate by its actions that trusteeship was a reality. Reiterating claims made during his deputation, he insisted that "the incidence of taxation is grossly unfair to the native" and "the Government of Kenya has displayed deplorable weakness in many respects where the settlers have pressed their interests against those of the natives."[14] He was reluctant to accept that a Labour Colonial Secretary would simply refuse to implement principles stated in the party platform. But it was all to no avail. Such failures caused Leonard later to question whether the immense amount of work undertaken by the advisory committees served a genuine purpose. He could console himself with the belief that they did occasionally have some impact:

> We spread through the Labour Party, and to some extent beyond it, some knowledge of the relations between the imperialist powers and the subject peoples of Asia and Africa and even some realization of the urgent need for revolutionary reform so that there would be a rapid and orderly transition from imperialist rule to self-government.
> (*Downhill*, 238)

Most of Leonard's early writings on imperialism were commissioned works, emanating from either the Fabian Society, the League of Nations Union, or the ACImpQ. In 1928 he published his most speculative treatment of the subject, *Imperialism and Civilization*, under the Hogarth imprint. Much of it recapitulates the discursive themes of his two earlier books, but it also anticipates the type of cultural criticism contained in *After the Deluge* (1931, 1939). In contrast to exhaustive studies, like *Empire and Commerce in Africa*, he was now able to write without constraint, accountable to no one but himself for its contents. Looking back through history, he observed that it was not until industrialization that Europe became "a belligerent, crusading, conquering, exploiting, proselytizing civilization" (*Imperialism*, 9). Asia and Africa were powerless to resist "ruthless world-conquest" on a scale previously "unknown in human history" (*Imperialism*, 11). But by the twentieth century imperial domination unleashed a world revolt against Europe as semi-independent states, especially in Asia, sought to escape from Western control. Imperialism, as it existed before 1914, was no longer possible. It was the collision of incompatible civilizations, rather than racial conflict, which inspired nationalist outbreaks in India, China, and the Islamic world, a belated reaction to imperial exploitation. Racial and religious conflict, he argued, emerged only once the clash of civilizations began, merely "a channel into which the waters of revolt against imperialism have run" (*Imperialism*, 27). Imperialism brought with it the seeds of its own destruction, when it imposed Western civilization on alien cultures. In India it was the British-educated elites who resorted to political agitation, developed in Europe, against their overlords. Writing in 1928, he expressed the view that "the revolt against Europe had already reached the stage at which it cannot be successfully resisted" (*Imperialism*, 70).

The situation in colonial Africa was different, since its more primitive inhabitants were able neither to withstand the European incursion, nor to assimilate its civilization. Yet, despite the unscrupulous methods of the conquerors, the absorption of African territory into European empires was "desirable" as a way to "protect the inhabitants from the merciless massacre and exploitation by private adventurers" (*Imperialism*, 76–7). Unless European settlers were restrained, the African, "a child in the hands of any European," would become the economic slave of the white capitalist (*Imperialism*, 82). Yet, even in Africa, where the white minority held sway, the revolt against foreign control would inevitably be repeated, its outbreak becoming "far more terrible than that of Asia" (*Imperialism*, 92). He was prescient in targeting East Africa as the site for future nationalist unrest, which exploded in the 1950s and 1960s. As Noel Annan observed, Harold Macmillan's notorious "winds of change" speech in 1960 echoed what had been Leonard's clarion call since the 1920s.[15]

In the book's most provocative chapter, "The Inverse of Imperialism," he probed the impact of Asians and Africans in countries primarily inhabited by white men. This offered an opportunity to look at the Negro[16] population in America and the immigration of Asians into the United States, Kenya, South Africa, and Australia, where their presence and economic competitiveness had aroused hostility. He cited the fierce antagonism of whites in America to the upward mobility of emancipated blacks who challenged their economic and political supremacy. While denying the ultimate viability of segregation, he held out little hope for assimilation, since hostile sentiment seemed unlikely to change. He claimed, without evidence, that racial conflicts were subordinate to political and economic ones, but that, once racist sentiments surfaced, they came to dominate the situation: "The presence of a large, homogeneous, unassimilated population belonging to one race and civilization in a State where the majority of the population belongs to another race and civilization creates a very difficult and dangerous situation" (*Imperialism*, 105).

To avoid replicating the American problem, he warned against unrestricted Japanese immigration to Australia or California. If the world were to prevent racial conflicts, it must avoid "these alien, unassimilated enclaves." He reserved his strongest condemnation, however, for South Africa, which was re-creating the American situation on "a colossal scale and in a form which must lead to appalling disaster" (*Imperialism*, 106–7). Once again, he looked to the League to extend genuine trusteeship to subject peoples, providing disinterested administrative and economic assistance. It was the only way to avoid strife, but it also required Asia—and somewhat later Africa—to learn the secrets of "stable government, honest administration, and sound finance" (*Imperialism*, 123). One might recognize this as a Fabian approach to the legacy of imperialism, but perhaps only a Fabian could find a glimmer of hope in the prospect. *Imperialism and Civilization* was less an anti-imperialist diatribe than a prophetic analysis of dangers that beset the increasingly unstable international scene. His sweeping judgments, often skirting the edge of unwitting racism, were uttered in a spirit of racial harmony. In the 1920s he envisaged a multiracial commonwealth without any notion of how to achieve it.

Labour adopted an updated policy for the colonial empire, which Leonard drafted, at the Hastings party conference in 1933. Its most notable feature was a new emphasis on socialization and self-government: "a continued effort should be made to develop the Empire into a real Commonwealth of self-governing and Socialist peoples" (*Colonial Empire*, 5). Nowhere in the empire had there been serious efforts on behalf of the native peoples, but this was the goal to which the party now committed itself. Labour promised to grant responsible government in Asia and Africa, provided that the franchise was given to native inhabitants on the same terms as European minorities. In the meantime, traditional village and tribal institutions would be preserved, with cooperative societies employed to train local leaders to become more democratic and efficient. Lest this appear to accelerate the process too hastily, the statement added: "In the more primitive communities of Africa and the Pacific, the British Government must still *for many years* be responsible for the difficult task of seeing that the economic life of the territory is adjusted to the economic life of the outside world without damage to the interests of the Native inhabitants" (*Colonial Empire*, 7). Obstacles to their advancement could be overcome by education "designed to assist even the more primitive type of Native to become a free citizen capable of efficient participation in and control of his industry and his Government" (*Colonial Empire*, 13).

Although he wrote less about it, Leonard was equally committed to promoting self-government in India. The ACImpQ included several ex-Indian civil servants, like Sir John Maynard, who took the lead in producing memoranda, twenty-three between 1924 and 1931. The concessions that had been offered were so grudging and incomplete that Indian nationalists could only conclude that "the alien rulers would release their hold on the subject people only if forced to do so by bloody violence" (*Downhill*, 226). Leonard joined a gathering of prominent Labour figures to meet Gandhi in December 1931 after the London Round Table Conference and enjoyed a memorable private conversation with Nehru in February 1936. Even though the party supported taking immediate steps to establish Dominion status, its leaders had no opportunity to realize the promise until after the war.

In November 1938 Leonard's memorandum on projected reforms to the Ceylon constitution for the ACImpQ advocated "an appreciable measure of responsible government" as the keystone of Labour policy for the island. In order to safeguard the Tamil minority from Sinhalese domination, he urged a federal solution on the Swiss model as a way to enable distinct communities to coexist peaceably in a democratic state.[17] He was the first person to propose a federal arrangement as a way to mitigate communal conflict in Ceylon, a solution that resurfaced fifty years later in the Indo-Sri Lanka accord of 1987. By making a number of concessions to Tamil demands, the accord temporarily brought an end to insurgent resistance, but it was not until 2009 that government forces finally defeated the diehard struggle of the Tamil Tigers.

The question of assimilation, a recurrent theme in *Imperialism and Civilization*, permeated Leonard's fragmentary writings about Palestine. In 1926 he had endorsed Palestinian self-government while acknowledging the Balfour Declaration as a stumbling block. During the interwar period the British mandatory authority dithered as to whether to implement the pledge to transform Palestine into a Jewish national homeland or admit the impossibility of complying with the provisions of both the mandate and the Balfour Declaration, a dilemma exacerbated by pro-Arab officials in the Palestinian administration. Despite efforts by historian Lewis Namier and by Chaim Weizmann, President of the World Zionist Organization, to convert Leonard to Zionism in the 1920s, he remained adamantly resistant. In his view, intermarriage and assimilation in Western Europe and America raised doubts about whether Jews would even continue as a distinct community, although he cited Nazi anti-Semitism as a factor militating against total integration. It was unfortunate that Palestine was the disputed territory, given the "indigenous nationalism everywhere in the Near East."[18] Just as he opposed Japanese migration to Australia or Indians to East Africa, he initially perceived Jews as an unassimilable element in the Arab world. Despite his Jewish heritage, he insisted that "the savage xenophobia of human beings is so great that the introduction of a large racial, economic, religious, or cultured minority always leads to hatred, violence, and political and social disaster" (*Journey*, 185). In 1941 it fell to Leonard to draft an ACImpQ report on Palestine whose aim was to make it possible for Jews and Arabs "to cooperate peacefully in a self-governing Palestine." Its key principle was to preserve territorial integrity and reject proposals for partition. The memorandum tried to grapple with the issue of Jewish immigration, advising some limitation in order to prevent Arabs from being reduced to a minority. While unrestricted immigration was unfeasible, it would be possible to admit more Jews without jeopardizing the Arab position. Within specified limits, "Jews should be allowed and encouraged to enter and develop the country."[19] By 1942 he held out some hope that a binational state might be created in Palestine, capable of providing for both a Jewish national home and its inclusion in a federation of Middle Eastern states.[20] Even after the war had ended, he was reconciled neither to Zionism nor to "the self-righteous sadism of both sides and of their supporters, masquerading in the hypocritical cloak of misery, patriotism, or impartiality." His seeming even-handedness prevented him from identifying any "peculiar nobility and righteousness" in the determination of the Jew in Palestine "to make life hell for everyone because everyone has made life a hell for him."[21] This was written shortly after the bombing of the King David Hotel killed more than ninety people, hardening British opinion against Jewish militancy. In view of earlier negative remarks about Palestine, his response to the creation of Israel marked a decided change in outlook. In 1949 he wrote that "our true interests are in a peaceful and prosperous Palestine and therefore in a peaceful and prosperous Israel." Reversing its "disastrous policy of encouraging the Arab League to liquidate the Jews," the British government should prove by its actions that "we desire friendship and cooperation with the new State."[22] After the Suez conflict in 1956, he extolled the Israelis' "determination to defend themselves. If efficiency, toughness, enthusiasm can save a people, Israel will survive." For a stable peace to be achieved in the Middle East, international action was required. To allow a "lawless attack upon Israel" would be "to endanger the future peace of the whole world."[23]

In 1940 the ACIntQ suspended operations until 1944, since Labour, junior partner in the coalition government, did not encourage the critical perspective that it had offered for more than two decades. After the Fabian Society and the New Fabian Research Bureau reunited in 1939, Leonard served on the Fabian Executive, helping to establish its Colonial Bureau. He transferred his foreign-policy initiatives to the International Bureau of the Fabian Research Department, becoming its chair from 1943 to 1953. The ACImpQ continued to function during the war under the auspices of the party's International Department, and Leonard dutifully attended its meetings as well as those of several Fabian groups, even after bombing of his Bloomsbury house in 1940 virtually marooned him in Rodmell. Eventually he acquired a London flat to avoid the protracted commutes from Sussex to Westminster under wartime conditions. He was the principal author of two major wartime reports on the future of the empire.[24] In view of the 1945 Labour victory and the appointment of Arthur Creech-Jones, chair of the Labour Party Reconstruction Committee and an ACImpQ stalwart, as Colonial Secretary in 1945, these documents were key markers in charting the direction of postwar imperial goals.

Much of their contents recapitulated manifestos of the 1920s, suggesting that Leonard's anti-imperialism had evolved to only a limited extent. Nearly all the colonies outside Africa were deemed "ripe for self-government," but most Africans were "not yet able to stand by themselves." European states needed to retain administrative control in trust for the native inhabitants, training them "in every possible way so that they may be able in the shortest possible time to govern themselves." Indirect rule must not be used as an excuse for reinforcing autocratic tribal rulers or denying access to education. Grants should be withheld from any colonial territory that refused to eliminate discriminatory practices in employment. The application of a color bar was "a negation of the idea of colonial administration as a trust in the interests of the native inhabitants." The reports called for economic planning coordinated by the Colonial Office, encouraging production by Africans, but also "imposing planned agriculture and production upon the inhabitants." The economic basis would remain agriculture; industry ought to be discouraged unless it benefited the native population. Exploitation of mineral wealth should be under state ownership and control rather than "private profit-making enterprise." The primary obligation of British administration must be educational, requiring substantially increased expenditure, to enable Africans to manage their own affairs. To develop the economic potential of African colonies and to improve living standards, large outlays of capital and loans were essential either from the metropole or from an international fund for development. These reports embodied a comprehensive scheme of political, social, and economic advancement, socialist in its focus on state planning, paternalistic in its reliance on supervision by officials and experts. They did not envisage African autonomy or even vernacular education. Instead, imperial authority would make restitution to their subjects for decades of neglect, doing for them what they could not yet do for themselves. The intention was to improve conditions, apply local revenue and government funding to the welfare of native inhabitants, and expand educational opportunity.

In August 1943 Leonard broadcast on the BBC Home Service on the responsibilities of colonial empire. He described extreme contrasts within the British Empire, ranging from Ceylon, whose people were "just as capable of managing their own affairs as we are," to Africa, where "millions of people are living in the most primitive conditions, uneducated and illiterate." If the empire was ever to become a Commonwealth of Free Peoples, then the "advanced" peoples should be given full self-government immediately after the war. He criticized those on the "extreme left" who wanted to grant self-government to

Africans as a way for the British to clear out of Africa. In his opinion this would be "disastrous for the Africans," likely to fall victim to profiteers. Instead colonial administrations should go "all out to devolve self-government" and provide "an enormous extension of elementary and secondary education." Native authorities needed to become "gradually democratized." In a strongly worded riposte, Elspeth Huxley, who had grown up in the white minority community in Kenya, chided Leonard for his outdated perspective. Criticizing him for referring to Africans as an undifferentiated, backward mass, she questioned whether the British record on education and self-government was as disgraceful as he claimed. Further, she doubted whether democracy would be appropriate where one tribe refused to be represented by another, a prospect that Leonard failed to anticipate.[25] He was prone to perceive colonial peoples as subsisting at different stages of development but equally capable of evolving to where they could manage their own affairs democratically. This led him to disregard traditional customs, tribal animosities, and social structure in Africa, despite available anthropological research. His years in Ceylon had helped him interpret similar factors in Asian cultures, but his lack of first-hand experience in Africa proved to be an abiding deficiency. In that sense *The Village in the Jungle* was a work of greater insight than *Empire and Commerce in Africa*.

Leonard pursued the themes of his talk in a 1945 essay on "The Political Advance of Backward Peoples" published in *Fabian Colonial Essays*. Once again, he claimed that "primitive or backward peoples" in their current state were incapable of coping with the political and economic problems that European civilization imposed, but he found no evidence to suggest any inherent racial incapacity. If the ultimate aim of colonial rule was democratic self-government of Africa by Africans, the primary duty of British authorities should be to train the native inhabitants so that they could administer their own countries as soon as possible. This could be accomplished only by educating the people: "universal education is a *sine qua non* of modern democracy." Yet, even while promoting schools for Africans, he retained an Anglo-centric perspective. If Africans were going to manage their own affairs, they needed to be given knowledge of Western civilization and "higher education on western lines." Training in democracy, necessarily gradual, need not be postponed until the population achieved the requisite educational standard. While native leaders would inevitably form the basis of local government, their institutions must become "fundamentally democratic in the western sense."[26] Leonard continued to doubt official commitment to preparing Africans for independence. As he lamented in 1959: "The sin and tragedy of our empire have been that we have never attempted to honor our promises and train brown and black subjects for self-government."[27] Elsewhere the outlook was more auspicious, and he applauded the concession of independence in India, Pakistan, Ceylon, and Burma. Labour in power after 1945 had implemented the postcolonial policy that he had advocated for a generation. No other figure on the Left had been so consistent a proponent of gradually dismantling the British Empire, nor so prescient in recognizing that emergent colonial nationalism made the transfer of power inevitable, whether by peaceful or by violent means. Still, he was encouraged by the fact that "everywhere the model for the liberated nations is the industrialized civilization of western Europe."[28]

Leonard's inability to visit many of the places he wrote about may have been a handicap in understanding native peoples and their readiness to govern themselves. As long as Virginia was alive, he was reluctant to leave her for any period of time. In the interwar years they regularly vacationed in France and took occasional trips to Spain, Italy, and Germany, but these travels were undertaken when Virginia's precarious health permitted. His political writings were based on information amassed at home, often the result of intensive reading, but never from actual observation, except when writing about Ceylon. After receiving a bequest in 1922 of several thousand pounds to promote socialism, Fabian leaders devised a plan to dispatch an investigator to Russia "to supplement documentary research into the Soviet system of government." Beatrice Webb asked Leonard whether "there was the remotest chance of your being able to do it."[29] He was the obvious candidate, having written "two books successfully for the F.S. and endless unpaid work for the Labour Party and the Co-operative movement." He had the advantage of familiarity with Russian language and literature. As Sidney told Fabian secretary Edward Pease: "This would be a big job, involving visiting Geneva and Moscow. Would you be disposed to spend out of the Atkinson Fund, say £250 for expenses and a fee of £250, the latter recoverable from royalties?"[30] Of course Leonard had to reject the proposal and, in fact, never visited the Soviet Union, about which he was to comment profusely in the coming years.

In later years he traveled more widely, usually in the company of his companion, Trekkie Parsons. In April 1957 they went to Israel for ten days, a visit that caused him to repudiate his earlier anti-Zionist views. Although he arrived "with a comparatively open mind," nothing prepared him for his delight in what he found. "I have never felt so exhilarated by the physical climate of a country and the mental climate of its inhabitants," he later wrote. What astonished him most was "the immense energy, friendliness, and intelligence of these people" (*Journey*, 186–7). The sense of common danger reminded him of the atmosphere in London during the Blitz, since the small country was besieged by hostile Arab states. Three years later he returned to Ceylon, which he had been keen to revisit since it became independent. He was warmly welcomed by Sinhalese authorities and the local press, quickly reminding readers of Leonard's support in 1916 after the British had cracked down on the riots. His public service was favorably recalled, and he was celebrated as the author of *The Village in the Jungle*. In honor of the visit, his official diaries were published, and he was escorted to the four regions of the island where he had worked as a colonial official. He admitted "to the discreditable enjoyment of being treated as a V.I.P. all over Ceylon" (*Journey*, 199). It was also gratifying to find ordinary people and officials going out of their way to praise the British administrators of Leonard's day, even if their words contained more than a hint of flattery. He was pleased to see that the people of Ceylon now governed themselves at every level: "you feel both in the streets of towns and in villages a breeze of independence blowing through men's minds, quickening their lives."[31] The most startling change, however, was the impact of the motorized bus. When Leonard had served in Ceylon, travel had been on foot, on horseback, and by ox cart. It often took him several days of laborious effort, penetrating the dense jungle, to reach more distant parts. But speed, while seeming to shorten distance, came at a price. As a civil servant he had gotten to know villagers by walking among them or stopping to hear their complaints, but this was less likely to transpire when officials could drive quickly from one place to another. Modernity had undermined that aspect of the relations between the governed and their rulers, and he lamented its loss. He found less poverty than he remembered, even though Ceylon remained predominately agricultural, with growth in rice and cotton production aided by large-scale irrigation.

By 1960 Leonard, 80 years old, was beginning to slow down. With the trip to Ceylon, almost fifty years after his resignation from the colonial service, his professional life had come full circle. After decades of anti-imperial activity, filled with books and articles, meetings and deputations, his own imperial past was vindicated. He had always been proud of his accomplishments in Ceylon, and now, instead of being maligned as an imperialist or dismissed as a relic of the past, he was hailed as a hero. How satisfying to discover that the affection he felt for his former subjects was reciprocated by their descendants a half century later.

Notes

1. After Fifty Years," *New Statesman*, 23 April 1960.
2. "The Colour of our Mammies," *Encounter* (July 1959).
3. Peter Wilson, "Leonard Woolf still not out of the Jungle?" *Round Table*, 97/394 (2008), 154.
4. Leonard had recurrent episodes of malaria as late as December 1919.
5. Memorandum to the Parliamentary Labour Party, 8 November 1918, Spotts, 388–9.
6. See J. A. Hobson, *Imperialism: A Study* (1902), and H. N. Brailsford, *The War of Steel and Gold* (1914).
7. Sidney Webb to LW, 11 March 1918, *Letters of Sidney and Beatrice Webb*, iii. 103; Glendinning, 192.
8. VW, *Diary*, 7 March 1919, i. 250.
9. LW, "Subject Peoples of the Empire," in H. B. Lees-Smith (ed.), *Encyclopedia of the Labour Movement* (1928), 257.
10. *New Statesman*, 1 May 1920.
11. *New Statesman*, 10 January 1969.
12. *Diary of Beatrice Webb*, 6 February 1927, iv. 113.
13. AClmpQ Memorandum, January 1926, Spotts, 393–4.
14. LW to Sidney Webb, 24 October 1929, Spotts, 394–5.
15. Noel Annan, *Our Age* (New York: Random House, 1990), 357.
16. Writing in 1928, Leonard employed this now outdated word. African-American or black were not in current parlance when he produced *Imperialism and Civilization*.

17. Memorandum on the Demands for Reform of the Ceylon Constitution (November 1938), Spotts, 416–17.
18. Review of *England in Palestine* by Norman Bentwich, *Political Quarterly* (April–June 1932), 299.
19. Draft Report on Palestine (1941), Spotts, 429.
20. *New Statesman*, 18 April 1942.
21. Review of *Palestine Mission* by Richard Crossman, *Political Quarterly* (October–December 1947), 367.
22. *New Statesman*, 29 October 1949.
23. "Israel and the Middle East," *Political Quarterly* (July–September 1957), 210–11.
24. "Draft Memorandum Formulating a Colonial Policy for the Labour Party after the War;" Labour Party International Department, September 1941; "The Colonies: The Labour Party's Post War Policy," March 1943.
25. *Listener*, 12 August 1943.
26. LW, "The Political Advance of Backward Peoples," in Rita Hinden (ed.), *Fabian Colonial Essays* (1945), 85–98.
27. *Encounter* (July 1959).
28. "The Splendours and Miseries of Colonialism," *Political Quarterly* (July-Sept.1958), 211.
29. Beatrice Webb to LW, 26 June 1922, *Letters of Sidney and Beatrice Webb*, iii. 156.
30. Sidney Webb to Edward Pease, 1 February 1923, *Letters of Sidney and Beatrice Webb*, iii.169.
31. *New Statesman*, 23 April 1960.

7
The Wars for Peace

When Leonard reflected on the prewar world in which he had grown up, he tended to stress the social and intellectual progress his generation had enjoyed. Although his father's premature death had placed the family in straitened circumstances, he recalled his youth, especially his years at Cambridge, as a sort of golden age. As he later observed: "Anyone who was a young man at the beginning of this century will remember that at that time the future seemed to contain a real possibility of greater prosperity and happiness, of a wider and deeper civilization, for human beings than had ever existed in their previous history" (*War for Peace*, 236).

In these formative years he gained in self-confidence, no longer apprehensive that he would be stigmatized because of his Jewish background, his intellectuality, or his lack of social connections. As the first Jew to be elected to the elite Apostles, he found among its number kindred spirits who shared his enthusiasm for philosophical disputation and modern literature. The coming of war in 1914 transformed these optimistic expectations into a nightmare that permanently altered his perspective on the world. Always prone to epochal pronouncements, he came to believe that it destroyed "the bases of European civilization" (*Downhill*, 9) and "the hope that human beings were becoming civilized—a hope not unreasonable at the beginning of the twentieth century" (*Journey*, 10).

At first the ongoing disruptions in his domestic life overshadowed the war news. Virginia had attempted suicide in 1913, and her recovery was spasmodic at best over the next few years. "In many ways 1914 and 1915 were years which we simply lost out of our lives, for we lived them in the atmosphere of catastrophe or impending catastrophe" (*Beginning*, 166). International politics had never impinged on his personal life or his intellectual pursuits before 1914, and few of his

Cambridge contemporaries foresaw the events that now unfolded. Yet it was immediately after the war had begun that he embarked on his seminal analysis of international government for the Fabian Society, a project that dominated his professional life for the better part of two years and constituted his singular contribution to the postwar settlement.

Leonard was initially opposed to the war, viewing it as senseless, the result of miscalculations by diplomats and generals. Accustomed to a dangerous but relatively peaceful world, he found it difficult to comprehend why "millions of men, most of them young, suddenly began to try to kill one another" (*Deluge*, i. 19). He believed that British leaders, who might have averted its outbreak, should never have become involved. Failure to resolve the conflict quickly, as well as mounting casualties, ultimately convinced him that Germany should be resisted. In later recollections he was not as equivocal about his support for the war effort: "Many of us hold that it was right for the Empire to fight with France and Belgium against Germany in 1914" (*War for Peace*, 46). On a personal level, he was less sanguine about the role he might play. Never regarding himself as a total pacifist, he lacked a basis for claiming conscientious objection, as Bloomsbury friends such as Strachey and Duncan Grant did, once conscription was extended to include married men up to the age of 41. Four of his brothers joined up; Cecil and Philip served as cavalry officers in France, where Cecil was killed in November 1917 when a shell burst during an attempted rescue of a wounded soldier, and Leonard may have felt pangs of conscience about not having followed their example. Such feelings would have stemmed from family solidarity rather than patriotic sentiment. Rationalizing his response, he insisted that, "if I had not been married or even if Virginia had been well, I should probably have joined up, because, though I hated the war, I felt and still feel an irresistible desire to experience everything" (*Beginning*, 177). Or so he explained it in 1964. Such bravado, however, was less evident in the moment. Strachey found Leonard alarmed at the prospect of compulsory military service or jail, thus abandoning Virginia to the care of others. He confided to Margaret Llewellyn Davies: "I feel I am a conscientious objector—for I loathe the thought of taking any part in this war—& yet I feel very much the difficulty, from the point of view of reason."[1] Since he could not seek exemption on grounds of religious compunction or committed pacifist beliefs, he would attempt to evade conscription because of health—his and Virginia's. He approached Dr Maurice Wright, whom he had consulted in 1914 about his trembling hands and Virginia's mental condition. Having treated him unsuccessfully for a congenital tremor and nervous exhaustion, the physician never doubted that Leonard was unfit for military service and readily furnished a statement for submission at his military examination. He also alluded to Virginia's history of mental breakdowns and Leonard's pivotal role in nursing her during these crises. As a result of a medical examination and Wright's testimonial, he was temporarily exempted in May 1916.[2] He told Violet Dickinson that "His Majesty's Army has decided that I am totally unfit to be used in any way by my country."[3] His relief was mingled with humiliation at having his familial trembling hands referred to as "senile tremor." When he was summoned again before the tribunal in October 1917, Wright testified that his nervous condition and low body weight (132 pounds) would render him incapable of enduring mental or physical fatigue without his health failing. Recurrent bouts of malaria and stress-induced, crippling headaches may have contributed to the diagnosis of ill health, although Leonard was physically resilient and athletic. In November, just before his thirty-seventh birthday, he was granted a total exemption from military service.

Once *International Government* was published, two months after Leonard had received his provisional military exemption, his growing reputation created opportunities in the world of political journalism. Writing on international affairs for such progressive periodicals as *War and Peace*, *International Review*, and *Contemporary Review* increased his visibility and led to regular employment as a reviewer for the *New Statesman* and for the *Nation*. His Labour Party activity was expanding, especially after his appointment in the spring of 1918 as secretary of the Advisory Committee on International Questions (ACIntQ). The First World War, in which he played no military role, ultimately shaped his career—as an authority on international relations, as a political journalist, and as a Labour Party functionary. At the same time he and Virginia busied themselves with the Hogarth Press, launched in 1917 as an avocation, but ultimately entailing a serious professional commitment. He had found his footing while losing the exuberant optimism of the prewar decades. The advent of peace signaled for him the end of civilization as he knew it: "In 1914 in the background of one's life and one's mind there were light and hope; by 1918 one had unconsciously accepted a perpetual public menace and darkness and had admitted into the privacy of one's mind or soul an iron fatalistic acquiescence in insecurity and barbarism" (*Downhill*, 9). Nor was this merely a subjective response. His psychological reaction paled when compared to the human consequences: "the sum of concentrated human misery was during those years probably greater than human beings had ever experienced before" (*Deluge*, i. 22).

Although advocacy of the League of Nations in the 1920s stemmed from his conviction about the inherent value of an international system, it remained at its core a means to avoid the recurrence of war by resolving disputes peaceably. While he continued to regard prewar German policy as "indefensible," his reading of self-exculpatory memoirs by European statesmen reaffirmed his sense that "they were all of them responsible for the war, and that if they or people like them are allowed to control policy again, the same thing will happen again."[4] Despite inability to realize its potential, Leonard never relinquished his belief that the League or an equivalent structure was the only means of saving the world from the catastrophe of war or repairing it after destructive conflict. Until the rise of Hitler he continued to stress that it was imperative to strengthen the League in order to curb potential aggressors. Few British writers on foreign affairs recognized as early as Leonard the true nature of the Nazi regime. Germany, he proclaimed within months of Hitler's ascent to power, had become "one of the most savage and senseless dictatorships that has been tolerated by a civilized European population for at least two centuries."[5]

A gloomy prognosis permeated his introduction to the edited volume *The Intelligent Man's Way to Prevent War*, published by Victor Gollancz in 1933, a precursor of the Left Book Club, launched three years later. Here Leonard described the war of 1914–18 as "a big step on the road back to barbarism." Despite a temporary reprieve in the 1920s, the barbarians had breached the frontiers of civilization and were destroying it from within. He warned that civilization could not survive another world war: "If there is another war, the barbarians will finally triumph."[6] The book's contributors, including Norman Angell, Will Arnold-Forster, and Viscount Cecil, offered ideas about how to prevent war by subjecting sovereign nations to international law and pooled security. All of them feared the rise of virulent nationalism and dictatorship as an obstacle to a peaceful resolution of conflict. If the self-sufficient state and economic nationalism prevail, "pacifism, liberty, democracy, socialism can have no place." Yet, so long as the majority of people were opposed to war, they had the power to prevent it by opting for those policies elucidated in the book: conciliation, disarmament, collective security, and adherence to international law.[7] To be sure, these exhortations were addressed to "the intelligent man" in Britain, presumably a League supporter with progressive inclinations, not designed for consumption in the Fascist states. Two years later he intervened in a *New Statesman* debate, chiefly between Angell and Brailsford, about the causes of war. While Angell blamed psychological delusions, Brailsford identified capitalism as the culprit. Leonard, eschewing mono-causal explanations, observed that "the causes of war are much too complex and multifarious to be covered exclusively either by economics or by psychology." Socialists needed to acknowledge the psychological factors that prompted millions to fight against their own economic interests. Whatever motivated combatants, "the imperialist structure of capitalist society must almost inevitably sooner or later produce war."[8]

Clear-eyed about the prospects for war, Leonard remained in a quandary about national armaments, which the League was intended either to eliminate or to internationalize. Collective security, and, even more, military sanctions, required weapons, but far from relinquishing their stockpiles, many states were competing to outpace rivals, and Germany was openly violating imposed strictures against rearmament. Unregulated armaments were a prescription for catastrophe. When Stephen Spender asked in 1934 whether he thought war was coming, Leonard replied: "Yes, of course. Because when the nations enter into an armaments race, as they are doing at present, no other end is possible."[9] For him, the disarmament problem was "the pivot of the movement away from international government and peace.... The world can choose between armed nationalism and disarmed internationalism; it cannot have both at the same time."[10] He attributed the growth of Hitlerism to the refusal of the major powers to reach an agreement on arms control and continued to view disarmament as the precondition for preventing war. Leonard rejected unilateral British disarmament and isolation, as proposed by Frank Hardie, the organizer of the Oxford Union "King and Country" debate, but conceded that mandatory sanctions against an aggressor was "much too dangerous in the world of today."[11] As he told Noel-Baker:

> You know that I entirely agree with you about collective security and that nothing but it can stand between the world and war. The disorientation in the forces on the Left with regard to the League is appalling. The sanctions madmen I have never been able to understand: they are people who believe in political absolute truths and like all absolutists end in the clouds or the mire.[12]

With the League's failure to constrain Japanese expansion and the collapse of the Disarmament Conference, he warned that "only a drastic revolution in the League itself, in the aims and policies of the existing governments, and in the whole European situation could make the League of today an effective instrument for peace and justice." Labour's foreign policy should aim at restoring a system for ensuring international accord by avoiding reliance on national armaments. To pursue a policy of rearmament in the face of League impotence would be to "throw power into the hands not of socialists, but of fascists."[13] Defending collective security to the point of armed sanctions against an aggressor, Leonard quarreled with Kingsley Martin, who was apprehensive lest military action, even under League auspices, degenerate into a capitalist, imperialist war. Having long argued that pooled force did not constitute old-fashioned war, he admonished the pacifist left for its lack of realism. The notion that it was possible to select a policy that would result in absolute good was absurd: "in 999,999 cases out of a million, the choice is between two evils and two courses both of which will lead to evil..."[14]

During the autumn of 1934 Leonard embarked on the first of several polemical books, *Quack, Quack!*, striking a far more satirical tone than earlier works on international government or economic imperialism. Sparked by the Nazi rise to power and such alarming events as the recent Nuremberg rally, he drew an analogy between Hitler and Mussolini and witch doctors who utilized magic and animal savagery to control primitive peoples. He included photographs of the two dictators, declaiming their political quackery, alongside effigies of the Polynesian war god Kukailimoko to show a remarkable resemblance. During periods in which civilized values were cherished, reason and knowledge predominated, but when war or economic crisis produced communal misery, "the superstitions of the savage creep back into popularity ... and everywhere is heard the great quacking of the quacks" (*Quack*, 19). This belief in the efficacy of magic, emblematic of primitive society, contained by civilization, was never far below the surface. Even in the most civilized societies there was a "submerged army of primitive men" ready to throw their weight on the side of unreason. The refusal of the cultured elite to share their advantages with the masses turned many who might have upheld civilized values into an "unholy alliance with the barbarians" (*Quack*, 25–7). It was the assertion not merely of reason against quackery and freedom against despotism, but of equality against privilege that was essential to sustain civilization in the face of barbarism. Fascism, the supreme example of the revival of savagery and magic, exploited the herd instinct of the populace, intoxicated "by the incantations of charlatans and fanatics, by the persecution of defenseless people, by the frenzy of military bands, marches, processions, goose-steps, and the ceaseless bull-roaring of the radio" (*Quack*, 44). Nor should these dictators be dismissed as cynical egoists: it was "the quack who believes in his quackery who does the damage and can destroy a whole civilization." Fascist Italy scarcely differed from past despotic oligarchies; Hitlerism, similarly irrational, was "more brutal, more efficient, and more uncompromisingly stupid." *Mein Kampf,* a "clarion call to the emotions of violent militant nationalism," was a manifesto that employed fear and hatred as means to destroy political reason. The corollary of barbarism was the suppression of dissent by imprisoning or executing opponents. He warned that a people cannot be savage in politics while remaining civilized in their social life (*Quack*, 69–72).

In *Quack, Quack!* Leonard broached the subject of anti-Semitism for the first time since his early fictional writings. The Nazi persecution of Jews, the most flagrant form of the "irrational, uncivilized, scapegoat-hunting psychology," marked a reversion to savagery, epitomized in the doctrine of Aryan superiority. He compared it, rather paradoxically, to the Soviet attack on the capitalist and the bourgeoisie, concluding that "in this hunting and persecution of public scapegoats we have reached the nadir of political quackery and the present revolt against civilization" (*Quack*, 103–5). Anti-Semitism, treated only obliquely in the text, received a more trenchant critique in a separate appendix. The Hogarth edition of 2,000 copies, published in May 1935 and favorably reviewed in the *Times Literary Supplement*,[15] nearly sold out within the first year; an American edition, published by Harcourt, Brace appeared in September, making this commercially his most successful book to date.

Why did Leonard relegate anti-Semitism to a special "Note" at the end of his book? Perhaps it was because he felt that it transcended his denunciation of Nazi propaganda; if he, as a Jew, were finally to address a problem he had so long avoided, it needed to be considered in a broader historical context. He questioned whether Hitler could succeed where Nebuchadnezzar and so many others had failed. The Jew had "become a professional world scapegoat and has instinctively acquired a technique of resistance to persecution and annihilation." Jews could not fail to recognize that the racial indictment represented a "revolt against civilization, a reversion to the primitive quackery of superstition." Nor was it surprising that the Jew was stigmatized, given that his cultural roots stretched back long before the Aryans emerged:

> For two thousand years they have been the traditions, not of the jungle and the tribe, not of hatred and savagery, but of civilization. Wherever a civilization has flourished for a short time in Europe, the Jew has lived close to it and in it, has thrown himself into it with energy and enthusiasm. Therefore the Jew has, not in his blood, but in his mind, the traditions both of his own and of a world civilization.
>
> (*Quack*, 196–7)

Even if the Jew were to accept the "superstitious nonsense about race and blood," he could demonstrate that in a world of mongrels, his blood was purer than most. "He belongs to a 'race' which was building a civilization in the valley of the Tigris and Euphrates thousands of years before the 'Aryan' had emerged from the squalor and savagery of his jungle or steppe" (*Quack*, 198). Despite his ancestors' belief in a savage tribal God and in themselves as a chosen people, they "reached a stage of civilization at which they understood the supreme obligation to pursue knowledge and use reason and to value them socially above wealth and power" (*Quack*, 200).

No Jew need feel shame in belonging to a lineage responsible for the Ten Commandments, Ecclesiastes, and the Psalms, Isaiah, Christ, Montaigne, Spinoza, Heine, Marx, Einstein, Proust, and Freud. Through the centuries Jews had been scattered "like dust over the face of the earth," sometimes abandoning their religious beliefs or racial consciousness, but the ingrained traditions of their own civilization survived:

> They have learnt in the ghettos of Europe the meaning of quackery and superstition, the effect of hatred, the value of reason, tolerance, and humanity. The Jew may indeed feel that perhaps after all, as a civilized man, a man into whose mind the lessons of civilization have been burnt by bitter experience, he is an appropriate victim when unfortunate people in the state of mind of the German Nazis are searching for a scapegoat. (*Quack*, 201)

It would be difficult to find anywhere in Leonard's writing a more poignant credo, reflecting an identity intrinsic to his very being. He was 55 when he wrote this defense of the Jew in a Christian world, threatened by Nazi persecution, if not yet by genocide. It took a concerted effort on his part to shed his assimilationist carapace and to avow pride in his heritage. Although he rarely mentions anti-Semitism in his autobiography or in his other books, he was impelled in 1935 to denounce it, not merely as a cultivated Englishman or as an internationalist, but as a Jew.

Charles Singer, a Jewish physician and professor at the University of London active in assisting academic victims of Nazi persecution, wrote to him to praise *Quack, Quack!* Calling for the publication of a cheap edition likely to attract a wider audience, he urged Leonard to lessen its criticism of the British monarchy and to eliminate the appendix on anti-Semitism as a way of appealing to conservatives. Leonard initially rejected any suggestion that he temper his more controversial remarks in a second edition, published only a year later, lest it appear that he had changed his mind. "My experience," he responded, "is that it is fatal to cut out arguments which people will not like.... If I write about the German quackery and cut out all reference to the English, I only bolster up and cover up the very thing which it was my purpose to uncover."[16] Upon reconsideration, however, he conceded that "the more one disagrees with criticism of one's own writing, the more likely one is to be wrong."[17] Without altering the text appreciably, he softened his ridicule of deference to the royal family and, more surprisingly, omitted the appendix on anti-Semitism in the later edition. Whether he had second thoughts about such avowed self-exposure, or feared that his remarks might offend British sensibilities, or because the milder manifestations of anti-Semitism he had witnessed in England paled beside the virulent race hatred prevalent in Nazi Germany remains enigmatic.[18] Whatever the reason, the cheap edition of 1936 sold well enough to warrant a reprint the next year.

With the manuscript of *Quack, Quack!* finished by the beginning of March, 1935, it seems barely credible that only two months later the Woolfs, planning to drive in their Lanchester convertible to Rome, where Vanessa Bell had rented a house, should have chosen a route through Germany. Harold Nicolson informed Leonard that the Foreign Office recommended that Jews avoid travel in Germany. He also consulted Foreign Office counsellor Ralph Wigram, a Sussex neighbor, who, while concurring with Nicolson, added privately that the Woolfs need not fear to go to Germany as long as they did not get mixed up in a Nazi procession or public ceremony. Wigram introduced him to Prince Bismarck at the German Embassy, who supplied a letter calling on German officials to show every courtesy to the distinguished visitors. Leonard found it "absurd that any Englishman, whether Jew or Gentile, should hesitate to enter a European country," on the presumption that British authorities would ensure that an English Jew would be treated no differently from any other subject (*Downhill*, 185). They traveled with his pet marmoset, Mitz, who often perched on his shoulder as they drove through several German cities and on to Austria and Italy. Although they encountered a procession in Bonn, where Nazi storm troopers were as prolific as anti-Jewish banners, the marmoset—*das liebe kleine Ding*—proved a goodwill emissary, captivating crowds of Hitler's supporters as they passed by. Firsthand observations of the way that the Nazi regime had transformed the populace reinforced the impressions conveyed in *Quack, Quack!* As he commented in the *New Statesman*: "You cannot be 24 hours in a totalitarian or fascist state without realizing that there is a psychological relationship between the rulers and the ruled which does not exist—except in war time—in democratic countries."[19]

While managing to avoid any direct confrontation, Leonard perceived "something sinister and menacing in the Germany of 1935" (*Downhill*, 192). He was never to visit Germany again. By way of contrast, Italy seemed to have reached a critical point, with patriotic enthusiasm and the veneer of efficiency crumbling. The moment would inevitably come when the dictator, whether Mussolini or Hitler, would be "faced by the emotional deflation of his subjects and his only chance of reinflating them and himself is by war."[20]

It was the duplicity of Britain and France in failing to impose effective sanctions against Italy after its invasion of Abyssinia that convinced Leonard of the League's fatal debility. An embargo on oil shipments would have halted Italian aggression, revitalizing the mechanism of collective security. As late as November 1935 he could still write to his nephew, Julian Bell, then in China, that "the League is the only last possible faint hope of preventing a world war."[21] Four months later that hope had evaporated: a prophetic letter to Julian warned: "It is now going to be simply a race between the economic breakdown of the Fascist governments and a European war.... The [British] Govt has to all intents and purposes destroyed the collective security system."[22] In a pamphlet published in a Hogarth series, Leonard decried British foreign policy as "muddle-headed, vacillating, inconsistent, paying lip-service to the League and its system, but continually in practice repudiating the obligations the fulfilment of which could alone give reality to the League system of peace, disarmament, and collective security."[23] The only chance of forestalling war would be to guarantee that an act of war against one would be treated as an act of war against all. By proposing to limit commitments, regionalizing the obligation to aid victims of aggression, British leaders adopted the best course "for wobbling along into the abyss." If it was not prepared to shoulder the burdens of collective security, the only viable alternative would be an alliance, but instead the Baldwin government chose rearmament, oblivious to evidence that "such competition in arming by Great Powers always has, and always will, lead to war between them."[24] Leonard refuted pacifist writer Helena Swanwick's rejection of sanctions, insisting that, "if the governments of Britain and France had set themselves to right wrongs, conditions would have been established in which the League would have worked and peace in Europe might not have been broken for 25 or 50 years."[25]

In July 1936 Leonard wrote a memorandum for the ACIntQ on the attitude Labour should adopt towards proposed League reforms. In his view the core of the covenant was the collective security system, whose ultimate test was the willingness of member states to disarm. The condition of League membership should be compliance with a mutually determined level of military and naval strength, consistent with the needs of collective defense, and the abolition of private manufacture of weapons. But he recognized that successive defeats in Manchuria and Abyssinia had undermined any belief that collective commitments would be fulfilled. This was why "governments are everywhere feverishly rearming and why in this country there is a movement towards isolation and extreme pacifism." Since denial of the universal obligation was a fait accompli, the most plausible alternative would probably be regional pacts, which Leonard had inveighed against earlier, committed to support militarily victims of aggression in limited areas. Whatever the intentions of the League's founders, small states were even hard pressed to participate in collective action in their own neighborhood, much less in distant corners of the world. He recognized that eliminating universality would destroy the system of collective security, enabling nations to decide that an act of war against one member was not within their sphere of interest. Nor should Labour expect decisive leadership from the National government, since "it will almost certainly either drift helplessly or entangle itself in commitments according as one or other view temporarily prevails in the Cabinet." If the party merely reaffirmed its longstanding ties to the League, "it will in effect be supporting a sham, an international system which no governments or peoples any longer believe to be operative or capable of assuring them defense against aggression."[26]

The Spanish Civil War convinced him that the League had been irretrievably damaged as an instrument for deterring aggression. Despairingly, he confided to Julian:

> I have come myself to be in favour of isolation at any rate as a temporary policy for this country. It is too late to stop a European war by an alliance; in fact it would probably precipitate a war.... The Labour Party does not know its own mind, and that is not a state of mind in which it can put forward a policy of alliance. The best that one

can hope is that we may stumble and stagger together into an ignoble policy of isolation, that the guns will not go off or the bombs begin to fall for a year or two, and that something meanwhile "may turn up".[27]

Obliged to veil his pessimism in print, he exhorted Labour to undertake "nothing less than a revision of its whole peace policy."[28] He favored a coalition of democratic and socialist states prepared not only to redress legitimate grievances of the Fascist powers, but also to counter any attack on unaligned states, such as Spain. When invited to participate in *Authors Take Sides on the Spanish War*, he responded tersely: "I am for the legal Government and people of Republican Spain and civilization; I am against Franco, Fascism, and barbarism."[29] Despite his antipathy toward the National Government for appeasing the dictators, he reluctantly conceded that mere negativity toward its rearmament program was futile. Without sufficient armaments, the policy of alliance would be a "policy of suicide." In this *Political Quarterly* article, while denoting the inevitability of war, he declared that it was not psychologically possible to stand aside and watch "the destruction of everything which one values in society."[30] Rejecting isolation was less a heroic stance than an admission of defeat: the international commonwealth for which he had striven for two decades was now on the edge of the precipice.

During the course of 1937 a more realistic tone crept into his pronouncements, although he held out little hope of achieving his goals. An April ACIntQ memorandum acknowledged that nations no longer based their policies on the League; they were instead trying to avoid war or be on the winning side by rearming and seeking allies. The immediate danger came solely from the Fascist powers, not just through overt aggression, but the prospect that some violent act by a dictator could precipitate a European war. Its prevention would depend on persuading the dictators that war would not pay. Agreement among the pacific powers should also be directed to reconstituting some kind of collective system including smaller states, none of whom would participate unless their security was guaranteed without a reciprocal obligation. In addition, Britain and France should aim at close cooperation with the Soviet Union, without including it in any security agreement to avoid alarming the smaller East European states.[31] Later in the year he noted a calmer spirit in Europe, a breathing space that might be used "to stop temporarily, or even perhaps permanently, the drift to war." The Fascist powers were not ready to risk war, enabling Britain and France to regain the initiative. He now envisaged a common front, in cooperation with the Soviet Union, which "would pursue the policy of resisting aggression, defending democracy, and resuscitating the League." There were, however, several obstacles to such a forward approach: first, "the hopeless fatalism of rearmament undirected by any policy but that of panic" and, second, the recognition that an international system to prevent war and the defense of the rights of democratic states was untenable under the present National government.[32] His short-lived flicker of optimism completely disappeared by the time of the *Anschluss* in March 1938. If there was still any chance of avoiding war, it required immediate drastic action on the part of Britain and France and a shift in Labour policy. Hitler must be warned that further aggression would be resisted, and Labour should offer to enter a coalition government under Churchill and support conscription and rearmament. Although Leonard's views were shared by younger Labour politicians, such as Hugh Gaitskell, Douglas Jay, and Evan Durbin, their emissary, A. V. Alexander, failed to overcome the resistance of the Parliamentary Labour Party. Even Leonard's militancy had its limits; he suffered from ambivalence throughout the Munich crisis, feeling "an immense relief, release, and reprieve, even though... the steps which have led to the avoidance of war... [were] shameful and morally and politically wrong" (*Journey*, 29).

The last years of peace were, Leonard later noted, "the most horrible period of my life" (*Journey*, 10). Virginia's mental state deteriorated again in 1936, as she struggled to complete *The Years*, which he deemed her worst book, and his own health was precarious in 1937 and 1938. Prostate trouble and diabetes were suspected, though neither was conclusively diagnosed. He was plagued by eczema and worsening tremor, for which he sought relief through Alexander technique treatment to no avail. He and Virginia were devastated by the death of their beloved nephew Julian in Spain in July 1937, needlessly sacrificed, the family believed, to the Republican cause. Above all, the ominous political scene, as well as intensifying Nazi persecution of Jews, took its toll on him psychologically, and for a time his literary output dwindled to little more than reviews and an occasional *Political Quarterly* article. As he later recalled: "Life became like one of those terrible nightmares in which one tries to flee from some malignant, nameless, formless horror, and one's legs refuse to work, so that one waits helpless and frozen with fear for inevitable annihilation" (*Journey*, 11).

For some years Leonard contemplated writing a play in the spirit of Bernard Shaw's parables about the collapse of civilization. He finally began it in the spring of 1938, as war clouds were darkening. Since he had never attempted a play before, he was sensitive about it, rebuffing Virginia's queries about when it would be completed. She recorded, somewhat spitefully, "L. writing his play—the one he's brewed these 10 years."[33] In October he read it to Maynard and Lydia Keynes, who thought it had merit, but repeated attempts to get it staged all proved abortive. *The Hotel* remains his least well-known published work, and he did not authorize a reprint until 1963. His introduction to the American edition observed that "it was written in the tension of those horrible years of Hitler's domination and of the feeling that he would inevitably destroy civilization" (*Hotel*, 5). Set in the foyer of the imaginary *Grand Hôtel de l'Univers et du Commerce*, the play was populated with stereotypical representatives of the European states and conflicting ideologies, including a British foreign secretary, a Russian communist agent, and a German and Italian Fascist duo. None of them, aside from the hotel proprietor's idealistic son and a quintessential Wandering Jew, has any redeeming features, as the characters wage a struggle to secure or withhold a consignment of arms for Spain. The cynical capitalist hotelier, Vajoff, oblivious to ideology and national rivalries, cares only for money: "I have no politics. Your fascism, your Nazism, your communism, what are they to me? My concern is business. If you want pianos or machine guns or frigidaires or bombs, I will supply you. But you must pay, gentlemen, you and your Führers and your Duces, you must pay the price" (*Hotel*, 29). The play, a cross between *Heartbreak House* and *Grand Hotel*, ends with concealed bombs exploding and destroying the building. The Jewish character, Jacoby, pathetic but indomitable, is a survivor who refuses to succumb to Nazi oppression:

> I was a good German.... I had fought for Germany, and I loved Germany and Breslau where I lived and my house there. Then

suddenly they took it all away from me. They drove me out of my profession—I was a lawyer. They drove me out of my house. They beat my son to death in a concentration camp.... I have said to myself, it's the end, there's nothing to live for, I shall commit suicide. And yet I don't. It's not fear. It's something inside me which just refuses to give in. Sometimes I say to myself, if Pharoah and old Nebuchadnezzar could not destroy us, I'm damned if I shall let Göring and Göbbels. There's no sense in it, of course; it's silly—but there it is.

(*Hotel*, 88–9)

Increasingly in the 1930s, especially during the Soviet purge trials, Leonard openly excoriated communism as no less a threat to Western culture than Fascism, notwithstanding his advocacy of an Anglo-Soviet military pact. Reviewing the Webbs' revised *Soviet Communism: A New Civilization*, he declared:

The Russian Government is a dictatorship and the excuses which the Webbs put forward for the dictatorship in Russia are precisely the same as those which the apologists of Fascism put forward for Hitler and Mussolini.... There is no possible reason why socialism should necessitate dictatorship. There is no such thing and never will be such a thing as dictatorship of the proletariat.[34]

Given his fulminations against Stalinism, it is implausible that in October 1938 Victor Gollancz commissioned him to write a defense of Western civilization for the avowedly pro-communist Left Book Club. Recanting his earlier indifference to Soviet repression, Gollancz, another Jewish Old Pauline, admitted in the weeks after Munich that his own views had "altered" and that liberal ideas needed to be "defended and preserved."[35] He could think of no one better suited to undertake the task than Leonard, a spokesman for democratic socialism, steeped in liberal values, rather than a typical fellow-travelling LBC author. Leonard was apprehensive, anticipating that his views would offend Gollancz's fellow directors, Harold Laski and John Strachey: "Some of the topics with which I would deal raise acute controversy among different sections of the Left and I daresay some of my opinions would be much disliked by a good many members of the Left Book Club. I assume I should have complete freedom in the expression of opinion within the law of libel."[36] Although it violated his customary practice, Gollancz consented, offering Leonard £500 for the book, which he completed in six months and submitted in May 1939 with the title *Barbarians at the Gate*.[37] The publisher's acquiescence did not preclude serious misgivings once he read the manuscript and had to withstand objections from Strachey and Laski. Gollancz claimed that it contained statements liable to be misconstrued by anti-Soviet propagandists.[38] If they could not halt publication of a commissioned book, the Left Book Club triumvirate sought to postpone it at least into the next year. What Virginia termed a "letter war" ensued, much to their frustration: "more time frittered, wasted. L. very calm; and how sane."[39] He responded to Gollancz's complaints by noting that the book had been written in response to an immediate crisis; delay might undermine the pertinence of his argument. What he had foreseen when agreeing to the publisher's terms had transpired:

> I am not hostile to the Soviet Government, but I know that any criticism of that Government or its policy is interpreted by many people as hostility.... I claim to be as good a socialist as any member of the selection committee of the Left Book Club and to be equally desirous with them of the success of the Soviet Union.... It is just because of this that I think it essential to point out errors in policy which seem to me fatal to the ultimate aim of socialism or communism.[40]

Unrepentant and obdurate, Leonard refused to alter his text on the pretext that criticism of the Soviet Union was inopportune. Nor was he dissuaded by speculation that his views might jeopardize delicate Anglo-Soviet negotiations or prompt resignations from disaffected Left Book Club members. Since Leonard would concede only minor revisions, after facing down his book club critics, who tried to persuade him that Stalin was motivated by the need to defend Soviet communism from internal and external threats, Gollancz could do little to prevent publication. In the end, once the Nazi–Soviet pact had been signed, the obstacles vanished, and the book, published in September 1939, was selected as the November monthly choice. *Barbarians at the Gate* was the first Left Book Club selection to criticize the Soviet Union openly. Strachey offered a stinging rebuke in the club's *Left News*, and Communist Pat Sloan trashed it in *Tribune*, a review that Leonard claimed "gave me no pain, but a little pleasure because it amused me."[41]

In the polemical style of *Quack, Quack!* the book denounced the resurgence of barbarism while distinguishing among the dictators. Stalin was the heir of Western civilization, embracing egalitarian ideals, whereas Hitler subjected the individual to the will of the leader. Leonard disclaimed any equivalence between the dictatorship of Stalin and those of Hitler and Mussolini: "The Soviet Government, whatever may be the results of its practice, is in its ultimate objective on the side of civilization, whereas Fascist dictatorships are on the side of barbarism" (*Barbarians*, 191). But if the Bolshevik revolution had been essential in order to impose socialism, the liquidation of capitalism and the triumph of the proletariat should have obviated the necessity of further autocracy. Instead, with the death of Lenin, the regime congealed as a tyrannical despotism. In its exercise of power rather than ultimate goals, there was little difference between the Soviet commissars and the Fascist rulers. The fault lay with Stalin and his subordinates, not with the underlying ideology. There was nothing intrinsic to Marxism that required that "there should be no communal control of the controllers of power or that personal liberty, freedom of speech, humanity and tolerance should not exist" (*Barbarians*, 190). The fundamental threat to Western culture stemmed from those who betrayed the ideals to which they owed allegiance. The greatest danger to civilization was

> not in Hitler, Mussolini, and the Nazi and Fascist systems, not in the barbarian at the gate, but within the citadel; it is in the economic barbarism of France and Britain and the ideological barbarism of Russia. For both these barbarisms destroy freedom and make the idea of a community in which the freedom of each is the condition of the freedom of all an illusion and a sham. (*Barbarians*, 219)

Once the war had begun, Leonard was unstinting in his support, while still claiming that, had British and French governments organized collective opposition to Hitler's ambitions, there would have been no war. Chamberlain's appeasement policies had left the nation without an alternative to resistance. He was doubtful as to whether victory in this war would be any more likely to achieve lasting peace and secure the rights of small nations than its predecessor: "Yet I believe that we were right to resist the Nazi policy of aggression against the small states of Europe even at the risk of war, and therefore we were right when that government accepted the challenge, to go to war" (*War for Peace*, 47–8). As long as Britain remained complicit in the system of power politics, force, and aggression—what had in previous decades been referred to as the international anarchy—the likelihood of transforming foreign relations was dubious. On the other hand, had Hitler not been resisted in 1939, "a vast area would be subjected to the most gruesome regime of violence, tyranny, and cruelty." Furthermore, he argued, it was not even Hitler, "a pitiable emigrant from the mental underworld of neurotic fear, envy, and sadism" who was wholly culpable, but rather the "system of power and force of which he is the disastrous *reductio ad absurdum*" (*Barbarians*, 53–4). From the outset Leonard was preoccupied with the components of a lasting settlement after Hitler's defeat. Responding to a *New Statesman* article on war and peace aims, he asserted that, if the British wanted to establish peace, they would have to "surrender the Empire," abandoning their strategic advantages in exchange for international tribunals, peaceful change, collective security, and disarmament.[42] European accord required a restriction of national sovereignty and the settlement of disputes on the basis of law and justice. In its existing form the British Empire was incompatible with a stable peace; in order to achieve economic justice within the community of nations, Britain would have to submit to radical changes in its economic organization.[43] If the old international system persisted, totalitarian war was inevitable; to avert future conflicts, states needed to renounce war as an instrument of national policy and reimpose a League system. In 1940 he looked ahead to a European union that would not only provide for collective security, but promote economic, social, and political cooperation (*Barbarians*, 106–7, 224).

On a more private level, Leonard's war was marked by tedium and inconvenience, punctuated by the tragedy of Virginia's suicide in March 1941. The destruction in the Blitz of his Tavistock Square and Mecklenburgh Square properties compelled him to spend those years primarily at Monks House, where, as an avid gardener, he was at least able to grow most of his own food. He and Virginia regularly witnessed German bombers heading toward London, and on one occasion German raiders flew so close to Monks House that they brushed a tree by the gate. The couple also attended first-aid classes and donated most of their saucepans for the war effort. In London they refused to enter shelters during bombing, thinking it "better to die, if that were to be our fate, in our beds" (*Journey*, 38). When the government appealed in May 1940 for Local Defence Volunteers to guard against parachutists, Leonard announced that he would join, even though he was nearly 60, five years short of the upper age limit. Virginia objected, and "an acid conversation" ensued: "Our nerves are harassed—mine at least: L. evidently relieved by the chance of doing something. Gun & uniform to me slightly ridiculous."[44] He acquiesced and remained aloof, but in 1941, shortly after her death, he volunteered for the Rodmell fire service, his duties consisting of night patrols in the village and helping to operate a pump, but incendiary bombs rarely fell in the vicinity. They had discussed what to do in the event of an invasion. Leonard imagined that the very least he could anticipate, as a Jew, was to be beaten up. As outspoken anti-Fascists, they suspected that they would be on the *Sonderfahndungliste* of political undesirables and consigned to a concentration camp should the Germans invade. Instead they proposed to commit suicide either by carbon monoxide from the car exhaust or by using the morphine that Virginia's brother, Adrian Stephen, prescribed for them. More characteristically, Leonard's chief recollection of the war was "its intolerable boredom." The endless delays in train service from Lewes to Victoria, as he struggled to meet his political commitments or cope with Hogarth Press business, the long walks when returning too late at night to find a taxi, the shortages of paper for book publishing, the restrictions of rationing, the blackouts, were continual irritants to someone impatient with obstacles, physical or bureaucratic. As he later remarked: "If I ever prayed, I would pray to be delivered, not so much from battle, murder, and sudden death, but rather from the boredom of war" (*Journey*, 65).

As early as 1940, Leonard began to renew his plea for international government. The League, he reiterated, had failed because states refused to fulfil their responsibilities, but that did not mean that only large-scale federation could prevent war. If an international authority was resuscitated, it must be able to enforce its decisions collectively, using peacekeeping forces. As a precondition, he noted unrealistically, it was imperative to abolish national air forces and to impose international control of armaments.[45] He envisaged a transition period between the end of war and the beginning of peace in order to lay the foundations for economic prosperity and political stability. This would not happen if "the political structure of Europe remains a chaos of independent sovereign states." Rather than focus on the unconditional surrender of Germany, he wanted the victors to assure the German people that, once they proved themselves as loyal and peaceful participants, they would be welcomed "as equal members of the new order." The main postwar challenges were the monumental task of feeding Europe and the shift from a war to a peace economy, a process that required an International Economic Commission under the direction of the United States, the British Empire, and the Soviet Union. But without political security, economic recovery was unachievable:

> Unless that political revolution is consciously controlled and directed by our "peace aims", the whole settlement will be jeopardized by internal struggles for political power by the staking out of international claims fatal to future peace, and by the automatic recreation of that system of international anarchy which, as soon as one great war is settled, makes another inevitable.[46]

He was prescient in foreseeing the risk of civil wars breaking out in liberated territories, causing "a war of ideologies" that would impede reconstruction and introduce "paralyzing discord" between the allies "upon whose cooperation economic reconstruction after the war must depend." In the face of territorial conflicts between communist and democratic states, the irreconcilable opponents of Russia would gain the upper hand, and the opportunity for accord between the United States, Britain, and the Soviet Union would disappear.[47]

Leonard took part in a conference on reconstruction, organized by the International Bureau of the Fabian Society in December 1942, and subsequently wrote the introduction to the published papers. Participants stressed international planning to relieve starvation, malnutrition, and disease, to restart the wheels of economic life, and to rebuild ruined cities. They recognized that millions of people would need to be repatriated, including prisoners of war, Jews driven by Nazis into foreign ghettoes, and civilians displaced to labor camps. Relief could be effective only as a prelude to reconstruction, planned and administered by international organs. Before the war ended, there must be an understanding about long-term economic and political policy, feasible only if the three powers pooled their resources and agreed about the objectives of international action.[48]

Ever since 1914 he had worried about the fate of small states in a multi-polar world order. Both world wars began after efforts by major powers to destroy their independence, yet the doctrine of self-determination was inextricably linked to the movement for democracy and liberty. Since there was scant evidence that nationalist passions had abated, any attempt to ignore such sentiment would undermine plans for postwar reconstruction. If the principle of self-determination survived, frontiers should be drawn to reduce ethnic minorities to a minimum. For the sake of international stability, a charter of rights for minorities should be adopted, and large-scale population transfer considered as an alternative to "the miseries of minority persecution." Even so, the existence of small nations would remain precarious as long as the international system was organized on the basis of power politics. Rather than consign small nations to dependence as clients of dominant powers, like the Soviet Union in Eastern Europe, he sought to curtail state sovereignty by means of a League type of international government or a more drastic system of federation: "There are no other known methods of substituting peace for violence and freedom for slavery."[49]

In 1943 Leonard was elected Chairman of the International Bureau of the Fabian Society and, as the war began to wind down, he put together a manifesto for Labour's postwar future, a preface to a distinctive socialist international policy in place of its former confusion and vacillation. It was essential for the party to define itself in contrast to Tory capitalism, which had produced economic bankruptcy and international anarchy in the interwar years: "We have to create an international authority in which national governments can cooperate for prosperity and through which the irresponsible use of national power as an instrument of national policy may be controlled."[50] The first task was to create an economic and political authority as the nucleus of international government, a radical change based on a universal renunciation of national sovereignty. This body would undertake the planning of production and consumption on a worldwide scale. Much of its power would inevitably be delegated to regional bodies; he cited, as examples, the application of the Tennessee Valley Authority concept to the Danube area or the organization of heavy industry on the Continent by the Germans irrespective of national frontiers, a daring suggestion while the allies were still at war with Hitler. Such proposals injected a stronger socialist perspective than he had previously evinced in his writings on world affairs. On the political side, he was inclined merely to reiterate ideas he had articulated since 1916. The maintenance of peace would depend on a potential aggressor recognizing that the international authority was able to mobilize militarily in defense of law and order. It was not insufficient force that made the League ineffective, but lack of will. For a renewed international organization to succeed, it must have real control of armed forces, in the form of either national contingents (a method later adopted by the UN) or an international air force. In addition, he called for the development of machinery for implementing international law, a proposition that harked back to his earlier writings. He conceded the difficulty of forging unity among the wartime allies once the common purpose of defeating Hitler had dissipated. No solemn treaty could prevent the alliance from falling apart, given the ideological and regional differences: "The United Nations will only remain united if they apply themselves to the definite task of planning an economic and political peace with the same will and international machinery and in the same detail as they have been planning war and the supply of planes, guns, and glass eyes."[51] Nor did the pamphlet avoid particular postwar problems that required practical solutions. On Germany, he asserted that its inhabitants should be condemned for willingly implementing Nazi barbarism, but insisted that "feelings of revenge and hatred are the worst possible foundations of a policy which aims at peace and prosperity."[52] Germany must be treated so as to ensure that it would no longer have the will or power to wage aggressive war, but instead would contribute to European economic cooperation. Initially, disarmament should be imposed, Nazi war criminals punished, and appropriate reparations levied, but the objective should be a democratic and pacific German government once the Nazi regime had been liquidated. Allied occupation must continue until democratic elements resurfaced. In the meantime, free political discussion and the revival of trade unions and cooperative societies needed to be fostered. He opposed any permanent dismemberment on the grounds that a settlement based on "penal truncation" was incompatible with peace. Revision of frontiers with

Poland and Czechoslovakia ought to be designed to minimize population transfers. If a peace settlement "entails the impoverishment of millions of Germans, it will entail impoverishment for ourselves and the rest of Europe."[53] Leonard said less about Palestine, but recognized that the transfer of Arab populations elsewhere was as inadvisable as it was in Germany. The only hope of reconciliation between Jews and Arabs was by means of a constitution that would "restore original frontiers" and safeguard the rights of both communities. He wanted an international body, rather than the British mandatory authority, to administer a "just settlement."[54] Once again, he demanded immediate self-government for India, Burma, and Ceylon, but continued to affirm that African territories must remain in the hands of the colonial powers, responsible for educating the people in self-government and facilitating economic development. Finally, he summoned socialist movements, which had established their *bona fides* through resistance activity throughout Europe, to unite in a new Labour and Socialist International, with the British contingent assuming a prominent role.

The detonation of atomic bombs over Japan threatened to shatter Leonard's hopes for a new international order based on cooperation among nations even before the war had ended. With its concentrated population, Britain was more vulnerable to the new weapon than other states. Should it be subjected to a nuclear attack, it would cease to exist as an inhabited country. Collective security made sense only as long as weapons were of limited destructiveness, but the situation changed with the advent of weapons capable of destroying the foundations of civilized existence. The solution was the international control of atomic energy and its restriction to industrial purposes. He argued in favor of concentrating all armaments other than those required for internal policing in the hands of the United Nations. Britain might set an example by offering to submit to national disarmament, whereas Soviet distrust might be allayed by sharing Anglo-American atomic energy information with them in order to forestall a Russian bomb.[55] He was not, however, prepared to remain silent about Soviet violations of human rights, a perpetual source of conflict with apologists, like Kingsley Martin. Until the cold war became intractable, Leonard remained sanguine about the likelihood of allied cooperation being sustained and nuclear proliferation averted, an expectation that was to prove woefully short-sighted.

By 1947 the mutual suspicions of the United States and the Soviet Union caused both to seek impregnable strategic positions. It was inevitable that Britain, financially dependent on American support, should align itself with American resistance to Russian expansion. While a totally independent British foreign policy was impracticable, Labour might at least seek to build the foundations of peace and security upon genuine impartiality, dissociated from super power maneuvers. Rejecting isolation or neutrality, he coupled reliance on the UN as an instrument of peace with a determined effort to lead non-aligned smaller states anxious to stand apart from power politics. While Britain had been justified in fighting Nazism, "we must not fight in the next war, because we cannot win it." Refusing to take part in an act of "national suicide" was the only way to evade a coming war. While still complying with collective security obligations, Britain should disengage from nuclear weapons research. Military strength need only be sufficient to deter an attack by a "minor state," and the government ought to reduce imperial commitments, as well as those in Palestine and Germany. Denying that he was an appeaser, a pacifist, or an isolationist, Leonard asserted that Britain had become a second-class power; refusal to admit this fact was either "sentimentality or blind stupidity." The only sensible course was to promote policies that ensure that

> Britain remains, in everything but military strength, a first-class power. Far from destroying the Commonwealth, it will consolidate and strengthen it as a Commonwealth of Free Nations based on international friendship and cooperation for economic and other peaceful ends, not upon subjection, domination, or military commitments which cannot possibly be fulfilled.[56]

When the war ended, Leonard resigned from his positions as secretary to the two Labour Party advisory committees. Although he continued to co-edit *Political Quarterly* with Robson (who returned to the journal after wartime service) until 1959, he contributed few additional articles. Having spent thirty years writing about foreign affairs, proclaiming the need for international government, he had nothing more to say publicly. Through two world wars he held to the view that peace could be attained only if states agreed to substitute collective security for national sovereignty:

> It is certain that it is within the power of human beings to prevent war, provided only that they have the will to create and the determination to maintain an international authority capable of imposing peace. But they cannot do that unless each is prepared to surrender to that authority some of the rights and powers of his own national state.[57]

This conviction infused all his books, articles, and reports from his first analysis of international government for the Fabian Society in 1916 to his last policy reports in the late 1940s. Perhaps he had been naively optimistic or maybe his pronouncements invoked magical thinking. If there was less international anarchy than in the past, power politics and nationalism were still prevalent. To be sure, nuclear conflagration was avoided, and UN peacekeeping operations testified to the viability of collective military action. Enduring peace and deference to international law, however, remained as elusive as they had been at the beginning of the century. Leonard turned his attention to explaining communal psychology, to protecting Virginia's reputation and literary legacy, and to writing his critically acclaimed, multi-volume autobiography. The polemicist and interpreter of world affairs, the inveterate political gadfly, the consummate committee man, settled uneasily into a role as a public intellectual, increasingly revered the more venerable he became.

Notes

1. LW to Margaret Llewelyn Davies [May 1916], Spotts, 214–15.
2. Virginia told James Strachey, "Leonard has got complete exemption owing to his tremor" (17 June 1916), VW, *Letters*, ii. 101.
3. LW to Violet Dickinson, 23 June 1916, quoted in Glendinning, 186.
4. LW, "Please, Sir, it was the other Fellow," *Essays on Literature, History, Politics* (1927), 211.
5. "Labour's Foreign Policy," *Political Quarterly* (October–December 1933), 507.
6. LW (ed.), *The Intelligent Man's Way to Prevent War* (1933), 7–9. The reversion to barbarism was a central theme of *Quack, Quack!*.
7. Ibid. 17–18.
8. Henry Brinton (ed.), *Does Capitalism Cause War* (1935), 22.

The Wars for Peace

9. Stephen Spender, *World within World* (London: Hamish Hamilton, 1951), 154.
10. "From Geneva to the Next War," *Political Quarterly* (January–March 1933), 35–6.
11. "Youth, Socialism and Peace," *Week-end Review*, 30 September 1933; LW to Frank Hardie, 29 November 1933, Hardie Papers, Bodleian Library, Oxford.
12. LW to Philip Noel-Baker, 11 March 1934, Noel-Baker Papers, Churchill College, Cambridge.
13. *A New Foreign Policy for Labour*, Report for the New Fabian Research Bureau (1934), 3–6.
14. LW to Kingsley Martin, 29 September 1935, Martin Papers, University of Sussex.
15. Its reviewer, H. M. Stannard, noted that Woolf "delivers a tremendous philippic" (*TLS*, 30 May 1935).
16. LW to Charles Singer, 25 September 1936, Spotts, 408.
17. LW to Charles Singer, 5 October 1936, Spotts, 408.
18. Glendinning (p. 282) contends that Leonard could not acknowledge the possibility of rejection in his own country.
19. *New Statesman*, 29 June 1935.
20. Ibid.
21. LW to Julian Bell, 24 November 1935, Spotts, 403.
22. LW to Julian Bell, 29 March 1936, Spotts, 406.
23. LW, *The League and Abyssinia* (1936), 17.
24. "The Ideal of the League Remains," *Political Quarterly* (July–September 1936), 342.
25. LW to H. M. Swanwick, 1 October 1937, Spotts, 412.
26. ACIntQ Memorandum No. 468 (July 1936).
27. LW to Julian Bell, 15 November 1936, Spotts, 410.
28. ACIntQ Memorandum No. 473a (December 1936).
29. *Left Review* (December 1937), 27.
30. "Arms and the Peace," *Political Quarterly* (January–March 1937), 34–5.
31. ACIntQ Memorandum No. 479A (April 1937).
32. "The Resurrection of the League," *Political Quarterly* (July–September 1937), 337–52.
33. VW, *Diary*, 31 March 1938, v. 133.
34. *Daily Herald*, 5 November 1937.
35. Victor Gollancz to LW, 19 October 1938, LW Papers.
36. LW to Victor Gollancz, 27 October 1938, Spotts, 416.
37. The American edition, published by Harcourt, Brace, was titled *Barbarians Within and Without*.

38. Victor Gollancz to LW, 22 June 1939, LW Papers.
39. VW, *Diary*, 29 June 1939, v. 223.
40. LW to Victor Gollancz, 23 June 1939, Spotts, 418–19.
41. LW to Aneurin Bevan, 28 September 1939, Spotts, 423.
42. *New Statesman*, 12 August 1939.
43. "De Profundis," *Political Quarterly* (October–December 1939), 470–1.
44. VW, *Diary*, 15 May 1940, v. 284.
45. LW, *The Future of International Government* (1940).
46. "How to Make the Peace," *Political Quarterly* (October–December 1941), 371–5.
47. "How to Make the Peace," 377–8.
48. *When Hostilities Cease: Papers on Relief and Reconstruction Prepared for the Fabian Society* (1943), 13–16.
49. "The Future of the Small State," *Political Quarterly* (July–September 1943), 217–21.
50. *International Post-War Settlement* (September 1944), 5.
51. Ibid. 13.
52. Ibid. 14.
53. Ibid. 17.
54. Ibid. 19.
55. "Britain in the Atomic Age," *Political Quarterly* (January–March 1946), 14–24.
56. LW, *Foreign Policy: The Labour Party's Dilemma* (November 1947), 19–26.
57. *International Post-War Settlement*, 8.

8
Socialism and Civilized Society

Although Leonard was an avowed socialist for most of his professional life, recognizably so in his political writings and affiliations, he was slow to assume that identity. His father, whom he revered, was a Liberal, "liberal-minded, intelligent, and humane" but not "politically or socially minded" (*Principia*, 30). Until Sidney Woolf's premature death, his family enjoyed financial security in a large house with numerous servants. Only occasionally did the "grumbling of the proletariat" in the late 1880s cause a slight tremor beneath the bourgeois comforts of the inhabitants of 101 Lexham Gardens (*Principia*, 33). Quoting W. S. Gilbert's *Iolanthe*, Leonard described himself as "born a little Liberal," although also "a little revolutionary," instinctively hostile to all authoritarians, aristocrats, or oligarchs (*Beginning*, 208). At Cambridge, his contemporaries, rebelling against religious dogma and stultifying Victorian morality, were impervious to radical politics. The iconoclasm of writers such as Ibsen and Shaw and the philosophical tenets of G. E. Moore inspired them, but they had little contact with either working-class protest or the writings of Marx. During the Ceylon years he was totally immersed in administrative responsibilities, and Lytton Strachey, his lifeline to events at home, disregarded politics in their extensive correspondence. When he returned in 1911, at the apex of New Liberalism and women's suffrage agitation, Leonard was "politically both ignorant and uncommitted." Looking back, he saw himself in 1912 as "a liberal, but not a Liberal, and half way to socialism" (*Beginning*, 99).[1]

His political initiation began during a brief involvement with the Charity Organisation Society in Hoxton, where exposure to poverty opened his eyes to the devastating impact of capitalism. Deploring paternalistic philanthropy as ineffectual, convinced that only social change could mitigate the problem, he pronounced himself a socialist.

It was not until he fell under the influence of Margaret Llewellyn Davies and the Women's Co-operative Guild (WCG) that his conversion was fully achieved, turning him into "a socialist of a rather peculiar sort" (*Beginning*, 105). He was not yet affiliated with the Independent Labour Party or the Fabian Society, although that would come shortly, but rather with an association of working-class women based largely in the industrial towns in the north of England. Attending its congresses, lecturing to its members, publicizing its activities, Leonard became a propagandist for the guild. Beyond its fundamental objective of non-competitive production and distribution, eliminating the profit motive, lay an ideal of democracy in which individual consumers, linked in self-governing cooperative societies, would determine what was produced. He envisaged the guild as an agency for educating working-class wives—few of whom he had previously come into contact with—and raising them from poverty. Although formerly indifferent to votes for women—his sister told him that "your suffrage sentiments are horrible"[2]—he developed a feminist vision of a socialist community, based on consumer control, liberating women not only from subjection to capitalist profit-seekers, but also from male-dominated trade unions. The social impulse resembled that of the later Family Allowances Act (1945), which paid a non-contributory child allowance to the mother. His experience with the organization, however, eventually dispelled initial enthusiasm, as he came to recognize "a narrow parochialism, a social and economic stuffiness, timidity, dreariness." The potential for a genuine alternative to capitalist production meant little to most members, concerned only with their dividends and shopping at "third-rate, badly arranged" cooperative stores, which offered inferior products (*Beginning*, 110).

Much of his journalism from 1912 to 1914, focused on the cooperative agenda, appeared in the *Co-operative News*. Even before Beatrice Webb enticed him into the Fabian inquiry that resulted in *International Government*, his major preoccupation until 1916, Leonard had suggested a short volume on the movement for inclusion in the Home University Library, a series of popular, non-fiction books launched in 1911, with Virginia's cousin, the historian H. A. L. Fisher, and Gilbert Murray as general editors. Strachey's first book, *Landmarks in French Literature*, and Moore's *Ethics* were among the earliest series titles, prompting Leonard to submit a proposal, possibly as soon as 1913, although no contract was signed until 1915. In another of what became a recurrent pattern of disputes with publishers,[3] Williams and Norgate, querying several passages and facing paper shortages, tried to withhold publication of *Co-operation and the Future of Industry*, initially scheduled for 1917, until after the war had ended. When Leonard threatened legal action, they agreed to cancel the contract, so that he could find a more compliant publisher. As Virginia described the situation:

> L. was as triumphant as a fighting beast who has driven his enemy to skulk in the bushes. I think he has reason to be. For one thing it looked as though [Williams] could still worry & impede it for some months to come; & L. might have been forced to arbitrate. As it is, the way is open, & instead of dealing with a surly unwilling spiteful mangy exasperating cur, he can make his own terms—which he is doing this afternoon with Allen & Unwin.[4]

It finally appeared in January 1919 under the imprint of George Allen & Unwin, responsible as well for the Fabian-sponsored *International Government* and his later *Empire and Commerce in Africa*. Leonard, increasingly disenchanted with the movement, took little pride in the book, never mentioning it in his autobiography, even though Allen & Unwin issued nearly 5,000 copies by 1928, far more than the influential *International Government*. Presumably most of them were distributed among loyal cooperators. After that experience, Hogarth Press would publish almost all his non-commissioned books.

Co-operation and the Future of Industry rehashed ideas from Leonard's earlier articles, adding an account of the movement's origins in the Rochdale Pioneers (1844) and its organizational structure. Much of the book seems aspirational, but its turgid style militated against attracting popular readership. The clarity and economy visible in more polemical works, such as *Imperialism and Civilization* or *Barbarians at the Gate*, are sadly deficient here. Tendentious pronouncements undermined his argument, as if readers could be swayed only by inflated claims:

> It is not production, but consumption which makes civilization differ from barbarism.... The most tremendous step in the world's progress would be taken if the community set itself to organize industry, not for providing work or making profits, but for the consumption of the community, for the consumers who are the community.
>
> (*Co-operation*, 3–4)

Cooperation could infuse the rank and file with "the real democratic spirit" once they learned to appreciate that it meant democratizing industry and not merely "a particular way of buying butter and tea" (*Co-operation*, 61). As constituted, the industrial system, based on class warfare, was a prescription for disaster, whereas cooperation presented a viable alternative. Yet, only if its principles were extended to industrial production, not limited to basic domestic items, would the movement achieve success. He conceded that this was unlikely so long as large segments of the nation refused to become co-operators.

While state socialism and cooperation both held that industry should function for the benefit of the whole community, the cooperative movement was more efficient, devising an organizational structure better adapted to control industry, unhampered by bureaucratic state or municipal enterprises. The book also deplored the syndicalist feature of Guild Socialism, based not on the production of goods for consumption but upon the provision of work and wages: "The motive and object of production must be the consumption of the community, and nothing else. That means that industry must be controlled democratically in the interests of the consuming community, and the unit in its organization and control must be the consumer" (*Co-operation*, 125).

In the concluding chapter he articulated his vision of a cooperative commonwealth in which membership in a consumer association would be compulsory for every citizen over 17. Since the state was an inappropriate agency for controlling industry, its functions would largely devolve upon the democratic consumer movement. In a reorganized labor market, every individual, male and female, would be obliged to perform an equal share of work. With the whole of the economy controlled democratically, class warfare would vanish, and extended leisure activity would replace superfluous productive work. His target seemed to be luxury as much as market glut, with a goal of "pure and simple food and all the simple clothing, houses, furniture, etc." (*Co-operation*, 137) His aim might have been to reshape society in his own abstemious self-image.

Disheartened by the limited horizons of the cooperative movement, he still believed that it had the potential to develop into something more ambitious. That may have been why he accepted an offer from Philip Snowden in 1920 to write a volume for the Social Studies Series, a collaboration between the Independent Labour Party and the National Labour Press. Originally promised £50 plus royalties, he found his fee reduced to £25 when the publisher encountered financial difficulties. By then Leonard had multiple socialist connections, including the Fabian Society (which he joined in 1913), the Independent Labour Party (in which he became active during the First World War), and, after 1918, the advisory committees of the Labour Party, but never felt compatible with the acerbic, anti-intellectual Snowden. Disinclined to refuse a commission, he managed to complete a short book by early 1921. As he wrote to Lord Robert Cecil on April 11, 1921:

> Personally I think the class war and the conflict of class interests are the greatest curses, and that the first thing that one should aim at is to abolish this conflict and class war. I think you want exactly the same kind of cooperation between individuals and classes in a nation as you want between nations, but that you cannot possibly get it so long as society is organized as it is today. I have just written a book which ought to be published in a week or so, dealing very largely with this point...[5]

Socialism and Co-operation, couched in more radical terms, claimed that the immediate object of socialism should be to abolish private ownership and capitalist control, substituting a partnership between consumers and producers. The state, purportedly embodying communal interests, had become "an engine of exploitation and tyranny" (*Socialism*, 28) Since the cooperative movement based industrial organization on consumption, shifting control to the community, it could become "the most powerful means for attaining the ideals of socialism" (*Socialism*, 35). Ultimately, the cooperative societies would encompass all aspects of production, supplanting trade unionism as the chief instrument for ensuring production for use within a socialist state. The aim of industry would no longer be to provide workers with an occupation but simply to furnish the necessities of life. While everyone needed to perform a share of "this unpleasant but necessary work," industrial production would be confined to a "minimum compatible with a comfortable existence" (*Socialism*, 66). In return for a specified amount of labor, each person would receive an equal share in commodities and services, and, as an active consumer, would motivate cooperative stores to supply what he or she wanted to consume. Any individual who refused to work would be debarred from receiving a share of industrial products, effectively ostracizing him or her from the community.

> The ideal society would be one in which this demand was only for commodities and services strictly useful, so that industry produced a high standard of material comfort combined with simplicity, and the community and individual were free to devote the greater part of their time and energy to activities other than those of industry.
>
> (*Socialism*, 82)

An efficient economy would require the individual to devote no more than three months to industrial production, leaving the remainder of the year for other pursuits. Under a cooperative system, utility, not luxury, would determine what articles would be produced. Objects of beauty would continue to be created in leisure time; art, literature, music, and sport, divorced from commercialism, would flourish. Cities and homes might become more attractive when ornamentation, redolent of Victorian excess, ceased to be manufactured. These goals resonated more closely with William Morris's *News from Nowhere* than with the outlook of the Co-operative Wholesale Society as he had known it. Such "heretical" ideas were just as unpalatable in Labour circles, making this "even more futile than most of my books" (*Downhill*, 85). He summed up his position by noting: "My vision of a socialist society [is] based on consumers' control" (*Beginning*, 106). Margaret Llewelyn Davies turned him into an adherent of cooperative principles, and he clung to them in the face of popular indifference. While Leonard was generally regarded as a moderate, middle-class, socialist intellectual, his idiosyncratic views at this time diverged from the mainstream. "I am aware that, although I call myself and think myself a socialist, many other socialists will deny that what I call socialism is really socialism" (*Socialism*, 3). In later years he was to refer to himself as "a Marxian Socialist—but only up to a point" (*Barbarians*, 123); his ideological orientation derived from involvement with cooperation, not from his reading of *Das Kapital*. Keeping his distance from Marxism was tied to his distaste for Soviet communism as well as residual liberal values. Cambridge and Bloomsbury were his cultural milieu, not the union meeting hall, although he excelled as a lecturer to working-class audiences. Virginia recounted a listener's comment after one of his WCG talks that "he was the only gentleman who spoke so that working

Socialism and Civilized Society 167

women could understand."[6] An outsider within the Labour Party, he gravitated towards kindred spirits among middle-class intellectuals and experts, such as Noel-Baker, C. R. Buxton, Brailsford, and Norman Leys, rather than MacDonald, Snowden, or trades unionists. Few within his immediate circle were ideological socialists or even politically minded, but socialist convictions infused all of his political writings, not to mention his activities, something Virginia learned to tolerate, if not wholly to support.

As Labour asserted its claim to compete nationally, it would have seemed natural for Leonard to seek a parliamentary seat. He had informed Virginia before their marriage that he wanted to "find out about labour & factories and to keep outside Government and do things on his own account,"[7] but opportunities beckoned that could not be easily resisted. A tentative approach in July 1918 failed to materialize. Then in the spring of 1920 the Seven Universities Democratic Association invited him again to stand as its candidate at the next general election for the double-seated Combined English Universities constituency.[8] Reluctantly yielding, he was adopted in May 1920, later claiming that he consented since he had no chance of actually being elected. The sitting MPs were H. A. L. Fisher, current President of the Board of Education, and the Tory, Sir Martin Conway. Leonard regarded Fisher, Virginia's cousin, as "the kind of respectable Liberal who made respectable liberalism stink in the nostrils of so many in my generation" (*Downhill*, 34). He had taken the precaution of contacting Sidney Webb to ensure that, were he to accept the association's offer, he would not be opposed by an official Labour candidate.[9] Webb reassured him, and he was indeed viewed as the Labour nominee.

Leonard's few speeches during the months before the 1922 General Election, in Manchester, Durham, Liverpool, and Newcastle, drew meager audiences of supporters, mostly women, although Conservative students tried to break up his meetings in Liverpool. He generally devoted his remarks to international politics or the cooperative movement, but his printed election address highlighted his left-leaning views at the time. Echoing a familiar trope, he warned that "there will be no change if the old men and the old methods are reinstated in Westminster, and if we want a change we must try a party with new principles and new men." On specific issues, he called for "a complete break with the dangerous and extravagant foreign policy" of the Lloyd George ministry, substituting reliance on the League of Nations, disarmament, and an equitable settlement of the reparations problem. The only hope for Europe consisted in closer understanding among Britain, France, and Germany, as well as diplomatic recognition of Soviet Russia and cooperation with the United States. He aimed to implement promises of self-government for India and Ceylon, and independence for Egypt, and to revise policies in Africa that exploited "so-called backward races." In home affairs he pledged equal opportunity to obtain elementary, secondary, and university education and a special levy upon fortunes exceeding £5,000. In conclusion, he declared:

> I believe in socialism and co-operation, but not in violent revolution; I believe that the resources of the community should be controlled by and in the interests of the whole community rather than small groups and classes. But the work of the next Parliament ought to consist neither in bolstering up the vested interests of the present economic system nor in immediately destroying it, but in laying the foundations of a real peace in Europe and of an educated democracy in this country. (*Downhill*, 36–40)

Leonard felt he had made a poor impression during his campaigning, unable to conceal his reluctance to become an MP. In Manchester he actually said as much, which "rather flabbergasted" his audience of elderly academics.[10] In the poll the two sitting members easily won, while he came in a distant fourth (out of six candidates) with 366 votes, relieved to have avoided a derisory result. In 1927 he was invited to contest the London University seat for Labour at the next election—when he might actually have stood a chance—but declined to become a candidate again.

The bulk of Leonard's writing during the interwar years dealt with international affairs, especially after the rise of totalitarianism in the Soviet Union, Italy, and Germany. For men of his generation, the traumatic event of their lives had been the First World War, causing countless deaths and shattering the illusion of progress. Even for those who did not experience combat, the loss of friends and relatives, the interminable slaughter of young men, provoked revulsion against militarism and a need to discover some justification for war. His contributions, notably *Empire and Commerce in Africa* and *International Government*, examined the factors that generated conflict and those that might prevent it. Yet, somehow that did not adequately explain why, despite the advance of democracy, wars recurred. Beginning around 1920, he commenced research on what became his notably unsuccessful *magnum opus*, the two-volume *After the Deluge* (1931, 1939) and its successor volume, *Principia Politica* (1953). He fastened onto the concept of communal psychology, the congeries of beliefs and values of the people, as the social force that could explain democratic progress and the persistence of war. To undertake such an investigation, tracing ideas back to the French Revolution and forward to the present, would have been a monumental task for an accomplished scholar unencumbered with other professional responsibilities. Leonard was remarkably well read in many areas and in several languages, even acquiring a rudimentary knowledge of Russian in the 1920s. His educational background, his incessant book reviewing, especially for the *Nation*, his irrepressible curiosity and eclectic cultural interests convinced him that such a project did not exceed his capabilities. While he was an undergraduate, after his immersion in the Greek classics, he had begun to explore modern European literature, and by 1924 Hogarth Press was publishing the papers of Sigmund Freud. He and Virginia coupled their days of writing with extensive reading. Yet, Leonard's knowledge was general, not specialized. He was, in Isaiah Berlin's terminology, a fox, not a hedgehog. His project would require the skills of an historian, an ethical philosopher, a social psychologist, and an anthropologist, qualifications that he could not claim. His self-confidence, rarely palpable in human relationships, was audacious in matters of the intellect, bred by the hermetic arrogance of Edwardian Cambridge and the Apostles, inculcating the notion that he could address almost any subject, invading the territory of the academic specialist with impunity. It was to prove his most profound disappointment.

Just prior to the publication of the first volume in the trilogy, Leonard, optimistic about the potential of broadcasting as an educational tool, delivered a series of six BBC talks on the modern state. It was a chance for him to rehearse some of the themes of the trilogy, utilizing his skill as a lecturer, honed in the League of Nations Society, the WCG, and as a parliamentary candidate. They were published in the *Listener*, reprinted in a volume entitled *The Modern State*, and reissued in 1945 for the armed forces.[11] Given their provenance, the tone was deliberately unthreatening, a modest testimonial to the ideals of liberal democracy, with the merest hint of socialist overtones. He observed that a decade after the Allies had fought a war to make the world safe for democracy, conservatives, who had once been hostile, were now its most ardent supporters, while communists had become its most bitter opponents. This gave rise to a widespread sense that democracy was failing. In order to resuscitate democratic sentiment, advocates needed to emphasize that the happiness of ordinary people was its motivating force. This idea, propagated throughout Western civilization, was now threatened by Fascists and communists, both contending that the happiness of the people should be subordinated to state authority. The essence of a democratic system, he affirmed, is that it treats everyone politically as an individual, ignoring distinctions of class and property. As a precondition of happiness, the government must provide universal education. While not every British child could enjoy similar educational advantages, access to secondary and university education had been extended. Belief in equal rights also led to the emancipation of women, which "may prove to be one of the greatest social revolutions in human history" (*Modern State*, 56). He went on to assert that "the ordinary lives of ordinary people are much happier today than they were thirty years ago and infinitely more happy than they were eighty years ago" (*Modern State*, 35). Harking back to a theme in his two books on cooperation, he suggested that the reduction in working hours generated the greatest measure of happiness and commended state action for providing public libraries, parks, adult education, and broadcasting to occupy leisure time.

Shifting his focus from happiness to equality, Leonard cited unequal distribution of wealth and income as an obstacle to a sustainable democracy. Only by eliminating the capitalist system and transferring control of finance, industry, and commerce to the whole community would social equality be achieved. The third component of democracy—liberty—required as little governmental interference with the individual as possible. Yet, he recognized that a balance needed to be struck: it was sometimes necessary to curtail individual liberty to protect the whole of society. Coupled with the increase in liberty was an expansion of state regulation to benefit the public. Of growing concern was that universal education and popular culture produced a standardized citizenry, what Mill called 'collective mediocrity': "It seems to me a kind of disease of democracy, for it destroys individuality and teaches people to follow one another like sheep instead of choosing for themselves. It is a real danger to the democratic ideal of liberty" (*Modern State*, 63). Standardization and mechanistic efficiency challenged the democratic vision of a "society of educated and intelligent people in which independence of thought and speech and every kind of freedom and initiative were encouraged" (*Modern State*, 65). In later years he faulted the media for weakening cultural standards, catering to the lowest common denominator rather than elevating the minds of the people:

> Those who control the popular press and the enormous machines of entertainment through sound broadcasting and television seem to be convinced that the "masses" must always be destitute of taste and intelligence, that they must be fed almost entirely upon "light" entertainment, and that they are totally incapable of understanding or appreciating anything new, serious or first rate in the realms of art and thought.[12]

While Leonard always contended that socialist and liberal values could be reconciled, he placed a higher value on individual rights than on collective needs. In the long run, democracy would survive only if people sought "the kind of civilization in which States and Governments exist to protect the happiness, equality, and liberty of ordinary persons. But if they prefer the ideals of nationalism and national glory and a narrow patriotism, democracy must inevitably perish" (*Modern State*, 81). This was a resounding defense of democratic values, increasingly precarious in the Anglo-American world, a touchstone for the more sustained analysis of *After the Deluge* and *Principia Politica*. Defiant in the face of encroaching authoritarianism, he upheld principles worth fighting for amid the darkening clouds.

Leonard produced only one book in the decade between 1921 and 1931, *Imperialism and Civilization* (1928), a concise synthesis of earlier research, originating in 1927 as six lectures under the auspices of the Union of Democratic Control. During those years and for more than two decades thereafter he labored over *After the Deluge*, an excessively ambitious project that spun out of control. Intending no less than an exploration of "the psychology of man as a social animal," he recognized that it would "require a good many volumes" (*Deluge*, i, p. v). It eventually became a trilogy, but even the third volume, *Principia Politica*, published in 1953, promised a sequel that would assess the viability of democracy. The critical response and advancing years ensured that a fourth volume was never written. Leonard did not explain why he chose the title *After the Deluge*, but the reference was clearly to the First World War, biblical allusions notwithstanding. Inadvertently perhaps, it also harked back to the celebrated aphorism attributed to the French king Louis XV: *Après moi le dèluge*. A central theme was the emergence of democratic ideas in England and France after the French Revolution in the face of upper-class resistance. While Leonard championed popular democracy, he was, at least in the 1930s, less sanguine about whether the masses would achieve or even aspire to the enlightened civilization whose roots he found in Athens during the age of Pericles. Culturally, he remained a Bloomsbury elitist, less empathetic toward ordinary human foibles than, for example, his friend, J. B. Priestley. Virginia, not always the most objective witness, confided in 1935 that Leonard was "very hard on people, especially on the servant class. No sympathy with them."[13]

Although the causes of the First World War had been discussed in several of his books, he felt that he had failed to delve below the surface to assess the impact of popular beliefs. He proposed to examine the interaction between general ideas about liberty, equality, and democracy and political events in the years between 1789 and 1914, though the first volume did not range much beyond the eighteenth century. From the outset *After the Deluge* became mired in terminological distinctions about the nature of history, the relation between political and economic ideas, and the meaning of civilization, a defect more pronounced because of his propensity for repetition and digression. The effort to determine the impact of communal beliefs upon historical events tended to dissolve into comparative analyses of the French and American revolutions. He claimed that the political ideas that motivated Europeans to fight between 1914 and 1918 could be summed up as freedom, nationality, and democracy, ideas that infused popular consciousness during the revolutionary era. The obstacle to their realization was the countervailing force of privilege and inheritance, the resistance first of the aristocracy and later of capitalists to extending popular rights. This implied a quasi-Marxist explanation for the defeat of popular aspirations: a rigid class structure obstructed the democratic impulse until the late nineteenth century. Less persuasively, Leonard tried to superimpose an alternative ideological interpretation, which he identifies as communal psychology:

> One finds in the mind of nearly everyone then living a background or network of what may be called fundamental ideas. These ideas may not often be consciously stated; they are often so wide or vague as to be in the nature of an intellectual attitude rather than of definite beliefs; but they are assumed as postulates by writers and thinkers, and in religious, political, or social controversies they are explicitly stated as conclusive reasons for acting in one way rather than another. (*Deluge*, i. 222–3)

This hypothesis rests on meager evidence, and these "fundamental ideas" are explicated only in generalities. Even granting the emergence of democratic sentiments, it would be impossible to substantiate a causal connection between them and political phenomena. Furthermore, he conceded that political ideas "are imposed by the past upon the present, by the dead upon the living" (*Deluge*, i. 41), a deterrent to fomenting a revolution in human consciousness.

Before 1789 political power was vested in property, and the general populace accepted privilege as an inherited right. Happiness was not yet a factor in the ordering of civil society. Somewhat bizarrely, he claimed that during the eighteenth century "political ideas hardly existed and were never operative" in Britain. It required the French Revolution and the subversive writings of Godwin, Paine, and Cobbett to turn the ordinary Englishman of the time into "a political animal" (*Deluge*, i. 114–15), a notion subsequently refuted by a generation of social historians, led by Christopher Hill and E. P. Thompson. By 1931 there were millions of people who "instinctively, unconsciously" held that happiness should be possessed "by all persons and all classes," but he ascribed such a belief to the American Declaration of Independence, the foundation of modern democracy, rather than to popular convictions dating back at least to the seventeenth-century Levellers (*Deluge*, i. 192).

Leonard's antipathy to religious faith provoked a gratuitous attack on Christianity for establishing "a framework for human society in which earthly miseries have a recognized, permanent, and honourable place" (*Deluge*, i. 219). Democracy, with its implicit commitment to an equal right to happiness, must therefore be essentially secular. Christian religious ideas were inimical to "the social network of ideas about happiness which lies behind democracy" (*Deluge*, i. 236). An additional target was the English public school, perpetuating a structure based on privilege. Here "everything is done to prevent the growth of any consciousness of individuality, to suppress the individual and turn him into an English gentleman" (*Deluge*, i. 249). Communal psychology in the public school imitated that of the regiment, cultivating *esprit de corps*, the psychology of the herd. The political concept of individuality was a disruptive challenge to authoritarian institutions, such as the Church, the army, and the public school; if the individual were recognized as the fundamental unit, it would necessitate the concession of social and political rights.

He derided those who doubted whether a society without aristocrats would be capable of maintaining the government, adding facetiously:

> there is not the slightest reason to believe that it is impossible for the man in the street to become in a few hundred years as cultured and intelligent and politically sagacious as any member of the present Cabinet or of any other Cabinet which has controlled our destinies in the last 200 years. What we have done with our pigs by breeding and environment we ought to be able also to do with our politicians.

Even if they proved to be mediocrities, it was preferable to choose politicians from ordinary mankind rather than from traditional elites. In an aristocratic social order, the base of the pyramid would consist of morons; a democratic society would reduce their number, although it could not guarantee a sufficient number of intelligent people to staff government functions (*Deluge*, i. 266–7).

The book suffers from its protracted composition, written in fits and starts over a decade. The framework promises more than it delivers, and idiosyncratic digressions interrupt the discursive flow. The reader, disturbed by its dogmatic tone or amused by prejudicial attitudes, might also find the unwieldy chapters and repetitiousness tedious. Leonard could dazzle with the breadth of his reading, his familiarity with a range of political philosophers, his mastery of detail, but in the end his thesis fails to convince. Goldie Dickinson, who read the manuscript, warned Leonard about "a certain excess of repetition," adding that "the reader's heart sinks before a long chunk like Chapter three" (186 pages in length).[14] Reviewers were respectful rather than laudatory, although Laski in the *New Statesman* termed it the most important book of its kind since Graham Wallas had published *Human Nature in Politics*, but admitted that it was "not easy to state briefly the thesis he is examining."[15] Lewis Namier, while admiring Leonard's "fundamentally hopeless attempt" to analyze the basic ideas in the general population, criticized the length and garrulous style. The argument could have been condensed and the structure more sharply defined.[16] Yet nothing was more distressing to the author than a belittling half-column review in the *Times Literary Supplement*. Virginia confided in her diary:

> L. says—& honestly believes—that this puts an end to the book.... He says his ten years work are wasted, & that he sees no use in going on.... However Laski & the experts may applaud, as they do in the serious weeklies, his book is dead; his work wasted.... Its his curious pessimistic temper: something deeper than reason.... liberating the irrational despondency which I see in all Woolves, & connect with centuries of oppression.[17]

Leonard conceded that his disappointment at the reception of *After the Deluge* (and subsequent volumes) "was fairly deep, though not very prolonged." A week later Virginia was relieved to note that the "morbidity of L's is over;"[18] in his autobiography he insisted that, once his books were published, he was not really concerned about other people's opinion of them. This attitude, disingenuous though it may have been, accorded with his oft-expressed mantra, "nothing matters." What he was attempting to do was, he asserted, "of immense importance to history and sociology," however contrary the view of scholars (*Downhill*, 204–5).

The second volume of *After the Deluge* does not delve deeply into the nineteenth century, despite a professed intention to extend its scope to the 1871 Paris Commune and Gladstone's 1894 retirement. Instead it traces the interaction of political leaders and the populace at the time of the 1832 Reform Act in England and the July 1830 revolution in France. Communal psychology is once again subordinated to narrative details. He described 1832 as "a real revolution, an English revolution, and therefore muddled, compromised, snugly wrapped up, and safely constitutionalized by the intellectual cotton-wool which we call English common sense" (*Deluge*, ii. 13). In England, bourgeois reformers preferred to retain the existing structure of property rather than "create a society of free and equal citizens governing themselves.... The desire for property and profits was stronger than the desire for freedom and equality" (*Deluge*, ii. 151). Political concessions in 1832 forestalled a more radical attack on the system. While the bourgeoisie achieved power, the aspirations for political equality were crushed. It is hardly surprising, in view of the tumultuous events of the 1930s, that he failed to complete the manuscript until the beginning of 1939. Published in in late September, several weeks after the war had started, it was generally ignored and sold poorly in both Britain and America, to his ineluctable dismay.

Leonard's perspective became clearer in *Barbarians at the Gate*, written as a defense of liberal democracy but underpinned by concessions to Marxist ideology. Published in the same year as the second part of *After the Deluge*, it was less constrained by the framework of communal psychology. He identified the transfer of economic and political power from the landed aristocracy to the middle class as the crucial transition in nineteenth-century civilization. New standards of social value, propagated by the American and French revolutions, envisaged a society in which the free development of each was the condition of the free development of all and in which every individual was guaranteed the same opportunity for happiness. Although gradual democratization took place, economic power was monopolized by manufacturers and financiers: "A society of free and equal citizens was no more possible without economic than it was without political democracy. The communal control of economic power was just as essential to it as the communal control of political power" (*Barbarians*, 153).

The resulting class war was the inevitable consequence of capitalist control of industry and finance. No society could be truly democratic unless it was grounded in liberty, equality, and tolerance. If democracy were linked to socialism, social relations would be based on cooperation, not privilege, and the role of the state subjected to popular will: "It is only when people begin to use the state and government, not as instruments of power or patriotism, but as part of the drainage system, that they begin to be civilized" (*War for Peace*, 91). Nor was there any reason to doubt that communal control over economic forces could be accomplished without violent revolution, transforming a capitalist system into a socialist one, in which common interests would supplant class conflict.

Leonard described *Principia Politica*, published in 1953, as the third volume of *After the Deluge*, but it differed in character from its predecessors. For one thing, the chronological framework was discarded, but it was also more autobiographical, emphasizing personal values, including the primacy of the "good" in society. In some ways it is the most readable of the trilogy, perhaps because it abandoned the communal psychology straitjacket for a more pertinent focus on "the eternal struggle between liberty and authoritarianism" (*Principia*, 6). Unfortunately, it was doomed from the outset by its title, suggested by Keynes, who told Leonard that what he was writing was an analysis of political principles, but the Latinate title proved commercially toxic, inviting an unintended comparison with Newton, Russell, and Moore.

He describes being "born into a society of which the foundations seemed, at least to the upper and middle classes, comfortably secure" (*Principia*, 48). His early social values, reflecting those of the affluent Victorian bourgeoisie, incorporated a distinct sense of social precedence, a reliance on deferential servants, and anxiety about working-class unrest. He grew up believing himself to be a gentleman in a world rigidly divided between gentlemen and cads; "we mixed and would mix only with our own class" (*Principia*, 34). Leonard identified 1832 as a crucial turning point in Britain, destroying "the past of the dinosaur." What replaced it was a bourgeois society that survived intact until 1914. The structure of society, subject to political and economic pressures, remained substantially unchanged while an intellectual revolution was taking place, "dividing me from the dead past of history." Its seminal figures were Darwin, Marx, and Freud, although Freud's impact was relevant only in his mature years. In *After the Deluge* Leonard had recounted historical milestones, but his attention now shifted to this cultural watershed: "the world was never the same after the publication of *The Communist Manifesto* and *The Origin of Species*" (*Principia*, 41–2).

Subordinating political ideas such as nationalism and imperialism, Leonard proceeded to exalt ethical standards of value, especially those reflecting his own ideals. The 1914 war challenged a complacent belief in progress by denying the value attached to human life. What he had recognized as a common body of ideas, a communal psychology, became more repugnant with the rise of Fascism, whose leaders "were almost all gangsters, perverts, or paranoiacs" and whose followers had turned into "sadistic savages" or worshippers of a "homicidal maniac" (*Principia*, 89). In an age which saw millions of people executed because of their religious identity or imprisoned as political dissidents, Leonard felt impelled to address good and evil:

> I have a social prejudice in favor of truth, freedom to pursue and express it, justice, tolerance, humanity and a prejudice against the use of force or violence, against cruelty, and against the killing or arbitrary persecution of human beings.... I consider a society good in proportion as its structure and motive power is based on and encourages human friendliness and cooperation, both communal and individual.... what determines whether a society is civilized is its material standards of life, its intellectual and spiritual standards of life, and its contributions to art, science, learning, philosophy or religion. (*Principia*, 51–3)

For Leonard, the source of these values could be ascribed to the ancient Hebrews and to fifth-century Athens. It was the Hebrews who first upheld the ethical value of the individual: the Ten Commandments made clear that "human life is a good thing and that to deprive an individual of it is an evil act." They never developed social standards of value because their religion and politics were indivisible, making it unacceptable to criticize government. Since a rationalized God was a precondition for a secular society, the Jews, "who were not an unintelligent people, never developed even the most rudimentary conception of politics" (*Principia*, 70). Instead it was the ancient Greeks who were the first to secularize government, a unique feat that made European civilization feasible:

> It was this religious or metaphysical attitude which, when combined with their intense curiosity, made it possible for the Greeks to liberate themselves from the spiritual prison of superstition which closed upon the human mind as soon as it took the fatal step of thinking and imagining. The Greeks became religiously and metaphysically sceptics without ever losing their belief in spiritual values. (*Principia*, 57)

They perceived the problem of sin, crime, and punishment in terms not of retribution, but of pity. Whereas the Hebrews submitted to a cruel and tyrannical God, the Greeks heralded the revolt of human reason against an irrational universe, affirming that distinctions between right and wrong applied to the gods no less than to mankind. For Leonard, absolving guilt and humanizing punishment were intrinsic ethical values: "to be a slave to [the sense of sin] is barbarism, to control it is civilization." Religion, whether Hebraic or its Christian offshoot, was "one of the greatest obstacles to a revaluation of standards in terms of truth and reason" (*Principi*a, 65, 68). By secularizing thought, the Greeks evolved a standard of value that was to become a vital component of European civilization.

Above all, it was the funeral oration of Pericles, as reported by Thucydides, that gave voice to Athenian social ideals and practices. For Leonard it had become totemic, ever since he first encountered it in a St Paul's schoolroom in the 1890s: "I can never read it even today, without an uplifting of the heart, the same purging of the passions which one gets in Greece itself... the creed of the civilized man and the civilized state in the language of bare beauty peculiar to the Greeks" (*Principi*a, 78). Nor was this merely hyperbolic or sentimental: throughout his life he returned to the classics, in their original language, as early morning reading, to restore his spirits and enlighten his mind. What was appealing in Pericles was the exaltation of freedom coupled with respect for law as the keystone of civilization, the pursuit of goals that had intrinsic value. The good state was "a community of free men, held together and directed, not by force and fear but by their voluntary acceptance of and obedience to law, laws made by themselves and based on reason, justice, and humanity." These guidelines, formulated by the ancient Greeks, were the ones "that personally I accept today." He juxtaposed Athenian ideals to "the primitive Semitic principle of retribution or vengeance" (*Principi*a, 80, 83), identifying himself with Hellenist rather than Hebraic values. The Greeks believed that the less compulsion there was in relations between the individual and society, the better the citizen. In choosing between two evils, the just man chooses the lesser, yet, if the good life were imperiled by external threat, choosing the lesser evil was consistent with a forceful response.

Leonard also cited the ancient Greeks during the Second World War when denigrating the distrust of the intellectual as the hallmark of British politics and a factor in ineffectual responses to the threat of

Fascism: "To think that it is possible for a nation to deal competently with such a world, either in peace or war, by instinct and improvisation is a suicidal delusion." The divorce of the man of action from the intellectual had become ingrained in Britain and "has brought us to the perilous position in which we stand." To the Greeks, the notion that the intellectual should be despised in the world of politics would have seemed ludicrous; Pericles, the "greatest of [their] statesmen, was also one of the greatest of [their] intellectuals."[19]

The second half of *Principia Politica* is a diatribe against modern authoritarianism, as represented by National Socialism and communism, elaborating themes developed earlier in *Quack, Quack!* and *Barbarians at the Gate*. What made the history of Nazi Germany so repugnant was not its sacrifice of civilized values, its repression of individuality, but the fact that "hundreds of thousands of ordinary, educated, apparently rational human beings accepted this repulsive nonsense as truth and condoned the barbarities and cruelties" (*Principia*, 167). In view of Hitler's demise, the brunt of Leonard's criticism was levelled at Soviet Russia. Reiterating his view that the communist regime perpetuated autocracy long after it could be justified by external pressures, he labelled it as "frigidly inhuman, as insanely irrational as that of the fascist or Nazi." Instead of empowering the workers, it created a dictatorship that violently suppressed all opposition and employed propaganda to convince the cowed masses that they were living in a free and democratic society. He was horrified by the liquidation of the kulaks, by Stalin's "perversion of reason," and by the "dialectical lunacy" of communism in practice (*Principia*, 211–12). Once again he emphasized the confusion between means and ends:

> the ruthless adoption of means which involve the certainty of great evils in order ultimately to attain a great social good is disastrous. It destroys or perverts our sense of social values and therefore the foundations of civilization.... What was regarded at first as a social evil is now regarded as a social good, and the civilized scale of values is contaminated and destroyed. (*Principia*, 223)

He conceded that Soviet industrialization in a single generation was a singular feat, the elimination of capitalism relieving workers from economic exploitation. Yet, despite more equitable distribution of wealth, the standard of living remained lamentably low. He doubted whether the Russian people could achieve a civilized life under a government that habitually suppressed and distorted the truth. He concluded that "in the last 500 years of European history there have been few periods and places in which the government has been worse, the lives which ordinary men and women were forced to live more degraded, the standards of social value more debased than they are in Russia today" (*Principia*, 234). Authoritarian regimes, ultimately incompatible with modern life, could not survive without provoking social disintegration or explosion, a prophetic observation, although Leonard never dared to predict when such a collapse might take place.

More definitively than was the case with *After the Deluge*, the publication of *Principia Politica* provoked a generally hostile response. The sharpest criticism came from a cluster of Oxford dons, including A. J. P. Taylor and Hugh Trevor-Roper, for once in agreement. Taylor labelled the attack on the Soviet Union as hysterical,[20] while Trevor-Roper dismissed its argument as irrelevant and incomprehensible.[21] What sparked their resentment was Leonard's pretense to mastery of his subject, ignoring the divide between the generalist and the academic specialist. Nowhere was this clearer than in a devastatingly condescending *New Statesman* review by the philosopher Stuart Hampshire, who complained that the book had been written "in the undistinguishing terms of common sense," free from the "apparatus of scholarship," venturing into historical and philosophical analysis "with the lightest possible equipment." In this third volume "indifference to specialized knowledge is carried to impossible lengths" and, in contrasting democracy with totalitarianism, the author was both "dogmatic and incoherent." Challenging the notion of Athenian society as a beacon of freedom, he refuted Leonard's idealized depiction as "imaginary" and dismissed his enumeration of democratic values as a litany of empty abstractions. In addition, he faulted his misunderstanding of "motives which are different from one's own and of the conditions of life which produce them."[22] After all that, it is little wonder that Leonard decided to abandon this kind of historical *cum* philosophical speculation to the experts and turned his attention instead to autobiography. It was to bring him greater critical and popular acclaim than any of his other publications.

The moral dilemma posed by means and ends, whether it was justifiable to commit a lesser evil in order to achieve a greater good, became a motif in Leonard's contentious correspondence with Kingsley Martin, editor of the *New Statesman* from 1930 to 1960. His connection with the weekly, beginning in 1913 and lasting until 1968, was never as intimate as in the Martin years, when he regularly contributed articles, reviews, leader columns, and letters to the editor. In addition, he occasionally deputized during the editor's absences in the 1940s and 1950s and served as a director from 1942 to 1965. Kingsley's own insecurity caused him to rely on others more confident of their views, less susceptible to his own crippling indecisiveness, and no one performed that role more consistently than Leonard. Where Kingsley was emotional, quixotic, and prone to self-reproach, Leonard was self-assured, forthright in his opinions. Martin's biographer acknowledged their "vitriolic quarrels" and "ferocious short-lived enmities."[23] While both ostensibly supported the League of Nations, the pacifist Kingsley never fully endorsed collective security or the application of sanctions against an aggressor, whereas for Leonard enforcing the League Covenant would lessen the probability of war. In what was to become a recurrent theme in their exchanges, he discounted Kingsley's moral qualms. The conviction that a choice could be made between entirely good and entirely evil actions is "an almost universal delusion and leads to political and social disaster." In nearly all cases the choice was between two evils and "the wise man is he who by reason or instinct chooses the less evil course leading to the lesser evil."[24] When the war began, Leonard faced it, if not with equanimity, at least fatalistically, while Kingsley was far more timorous, declaring that "it is criminal folly to support a war against Germany & Russia & that if it goes on we are likely to be defeated."[25] Leonard told Vita Sackville-West that Kingsley was "the worst scaremonger and rumour-monger in London, far worse in talk than in the [*New Statesman*]."[26] In June 1940, in the wake of the Dunkirk evacuation, he warned Leonard of an imminent invasion of Britain, precipitating a government withdrawal to Canada (*Journey*, 54).

While Leonard, having flirted with neutrality in the late 1940s, eventually embraced the Anglo-American alliance, Kingsley moved leftward, avowedly pro-Soviet and anti-American. In October 1949 he refused to censure Hungary for executing Lazlo Rajk, the Interior Minister, on trumped-up charges. When the editor, who observed that Christians were just as ready to act as if the end justified the means, added that those who applauded the indiscriminate bombing of cities should withhold their scorn, Leonard accused him of defending judicial murder. By comparing communist show trials to Christians massacring heretics, he seemed to intimate that "one wrong anywhere makes everything right for ever after." Clearly intending to provoke Kingsley, he concluded his published letter to the editor by saying: "I am one of those Rip van Winkles, who has always condemned the murders of Socrates, Christ, and Giordano Bruno as well as that of Mr Rajk."[27] An indignant Kingsley retorted that he failed to see how Leonard could say that "good ends can never justify bad means after we have thought the end of national safety justified fighting a world war."[28] In this exchange it was Leonard who had the last word and, as usual, the better of the argument:

> If our whole sense of justice had not been perverted in the last 30 years, I do not believe that you or anyone else would use that argument about a gang of low-class Hungarian politicians deliberately murdering by judicial process members of another gang, not with regard to a great issue but with regard to an internal struggle for power.[29]

During the Korean War Kingsley denounced American imperialists for striking a blow against China and the Soviet Union by attacking North Korea. His London Diary column, while commending China for "administrative honesty and efficiency," questioned whether the execution of a million and a half people had really been necessary.[30] This stirred Leonard to ask Critic [London Diary's *nom de plume*] "to give some indication... under what circumstances the execution of 1½ million persons by a Government is 'really necessary'."[31] The dispute reignited in the summer of 1956 when, after a heated verbal exchange, Leonard protested: "I don't think you realize how contemptuously (or should I say just rudely) you treat me the moment I disagree with anything you say in the *NS*—and though I intend to follow Christ's teaching, Jehovah always breaks through." The issue on this occasion was a reluctance to admit Nasser's threat to the Suez Canal and to international peace. He excoriated those on the Labour left, who found excuses for

> the sort of nationalist threatening of a Nasser which you would howl against if it was made by a miserable French or British Government or by the imperialist USA.... You never say what is true, that the

imperialism and nationalism of a communist Russian Government or a dago Egyptian Government is no better than and is today more dangerous than that of any British or American Government.[32]

A final rejoinder from Leonard in 1963 tried to resolve once and for all his views about means and ends:

> It is never right for an individual or a government to do any vast evil as a means to some hypothetical good. That is why the question "Is the execution of 1½ million subjects by the [Chinese] government really necessary?" is both shocking and ludicrous.... I am sorry, but I cannot pretend to believe what you believe or that anyone, individual or government, Jew, Arab, capitalist, or communist, is justified in doing immense evil immediately on the excuse that he thinks that it will hypothetically in the distant future prevent a greater evil or produce a very great absolute good.[33]

Despite their differences, Kingsley never renounced his more than thirty-year practice of turning to Leonard for political guidance, but it no longer reinforced his own convictions. Hence the angry letters, the injured feelings, the mutual recriminations. Their professional and personal relations survived to the end, but only just barely. By the 1960s they were elderly and weary combatants, ceasing to derive much pleasure from the rancorous political arguments in which they continued to engage. Leonard, seventeen years older, survived Kingsley by six months; his final publication was an obituary of his sometime friend and editor, who was "one of those people who always needed a father figure, and, in a small way, I figured as such in his life."[34] Kingsley, always "lamenting catastrophic evil and predicting disaster," was an easy target for Leonard, who exploited his vulnerability, partly in order to irritate him. They were longtime colleagues, and Kingsley eventually became a Sussex neighbor, perhaps in part because he craved Leonard's attention. "No one," he noted, "was ever so ready for argument and so obstinate and lovable."[35]

A very different epistolary quarrel was triggered by a letter in *The Times* in March 1968 by Rosamond Fisher, wife of the retired Archbishop of Canterbury. After an Israeli reprisal attack against Arab guerrillas, Lady Fisher likened the Arabs to the French resistance during the Second World War. Leonard's horrified response queried whether it was heroic to attack a bus containing children.[36] When

Geoffrey Fisher replied in defense of his wife, Leonard drew a sharp distinction between the Arabs and the French, who had acted against an army of occupation and did not blow up busloads of German children, observing as well that "this time Jesus Christ would agree with me and not with you and Lady Fisher." He was careful to note that, "though I am an (atheistical) Jew, I have no prejudice against Arabs."[37] An exchange of acrimonious letters ensued: Leonard recounted his initial misgivings about Zionism, his change of heart after millions of Jews were exterminated, and his support for "an established Israeli state with a large and immensely energetic population." Since the bloodshed would continue unless the Arabs could be induced to negotiate with Israel, he questioned whether it was appropriate to incite them to commit acts of violence, terror, and sabotage. To bolster his argument, he pointed to Christ's "uncompromising attitude towards violence and cruelty, the notion, for instance, that anything can be justified by anything, e.g. the massacre of children by the heroism and bravery of patriotism."[38] When Fisher retorted that terrorists were acting bravely on behalf of their homeland, Leonard demurred:

> I agree that it is a question purely of moral judgment. But my answer is the most emphatic NO, no matter who these terrorists may be—Jews, Arabs, French or British. To say yes is to make a moral judgment that the end justifies the means, a principle which, I think, is horribly immoral and has for thousands of years been used to justify every kind of evil and crime.... The end does not justify the means.[39]

Here again Leonard's moral barometer was in play: the core principle behind his strictures against Soviet and Chinese communism and his dissent from the views of men as different as Kingsley Martin and Geoffrey Fisher. He would neither compromise his integrity, nor bend to the prevailing political winds. He refused to remain silent when his indignation was aroused. His vision of liberty, justice, and tolerance would brook no exceptions, no accommodation to *realpolitik* or expediency. When socialist ideals were betrayed by authoritarian dictators or colonial freedom movements turned violent, he wrote in no uncertain terms to repudiate their actions. He advocated socialism and the liberation of subject peoples, but he believed in ethical values even more.

Notes

1. Leonard, subsequently denying his political roots, claimed in a letter to Gore Graham (17 November 1937), "I am not a liberal and never have been one" (Spotts, 414).
2. Flora Woolf to LW, 18 December 1908, Spotts, 143.
3. Edward Arnold, taking a dim view of sales prospects for *The Village in the Jungle*, offered ungenerous royalty terms and issued a small second printing.
4. VW, *Diary*, 8 March 1918, i. 124.
5. Spotts, 391.
6. VW, *Diary*, 7 January 1915, i. 10.
7. VW to Madge Vaughan, [June 1912], VW, *Letters*, i. 503.
8. The constituency, consisting of all English universities except Cambridge, Oxford, and London, was abolished in 1948.
9. LW to Sidney Webb, 31 May 1920, Spotts, 390. J. A. Hobson had contested the seat in similar circumstances in the 1918 election.
10. VW, *Diary*, 18 March 1922, ii. 103. In a television interview with Malcolm Muggeridge in March 1967, Leonard expressed regrets at never having been an MP. His father had offered himself as a candidate shortly before his premature death.
11. The volume, edited by Mary Adams, included other talks as well. These broadcasts took place in September and October 1931.
12. LW typescript [1958?], MS Eng 1663, Houghton Library, Harvard University.
13. VW, *Diary*, 25 June 1935, iv. 326.
14. G. Lowes Dickinson to LW, 29 October 1931, quoted in Duncan Wilson, *Leonard Woolf: A Political Biography* (1978), 224.
15. *New Statesman*, 17 October 1931.
16. *Observer*, 25 September 1932.
17. VW, *Diary*, 23 October 1931, iv. 51. The brief review by Harold Stannard was "The Social Animal", *TLS*, 22 October 1931. Virginia had just received a laudatory review of *The Waves* in the *Manchester Guardian*.
18. VW, *Diary*, 30 October 1931, iv. 51.
19. *New Statesman*, 20 July 1940.
20. *Observer*, 1 November 1953.
21. *Sunday Times*, 1 November 1953.
22. *New Statesman*, 14 November 1953.
23. C. H. Rolph, *Kingsley* (1973), 199–200.
24. LW to Kingsley Martin, 29 September 1935, Spotts, 401.
25. Kingsley Martin to LW, 17 September 1939, LW Papers.

26. Vita Sackville-West to Harold Nicolson, 28 September 1939, *Vita and Harold*, ed. Nigel Nicolson, 317.
27. *New Statesman*, 16 October 1949.
28. Kingsley Martin to LW, 23 October 1949, LW Papers.
29. LW to Kingsley Martin, 24 October 1949, Spotts, 435.
30. *New Statesman*, 30 August 1952.
31. *New Statesman*, 6 September 1952.
32. LW to Kingsley Martin, 3 August 1956, Martin Papers.
33. LW to Kingsley Martin, 7 and 10 May 1963, Martin Papers.
34. *Political Quarterly* (July–September 1969), 245.
35. Kingsley Martin, *Editor* (1968), 8.
36. *The Times*, 25 March 1968.
37. LW to Lord Fisher of Lambeth, 1 April 1968, Spotts, 454.
38. LW to Lord Fisher of Lambeth, 4 April 1968, Spotts, 454–6.
39. LW to Lord Fisher of Lambeth, 12 April 1968, Spotts, 457–8.

9
Journey's End

In *Culture and Anarchy* Matthew Arnold, extrapolating from Heinrich Heine's dictum that all men were either Jews or Greeks, identified two opposing forces, each striving for human salvation, which he described as Hebraism and Hellenism. Hebraism was concerned with obligation to duty, obedience, and strictness of conscience; Hellenism, by contrast, was associated with spontaneity of consciousness, with beauty, sweetness, and light. Whereas Hebraism, rooted in a sense of sinfulness, was dubious about the possibility of attaining perfection, Hellenism was imbued with an optimistic faith in individual reason as the basis for human progress. If Bloomsbury aspired to the Hellenist ideal of beauty, rationality, and spiritual fulfilment, Leonard embodied both Hebraism and Hellenism, and the tension between them provided the dynamic for his moral and spiritual evolution.

The Woolf family had been in London for several generations before Leonard's birth, probably dating back to the eighteenth century. His paternal grandfather, Benjamin, a traditionally observant Jew, bore the countenance of "stern rabbinical orthodoxy" (*Sowing*, 15), a description by his grandson based on a portrait that hung in the Woolf dining room. Benjamin, who worked his way up from Spitalfields to a prosperous Regent Street tailoring business, became a pillar of his congregation. Leonard's assimilated and only nominally religious father, Sidney, served as a warden in the Reform West London Synagogue in Mayfair. The Woolf children—at least the sons—received tutoring in Hebrew, enough to enable them to chant the prayers at synagogue. Virginia later commented, with more than a touch of exaggeration, that Leonard "was a strict Jew as a small boy, and he can still sing in Hebrew.[1] Although the family may not have kept a kosher home, they abstained from eating pork. Despite his confirmation at the West London Synagogue in 1893, the following year he disavowed all religious observance and affirmed his non-belief much to the dismay of his mother. That this took place soon after his father's death was perhaps no coincidence. Leonard idolized his father, who bequeathed to him an enduring ethical code, summarized in the words of the prophet Micah: "What doth the Lord require of thee, but to do justly, and to love mercy, and to walk humbly with thy God?" In later years he came to regard this "Semitic vision" of justice and mercy as "the foundation of all civilized life and society" (*Journey*, 167). To be sure, his rejection of religious practice was never as complete as Leonard claimed. As late as 1898 a diary entry indicated an entire day (presumably the Day of Atonement) spent at synagogue,[2] and there were other occasions in his life when his presence was obligatory. In his autobiography, Leonard disavowed any sense of sin or need to worship a deity:

> If Jehovah or almost any of the other major deities is our creator and ruler, the lot of man is hopeless, for he is subject to a "person" who is not only irrational, but cruel, vindictive and uncivilized. The only tolerable Gods were those of the Greeks because no sensible man had to take them seriously. (*Sowing*, 44)

In his dispute with Geoffrey Fisher he contended that "the real difference between us is that you believe that God made man in his image, while I believe that man made God in his image.[3] His denial of God was accompanied by a disdain for the "elaborate abracadabra of dogmas and fantasies." In later years he deplored the fact that civilized people still accepted "as divine truth the myths dreamed by Palestinian Jews two or three thousand years ago" (*Downhill*, 19).

The problem in comprehending Leonard's budding atheism and animus against religion is that the evidence comes largely from his autobiography or *Principia Politica*, all written when he was over 70. The death of an adored parent when he was only 11, rendering his father's legacy all the more precious, forestalled his generational rebelliousness towards Victorian values. Relating his own experience to Sophocles' recognition of reversal of fortune as the essence of tragedy, he recognized that

> his death meant not only the disaster of his death, the loss of him, but also the complete break-up and destruction of life as I had known it.... The reversal of fortune had had, I am sure, a darkening and permanent effect.

> In my own case I can only describe it as this sense of fundamental insecurity, and a fatalistic acceptance of instability and the impermanence of happiness. This fatalism has given me a philosophy of life, a sceptical faith which has stood me in good stead in the worst moments of life's horrors and miseries. (*Sowing*, 84, 6)

What he also derived from his father was a sense of Jewish identity. It was partly associated with an emphasis on education, inherited from his paternal grandfather as well, which turned Leonard into an incorrigible intellectual at a young age. Coupled with this commitment to learning was industriousness, a Victorian no less than a Jewish trait:

> To work and work hard was part of the religion of Jews of my father's and grandfather's generations.... I think that my father had absorbed this tradition and instinctively obeyed it, and that, young as I was when he died, I had observed it and again, in my turn, instinctively obeyed it. (*Journey*, 128–9)

Judaism, providing scant consolation for the loss of his father, might prove a potential handicap as he made his way at St Paul's and Cambridge. He admitted to being psychologically insecure, afraid of making a fool of himself, and lacking social confidence. It was during these years that he developed his "carapace" to shield himself from a hostile school environment, but never conceded that it was a defense against the shock of anti-Semitism. It might have been a way to achieve inclusion, avoiding slights as he forged a path into the intellectual elite world of the Apostles and as a newcomer in Ceylon. In a television interview in 1967, he insisted that he did not recognize that he was "different from anyone else for years." A derogatory remark at school was "the first time I realized that it wasn't merely that my religion was Jewish and somebody else's was Mohammedan".[4] When he went up to Trinity in 1899, he perceived himself as an outsider, "a mere spectator with my hands in my pockets".[5] Although his family belonged to the professional middle class, they had "only recently struggled up into it from the stratum of Jewish shopkeepers. We had no roots in it" (*Beginning*, 74). The Woolfs were *arrivistes*, their gentility lacking the patina of age that many of his contemporaries bore so effortlessly. When Vita Sackville-West took Leonard and Virginia to Penshurst in 1940, the incongruity of the aristocratic welcome accorded by its impecunious owner to "the descendants of the Scottish serf and the ghetto Jew" did not escape him (*Journey*, 58).

During his first years at Cambridge, where he suffered no apparent disability for being Jewish, Leonard underwent some kind of spiritual crisis, akin to that of Leslie Stephen forty years earlier, which had caused his wife's father to resign his Cambridge fellowship. Since he never addressed it directly in his autobiography, the clearest evidence can be found in a May 1901 letter from his older sister Bella, the sibling to whom he felt closest, lamenting that

> the "unanswerables" of life take such hold of you that for the time being you cannot see the sun because of the clouds. But I do believe you will rise triumphant from the Valley of the Shadow of "Doubt"—as all true "seekers after light" do. Only it's the transition which is a trial—both to you & to others.[6]

A further intimation of his spiritual anxiety emerges in a poem he wrote several months later:

> For soon Doubt came upon me black as Hell,
> And everything seemed slipping from my grasp
> And the whole world was vanity—I saw
> For the first time into the heart of things,
> Beneath the shining surface of this pool.[7]

His repudiation of religious doctrine left him bereft of moral signposts, a perception that in the end "nothing matters." This struggle with doubt was replaced by a "broken down" skepticism by which civilized men "learn to overcome this fear of mental vacuum, of uncertainty about the truth of things and the meaning of their own existence" (*Quack*, 180).

He was only gradually coming to terms with what it meant to be a Jew, how he might reconcile his defiant unbelief with recognition of his ethnic identity. Much as he shied away from both the Jewish community—even to some extent his own family—and any form of religious practice, he also felt pride in his heritage. "Most people," he later wrote, "are both proud and ashamed of their families, and nearly all Jews are proud and ashamed of being Jews. There is therefore always a bitterness and ambivalence in these loyalties" (*Sowing*, 196). A few months before Bella's letter, Leonard had pondered, in a missive to Lytton, whether "there really is Eastern blood in my veins which answers the cry of an ancestor—how splendid if one discovered that one was descended from Job"![8]

This moral void was supplanted by the intellectual ferment of Cambridge at the turn of the century, the intimate friendship of kindred spirits in the Apostles, the cultural iconoclasm, but perhaps most of all by the moral example and teachings of G. E. Moore, whose seminal *Principia Ethica*, published in 1903, had so great an impact on the future members of Bloomsbury. What attracted Leonard to Moore, whom he identified as "the only great man I have ever met," were his goodness and innocence, his pursuit of truth "with the tenacity of a bulldog and the integrity of a saint" (*Sowing*, 131, 4).[9] If Moore inspired his acolytes to question received truth, he was equally preoccupied with the problem of moral conduct and the consequences of actions. It was not that duty and virtue were irrelevant, but rather that they must be justified as a means towards the realization of ultimate ends. In Leonard's view, Moore "gave us a scientific basis for believing that some things were good in themselves," indefinable or intuited though they might be. They were "fascinated by questions of what was right and wrong, what one *ought* to do" (*Sowing*, 148–9). If such doctrines tempered Leonard's stern Hebraist conscience, they also convinced him that a life of public activity might be reconciled with the selfless pursuit of truth, a conviction that drew him back to his image of classical Greece. By the time he left Cambridge he had come to believe that it was "not merely my right, but my duty to question the truth of everything and the authority of everyone, to regard nothing as sacred and to hold nothing in religious respect" (*Sowing*, 153). While Judaism seemed still mired in antiquated tradition, the primitive Semitic adherence to the dictates of a retributive God, classical Greek civilization, liberated from a sense of sin, had revalued ethical standards to recognize that happiness, freedom, and tolerance were worthy goals for human society. It represented an ideal that resonated with Moore's teaching and provided Leonard with cultural mooring that he could not find in the Hebraic tradition. His conception of Greek culture, derived from years of academic immersion, transformed his outlook, shaping the evolution of his moral conscience in the years that followed. The pillars of his father's creed—justice and mercy—when coupled with the Greek emphasis on liberty and beauty remained his "vision of civilization" (*Journey*, 167), infusing his Hebraic cast of mind with Hellenist values.

In his early fictional depiction of Jews, Leonard, still ambivalent about his ethnicity, ironically exploited negative stereotypes. The young, materialistic anti-hero of *The Wise Virgins* says to the female character loosely based on Virginia:

> We aren't as pleasant or as beautiful as you are. We are hard and grasping, we're out after definite things, different things, which we think worth while.... Money, of course. That's the first article of our creed—money, and out of money, power. That's elementary. Then knowledge, intelligence, taste. We're always pouncing on them because they give power, power to *do* things, influence people. That's what really we want, to feel ourselves working on people, in any way, it doesn't matter. (*Wise Virgins*, 111–12)

In his story entitled "Three Jews," he comments tellingly: "Yes, they don't like us. We're too clever perhaps, too sharp, too go-ahead".[10] Even when he abandoned fiction, Leonard occasionally seized upon Jewish characteristics as he came to terms with his own background, eventually celebrating rather than denigrating them. A 1920 review noted that "the Jew has for centuries been able to meet his environment with a granite resistance. It is that he creates his own environment out of his past".[11]

In marrying Virginia, he had to reconcile himself not only to her snobbery, but also to her anti-Semitic traits. Her attitude was not malicious, except where her in-laws were concerned, but even with Leonard her jibes could wound. On one memorable occasion at Charleston, in response to a question, Virginia exclaimed, "Let the Jew answer," provoking Leonard to retort, "I won't answer until you ask me properly".[12] Certainly, as far as her husband was concerned, Virginia surmounted her innate prejudice to the point that by the late 1930s she identified both Leonard and herself as Jews, albeit not practitioners of the faith. Still, as late as 1930, she could write in confidence to Ethel Smyth: "How I hated marrying a Jew—how I hated their nasal voices, and their oriental jewellery, and their noses and their wattles—what a snob I was: for they have immense vitality, and I think I like that quality best of all".[13]

Virginia was hardly the only member of their circle to express anti-Semitic sentiments, although rarely in Leonard's presence. If he was not oblivious to these slights, he seems to have been indifferent to them, deliberately ignoring British anti-Semitism in his autobiography. His Judaism was not held against him by his friends, who invariably valued him as a central figure in the Bloomsbury Group. He told one correspondent that T. S. Eliot, known to harbor anti-Semitic propensities, "did not in my presence at any rate ever show any signs of it".[14] On the other hand, he did not hesitate to denounce Bertrand Russell's "aristocratic anti-Semitism," comparing it to the "snobbish anti-Americanism habitual in the British upper class in which he was born".[15]

In reviewing *Downhill All the Way*, Dan Jacobson, the South African Jewish novelist, was perplexed by its author's reticence about anti-Semitism. Leonard, who praised Jacobson's own memoir, *Time of Arrival*, felt impelled to respond:

> As regards my Judaism, I know that it is strange that it should have had so little effect upon my life. I have always been conscious of being a Jew, but in a way in which, I imagine, a Catholic is conscious of being a Catholic in England or someone else of being of Huguenot descent, or even in the way a man is conscious of having been at Cambridge and not Oxford. I have always been conscious of being primarily British and have lived among people who without question accepted me as such. Of course I have all through my life come up against the common or garden antisemitism, from the Mosley type to "some of my best friends have been Jews." But it has not touched me personally and only very peripherally.[16]

Leonard's antipathy to all religion made him intolerant toward believers. He was repelled by bearded, long-haired orthodox Jews when he visited Israel, but equally refused to sanction a Roman Catholic as editor of the *New Statesman*, just as he would "a communist or any other denominationalist who subjects his will and actions in principle absolutely to an organization or party".[17] Beatrice Webb deplored his militant secularism and hostility to denominational education: "Here his Jewish blood comes in ... the anger of a Jew and an apostate from the Judaic faith".[18] Her judgment softened when assessing him a few years later: "Leonard a distinguished Jew—a saint with very considerable intelligence; a man without vanity or guile, wholly public-spirited, lacking perhaps in humour or brilliancy but original in thought and always interesting".[19]

In many writings, such as *After the Deluge*, his animus against organized religion was blatant, and he certainly did not exempt Judaism from his strictures. Although he avoided religious services, obligatory attendance at funerals of Rodmell villagers prompted his comment that "what the Mormons believe is chickenfeed for the gullible compared to what the parson tells us to believe on the authority of savage Semitic tribesmen who wandered about Mount Sinai 3000 years ago".[20] The notion of divine worship seemed to him an irrational fantasy, a pathetic search for consolation, linked to a fallacious belief in immortality. As he told J. B. Priestley: "I do not, of course say that it is totally impossible for there to be an afterlife; what I say is that there is absolutely no evidence that there is an afterlife".[21]

His intellectual heroes included figures such as Erasmus and Montaigne, who challenged authority in the search for truth. That Montaigne clung to Catholicism was less pertinent to Leonard than his rejection of cruelty and intolerance. Cruelty, whether imposed by an individual or a state, fostered violence, which was incompatible with civilization. From his early days he felt empathy for victims of cruelty or prejudice, as his strong identification with Dreyfus revealed. The fact that Dreyfus was a Jew may have heightened his feelings, but he was sympathetic toward any group suffering discrimination, from Armenians in the Ottoman Empire, to Tamils in Ceylon, to Africans under colonial oppression, to British women enduring economic and political disabilities in the early twentieth century. V. S. Pritchett viewed him as one of the "rationalist saints of our time with the Jewish feeling for justice and mercy, enlarged by the half-Jewish Montaigne's hatred of cruelty".[22] One characteristic incident demonstrates Leonard's instinctual defense of victims of authority. In *Downhill All the Way* he recalled, after an evening at Vanessa's studio in Fitzroy Street, encountering a drunken prostitute in the street who, being verbally abused by several jeering passers-by, responded with profanity. A policeman appeared to be provoking her in order to warrant an arrest for disorderly conduct. His temper aroused, Leonard upbraided the officer: "Why don't you go for the men who began it? My name's Woolf, and I can take my oath the woman's not to blame".[23] Sensing the evanescent support of the gathering crowd, the abject policeman disavowed any intention to charge the woman, who was then peaceably escorted from the scene. What Leonard neglected to mention was that he and Virginia had just left Angelica Bell's eleventh birthday party, where guests were invited to dress as characters in *Alice in Wonderland*. When he stepped forward to chastise the policeman, wearing a green baize apron and a pair of chisels as the Carpenter, he was so indignant that he was heedless of his ludicrous appearance. Willie Robson, a colleague for more than three decades, remarked in a memorial broadcast that he was "a tremendously passionate man" whose reason was "harnessed to the most profound and turbulent emotions".[24]

Leonard commented very little about the Holocaust until the later volumes of his autobiography, when he discussed it in the context of the barbarism that had engulfed Europe, the threat to civilization that had been the focus of *Quack, Quack!* and *Barbarians at the Gate*. Yet, not even his most pessimistic apprehension matched the senseless savagery of totalitarian regimes:

> When one reads that a million kulaks have been ruined or done to death because they were rather prosperous peasants, or 500,000 Russian communists have been killed by Russian communists because they were either right deviationists or left deviationists, or six million German [*sic*] Jews have been killed by German Christians because they were Jews, one cannot [but] feel that ... each of those six million Jews when he found himself being driven naked by nazi guards into the gas chamber, suffered, before the annihilation of death, the same agony which you or I would suffer if it happened to us.   (*Downhill*, 22–3)

The mingling of empathy and horror, compounded by Jewish self-awareness, lingered to the end of his life. Given his family's long-established residence in England, he does not appear to have had any relatives who perished in the Holocaust, but some Russian acquaintances fell victim to Soviet purges.

Frederic Spotts contends that Leonard's state of mind at Cambridge—skeptical and irreverent—not only precluded any religious belief but also left him devoid of ambition for power, wealth, and success. To this can be attributed his austerity, his contempt for money, and indifference to popular esteem. He shunned public honors as he shunned religious worship and was contemptuous of those who accepted titles. Fame and faith were both illusions, inimical to his rationalist outlook. It was his intellectual mentor, Moore, who instilled the conviction that what mattered was employing one's creative talent in the world of ideas, to produce works that were socially beneficial, that contributed in some way to improving lives, however meager the rewards. Leonard knew that he lacked genius but recognized it in Virginia and sought to nurture it by encouraging her originality, protecting her health, and safeguarding her reputation after her death. Their marriage endured for the most part happily, despite her mental instability, her lesbian proclivities, and the obsessive quality of her literary endeavors. She needed him to validate her writing, and, as her first and most important reader, he confirmed her achievement, even though his judgments were not invariably positive. Leonard adored Virginia unconditionally, believing that by marrying him she had bestowed the greatest gift, and she reciprocated his feelings in her own way, confessing, somewhat obliquely in her diary: "I have no circumference; only my inviolable centre: L. to wit".[25]

Although he never denied his ethnic background, it may not have been central to his identity. Cambridge, the Apostles, Bloomsbury, and rural Sussex were the core of his being, and whatever spiritual existence he possessed grew out of his affinities with Moore's ideas and Athenian culture, with animals and with gardening. Peering out of the window at Monks House, he affirmed that

> my roots are here and in the Greece of Herodotus, Thucydides, Aristophanes and Pericles. I have always felt in my bones and brain and heart English, and more narrowly a Londoner, but with a nostalgic love of the city and civilization of ancient Athens.... When my Rodmell neighbours' forefathers were herding swine on the plains of eastern Europe and the Athenians were building the Acropolis, my Semitic ancestors, with the days of their national greatness, such as it was, already behind them, were in Persia or Palestine. And they were already prisoners of war, displaced persons, refugees, having begun that unending pilgrimage as the world's official fugitives and scapegoats which has brought one of their descendants to live, and probably die, Parish Clerk of Rodmell in the County of Sussex. (*Sowing*, 13)

If Virginia's suicide was not entirely surprising—she had contemplated it for years and attempted it before—it left Leonard inconsolable and desperately lonely. That he survived without spiritual desolation he attributed to his "full share of the inveterate, the immemorial fatalism of the Jew" (*Journey*, 127). Disingenuously, he insisted that until he began to grow old, he hardly ever thought about death. Yet her tragic end was only one, if by far the most important, of the deaths that figured so prominently in his life, beginning with those of his father, Thoby Stephen, his brother Cecil, and later Lytton and Julian. Leonard regularly adjusted to untimely death among those to whom he was most deeply attached:

> I knew that it is the inevitable end, but fundamentally I am a complete fatalist. It is in part perhaps due to the Jewish tradition, the sceptical fatalism that undermines even Jehovah in *Ecclesiastes* and deep down in *Job*; and later in nearly two thousand years of persecution and the ghettoes of Europe the Jews have learnt that it is a full-time job to fight or evade life's avoidable evils, the wise man does not worry about the inevitable. (*Journey*, 73)

Still, he admitted, "I deplore the fact that I shall have to die and be annihilated; I should like to live personally forever" (*Journey*, 123). That this was written only months before his death at nearly 89 hardly suggests that he was sanguine about his demise, calmly resigned to the termination of life. Occasionally he found himself trying to reconcile fatalism, even indifference, toward the prospect of death with outright defiance. In 1943, two years after Virginia's suicide, he told Trekkie:

> the moment comes when one must stand up and defy fate. And that, I believe, is really the only way to meet it and to deal with God, death, and life. If one can recognize fate as fate, the inevitable as inevitable, even one's own fate becomes impersonal. Then you can stand up and defy the universe, which is the only right attitude for a human being; "I don't like you," you can say, "don't like what you do and are going to do to me; I despise you and your ways; but the responsibility is yours, not mine; so go ahead, go your way, and while there is still time, I propose to go mine".[26]

Such sentiments were reminiscent of the concluding sentence of *The Waves*, Leonard's favorite among Virginia's novels: "Against you I will fling myself, unvanquished and unyielding, O Death!"[27]

As the end drew nearer, Leonard attempted to take stock of his accomplishments. Looking back in 1968 in the aptly-titled *The Journey*

Not the Arrival Matters, borrowed from Montaigne, "the first civilized modern man," he concluded that, in more than fifty-seven years of political work in England, he had "achieved practically nothing." During his long career he estimated that he had "ground through between 150,000 and 200,000 hours of perfectly useless work" (*Journey*, 158). He was well suited to the kind of political work he undertook: conscientious, meticulous about detail, dispassionate, diligent in research, quick to grasp practical problems, prepared to shoulder tedious burdens without complaint. He combined leadership of Labour and Fabian committees with more prosaic activities, such as Clerk of the Parish Council, President of the Rodmell Horticultural Society, and membership of the Civil Service Arbitration Tribunal. Political expediency had frustrated the hopes of enlightened idealists like Leonard, aiming to implement plans for collective international institutions, egalitarian social policies, and emergent democracy in former colonies. Despite his best efforts to promote collective security, he was unable to prevent Europe from destroying itself after 1918. Even so, Leonard could never resign himself to defeat: "if at any moment I had become convinced that my political work produced absolutely no effect at all in any direction, I would have stopped it altogether and have retired to cultivate my garden—the last refuge of disillusion." However futile his endeavors, "for me personally it was right and important that I should do it." He recognized that on a universal scale, nothing really mattered, but "in one's own personal life, in terms of humanity and human history, certain things are of immense importance: human relations, happiness, truth, beauty or art, justice and mercy" (*Journey*, 171–2). The Hellenist ideals endured without effacing his Hebraic code of conduct. As Malcom Muggeridge observed in a remembrance:

> He believed in his heart that all the liberal hopes plausibly entertained for our Western civilization expired in the First World War, never to be seriously revived. Even so, he worked on, to the very last day of his life, concerned about injustice, cruelty, oppression and all other impediments to ameliorating our human condition.[28]

In the end, we must reject Leonard's self-estimation: his significance was more palpable than modesty allowed. As one of the last survivors of the Bloomsbury Group, he was instrumental in shaping its retrospective image, refuting the notion of an exclusive clique that sought to dominate interwar British culture. Although the League of Nations ultimately failed to realize its goals, Leonard became one of its principal publicists, and it might be appropriate to regard his many years of advocacy as bearing fruit in the United Nations. No Labour activist contributed more to undermining faith in the triumphs of British imperialism or to informing the public about the need to implement African self-government gradually. He was a friend to the peoples of Ceylon and India, insisting upon education and training as a precondition for democratic evolution. In partnership with his wife, he launched one of the most successful independent publishing houses in England, the Hogarth Press, which, defying all expectations, survived for several decades before he resolved to merge it with another publisher. Finally, he provided the domestic context, the security, and the understanding in which Virginia could flourish as a writer. No one, apart from her sister Vanessa, was as essential to her during their twenty-eight years together or contributed as much to her professional success as a writer. His own accomplishments were multifaceted—personal, political, literary, commercial—not least the enduring friendships that knit his life together from his early days in Cambridge to his declining years as a solitary gardener, competitive bowls player, and luminary in rural Sussex, the acknowledged sage of Rodmell.

Like others who lived eventful lives, he spent his final decade composing his memoirs, a selective, sometimes self-deprecatory, yet unfailingly honest, five-volume autobiography that illuminates a life relentlessly striving for a civilized society. The occasional misstatements or chronological errors testify to the faulty memory of an octogenarian, but also to the remarkable fact that it was published just as he wrote it, without the intervention of editorial mediators. As an inveterate writer and professional publisher, he knew what he wanted to say and how to say it. It is this that makes it so revealing of Leonard's personality: his moral integrity and generosity of spirit, his lack of pretension, his austere and irascible persona, his stoicism and probity. Some found him granitic and obdurate, especially those Hogarth Press employees expected to meet his rigorous standards of conduct and work ethic. It was said that he related more easily to animals than to people, finding them more tractable. He developed the punctilious habit of recording every detail of his life—the yield of his fruit trees, the earnings of Hogarth books, the daily count of words written, his bowls game scores, the state of Virginia's health. His legendary frugality with money occasionally triggered disputes with his wife, who was inclined to be more extravagant in spending their income. The authors of this biography delighted in receiving letters from Leonard many years ago, mailed in previously used envelopes, in which his own name and address as recipient were crossed out and the new name and address written in. Persistently believing in the correctness of his opinion, he rarely considered the possibility of contrary perspectives. If this irritated some, others found much to admire. The writer Peter Calvocoressi, who encountered Leonard in the 1950s, after Hogarth merged with Chatto & Windus, recalled his

> unusual trait of yoking strong commitment with balanced judgment and... the patience to understand and sympathise with different kinds of people. His wit was precise, inclined to the ironical, fierce only against humbug. He was the only man I ever met who seemed to me to be right about everything that matters.[29]

Eric Hobsbawm, acknowledging his "air of total incorruptibility and uprightness," identified him as "the example of a man of integrity and unselfishness."[30]

Over a very long life, which brought him into contact with the powerful and the humble, he recognized only one great man— G. E. Moore. We would not claim that Leonard deserved such an accolade, but he was much more than merely Virginia's husband, the role for which he is most readily remembered. A man of formidable intellect and strong convictions who left behind a significant body of published work on international relations, imperialism, and democratic socialism, his humanity and nobility of vision merit greater recognition. As E. M. Forster, a friend since Cambridge days who survived him by only a few months, declared: "What a life he has led and how well he has led it."[31]

Notes

1. VW to Margaret Llewelyn Davies, *Letters*, ii. 85.
2. George Spater and Ian Parsons, *A Marriage of True Minds* (New York: Harcourt Brace Jovanovich, 1977), 154.

3. LW to Lord Fisher of Lambeth, 12 March 1967, Spotts, 554.
4. Sound recording of BBC TV interview with Malcolm Muggeridge, September 1967, British Library.
5. LW to Lytton Strachey, 25 June 1903, Spotts, 31.
6. Bella Woolf to LW, 4 May 1901, Spotts, 16.
7. Quoted in Spotts, 7.
8. LW to Lytton Strachey, 20 March 1901, Spotts, 13.
9. S. P. Rosenbaum maintains that Leonard was "the most worshipful of Moore" among the Cambridge Apostles of his generation. Rosenbaum, *Victorian Bloomsbury*, 197.
10. LW, *Two Stories* (London: Hogarth Press, 1917).
11. *New Statesman*, 13 March 1920.
12. Spotts, 470.
13. VW to Ethel Smyth, 2 August 1930, *Letters*, iv. 195–6.
14. LW to Lyall Wilkes, 13 January 1968, Spotts, 562.
15. *Political Quarterly* (July–September 1968), 345.
16. LW to Dan Jacobson, 3 June 1968, Spotts, 565–6.
17. LW to John Campbell, 18 June 1965, Spotts, 362.
18. Beatrice Webb, *Diary*, 6 February 1927, iv. 131.
19. Ibid., 1 April 1931, iv. 243.
20. LW to Sylvia Townend Warner, 4 September 1964, Spotts, 533.
21. LW to J. B. Priestley, 15 March 1967, Spotts, 554–5.
22. *New Statesman*, 24 October 1969.
23. VW to Clive Bell, 18 January 1930, VW, *Letters*, iv. 129.
24. Robson, "Leonard Woolf 1880–1969," BBC Radio 3, 17 February 1970, quoted in Glendinning, 332.
25. VW, *Diary*, 30 October 1938, v. 183.
26. LW to Trekkie Parsons, 29 March 1943, *Love Letters: Leonard Woolf and Trekkie Ritchie Parsons (1941–1968)*, 25–6.
27. VW, *The Waves* (London: Hogarth Press, 1931), 220. It was also inscribed on the memorial plaque at Rodmell, where her ashes were interred.
28. Malcolm Muggeridge, *Observer*, 17 August 1969.
29. Peter Calvocoressi, *Threading My Way* (London: Duckworth, 1994), 173.
30. Eric Hobsbawm, *Virginia Woolf Bulletin*, 21 (January 2006), 29.
31. Quoted in Quentin Bell, *Elders and Betters*, 128.

Select Bibliography

Books and Pamphlets by Leonard Woolf

The Village in the Jungle (London: Edward Arnold, 1913).
The Wise Virgins (London: Edward Arnold, 1914).
International Government (London: George Allen & Unwin/Fabian Society, 1916).
The Future of Constantinople (London: George Allen & Unwin, 1917).
Co-operation and the Future of Industry (London: George Allen & Unwin, 1919).
Empire and Commerce in Africa (London: Labour Research Department/George Allen & Unwin, 1920).
Mandates and Empire (London: League of Nations Union, 1920).
Economic Imperialism (London: Swarthmore Press, 1920).
Socialism and Co-operation (London and Manchester: National Labour Press, 1921).
Stories of the East (London: Hogarth Press, 1921).
International Co-operative Trade (London: Fabian Society, 1922).
Fear and Politics: A Debate at the Zoo (London: Hogarth Press, 1925).
Hunting the Highbrow (London: Hogarth Press, 1927).
Essays on Literature, History, Politics, Etc. (London: Hogarth Press, 1927).
Imperialism and Civilization (London: Hogarth Press, 1928).
The Way of Peace (London: Ernest Benn, 1928).
After the Deluge, vol. i (London: Hogarth Press, 1931).
Quack, Quack! (London: Hogarth Press, 1935).
The League and Abyssinia (London: Hogarth Press, 1936).
The Hotel (London: Hogarth Press, 1939).
After the Deluge, vol. ii (London: Hogarth Press, 1939).
Barbarians at the Gate (London: Left Book Club/Victor Gollancz, 1939).
The War for Peace (London: George Routledge & Sons, 1940).
The International Post-War Settlement (London: Fabian Research Series/Victor Gollancz, 1944).
Foreign Policy: The Labour Party's Dilemma (London: Fabian Research Series/Victor Gollancz, 1947).
Principia Politica: A Study of Communal Psychology (London: Hogarth Press, 1953).
Sowing: An Autobiography of the Years 1880–1904 (London: Hogarth Press, 1960).
Growing: An Autobiography of the Years 1904–1911 (London: Hogarth Press, 1961).
Diaries in Ceylon 1908–1911 (London: Hogarth Press, 1963).

Beginning Again: An Autobiography of the Years 1911–1918 (London: Hogarth Press, 1964).

Downhill All the Way: An Autobiography of the Years 1919–1939 (London: Hogarth Press, 1967).

The Journey Not the Arrival Matters: An Autobiography of the Years 1939–1969 (London: Hogarth Press, 1969).

Letters of Leonard Woolf, ed. Frederic Spotts (London: Weidenfeld and Nicolson, 1990).

Love Letters: Leonard Woolf and Trekkie Ritchie Parsons (1941–1968), ed. Judith Adamson (London: Chatto & Windus, 2001).

Books and Pamphlets to which Leonard Woolf Contributed

Woolf, Leonard, *et al.*, *The Modern State*, ed. Mary Adams (London: George Allen & Unwin, 1933).

Brinton, Henry (ed.), *Does Capitalism Cause War?* (London: H. & E. R. Brinton, 1935).

Cole, Margaret (ed.), *The Webbs and their Work* (London: Frederick Muller, 1949).

Hinden, Rita (ed.), *Fabian Colonial Essays* (London: George Allen & Unwin, 1945).

Woolf, Leonard (ed.), *The Framework of a Lasting Peace* (London: George Allen & Unwin, 1917).

Woolf, Leonard (ed.), *The Intelligent Man's Way to Prevent War* (London: Victor Gollancz, 1933).

Woolf, Leonard, and Virginia Woolf, *Two Stories* (London: Hogarth Press, 1917).

Additional Published Sources concerning the Woolfs

Bell, Quentin, *Virginia Woolf: A Biography* (New York: Harcourt Brace Jovanovich, 1972).

Glendinning, Victoria, *Leonard Woolf: A Biography* (New York: Free Press, 2006).

Lee, Hermione, *Virginia Woolf* (London: Chatto & Windus, 1996).

Luedeking, Leila, and Michael Edmonds, *Leonard Woolf: A Bibliography* (Winchester: St Paul's Bibliographies, 1992).

Manson, Janet M., and Wayne K. Chapman, *An Annotated Guide to the Writings and Papers of Leonard Woolf* (Clemson, SC: Clemson University Press, 2017).

Spater, George, and Ian Parsons, *A Marriage of True Minds: An Intimate Portrait of Leonard and Virginia Woolf* (New York: Harcourt Brace Jovanovich, 1977).

Select Bibliography 205

Strachey, Lytton, *The Letters of Lytton Strachey*, ed. Paul Levy (New York: Viking, 2005).
Wilson, Duncan, *Leonard Woolf: A Political Biography* (New York: St Martin's Press, 1978).
Wilson, Peter, *The International Theory of Leonard Woolf* (New York: Palgrave Macmillan, 2003).
Woolf, Virginia, *The Diary of Virginia Woolf*, ed. Anne Olivier Bell, 5 vols (New York: Harcourt Brace Jovanovich 1977–84).
Woolf, Virginia, *The Letters of Virginia Woolf*, ed. Nigel Nicolson and Joanne Trautmann, 6 vols (New York: Harcourt Brace Jovanovich 1975–80).

Other Works Consulted

Ashworth, Lucian M., *International Relations and the Labour Party: Intellectuals and Policy Making from 1918–1945* (London: I. B. Tauris, 2007).
Barron, T. J., "Before the Deluge: Leonard Woolf in Ceylon," *Journal of Imperial and Commonwealth History*, 6/1 (1977), 47–63.
Bell, Clive, *Old Friends* (London: Chatto & Windus,1956).
Bell, Quentin, *Elders and Betters* (London: J. Murray, 1995).
Edwards, Ruth Dudley, *Victor Gollancz: A Biography* (London: Victor Gollancz Ltd, 1987).
Gamble, Andrew, and Tony Wright (eds), *The Progressive Tradition: Eighty Years of The Political Quarterly* (Oxford: Wiley-Blackwell, 2011).
Gottlieb, Freema, "Leonard Woolf's Attitudes to his Jewish Background and to Judaism," *Transactions & Miscellanies (Jewish Historical Society of England)*, 25 (1973–5), 25–37.
Holroyd, Michael, *Lytton Strachey: A Critical Biography* (London: Heinemann, 1967–8).
Hyams, Edward, *The New Statesman: The History of the First Fifty Years 1913–1963* (London: Longmans, 1963).
Keynes, John Maynard, *Two Memoirs* (London: Rupert Hart-Davies, 1949).
Lehmann, John, *Thrown to the Woolfs: Leonard and Virginia Woolf and the Hogarth Press* (London: Weidenfeld and Nicolson, 1978).
Leventhal, F. M., *The Last Dissenter: H. N. Brailsford and his World* (Oxford: Clarendon Press, 1985).
Leventhal, F. M., "Leonard Woolf and Kingsley Martin: Creative Tension on the Left," *Albion*, 24/2 (1992), 279–94.
Leventhal, F. M., "Leonard Woolf: The Conscience of a Bloomsbury Socialist," in Susan Pedersen and Peter Mandler (eds), *After the Victorians: Private Conscience and Public Duty in Modern Britain* (London: Routledge, 1994), 149–68.
Levy, Paul, *Moore: G. E. Moore and the Cambridge Apostles* (London: Weidenfeld and Nicolson, 1979).

Light, Alison, *Mrs Woolf and the Servants* (New York: Bloomsbury Press, 2008).
Lubenow, William C., *The Cambridge Apostles, 1820–1914* (Cambridge: Cambridge University Press, 1998).
Martin, Kingsley, *Editor: A Second Volume of Autobiography 1931–1945* (London: Hutchinson, 1968).
Ondaatje, Christopher, *Woolf in Ceylon: An Imperial Journey in the Shadow of Leonard Woolf, 1904–1911* (Toronto: Harper Collins, 2005).
Robson, William A., *The Political Quarterly in the Thirties* (London: Allen Lane, 1971).
Rolph, C. H., *Kingsley: The Life, Letters and Diaries of Kingsley Martin* (London: Victor Gollancz Ltd, 1973).
Rosenbaum, S. P., *Victorian Bloomsbury* (Houndmills: Macmillan, 1987).
Sackville-West, Vita, and Harold Nicolson, *Vita and Harold: The Letters of Vita Sackville-West and Harold Nicolson*, ed. Nigel Nicolson (New York: G. P. Putnam's Sons, 1992).
Snaith, Anna, "Leonard and Virginia Woolf: Writing against Empire," *Journal of Commonwealth Literature*, 50/1 (2014), 19–32.
Spalding, Frances, *Vanessa Bell* (London: Weidenfeld and Nicolson, 1983).
Stansky, Peter, *On or about December 1910: Early Bloomsbury and its Intimate World* (Cambridge, MA: Harvard University Press, 1996).
Stansky Peter, *Excursion to Empire: Finding Bloomsbury in Ceylon* (Menlo Park, CA: Occasional Works, 2004).
Stansky, Peter, and William Abrahams, *Journey to the Frontier: Julian Bell and John Cornford: Their Lives and the 1930s* (London: Constable, 1966).
Stansky, Peter, and William Abrahams, *Julian Bell: From Bloomsbury to the Spanish Civil War* (Stanford: Stanford University Press, 2012).
Webb, Beatrice, *The Diary of Beatrice Webb*, ed. Norman MacKenzie and Jeanne MacKenzie, 4 vols (Cambridge, MA: Harvard University Press, 1982–5).
Webb, Sidney, and Beatrice Webb, *The Letters of Sidney and Beatrice Webb*, ed. Norman MacKenzie, 3 vols (Cambridge: Cambridge University Press, 1978).
Willis, J. H., *Leonard and Virginia Woolf as Publishers: The Hogarth Press, 1917–1941* (Charlottesville: University Press of Virginia, 1992).
Winkler, Henry R., *The League of Nations Movement in Great Britain 1914–1919* (New Brunswick: Rutgers University Press, 1952).

Unpublished Dissertation:

Reader, Luke James, "Socialized Imperialism: Leonard Woolf and the Legacy of Empire in British Public Life, 1914–1945," Ph.D. dissertation, University of California, Irvine (2013).

Index

Advisory Committee on Imperial Questions (ACImpQ) 112, 117, 118, 119, 120, 121, 124, 125, 126, 157
Advisory Committee on International Questions (ACIntQ) 100–2, 106, 110, 112, 117, 126, 135, 144, 145, 157
aesthetics 24, 63–4
Alexander, A. V. 146
Aliens Act 5
Angell, Norman 98, 136, 137
Annan, Noel 122
anti-imperialism 109–31, 151, 156
  Economic Imperialism 116
  Empire and Commerce in Africa 111–16, 119, 121, 128, 163, 169
  Imperialism and Civilization 121–3, 124, 163, 171
  Mandates and Empire 116–17
  paternalism 110, 120, 127
  self-determination 154, 156, 168
anti-Semitism 5, 6, 7, 9, 10, 13, 53, 55–7, 95, 125, 190, 193–4
  Nazi persecution 139, 146, 153
  Quack, Quack! 139–42
Anti-Slavery and Aborigines Protection Society 110
Apostles 14, 17, 18, 19, 20, 21–3, 26, 33, 50, 84, 86, 97, 133, 169, 190, 192, 197
Arab League 126
Arnold, Matthew 188
Arnold-Forster, Will 102, 136
Arts and Crafts movement 61
atheism 6, 185, 189
atomic bombs 156
Auden, W. H. 69

Baldwin, Stanley 143
Balfour Declaration 119, 124, 125
BBC talks 127, 169–70
Bell, Angelica 196

Bell, Clive 7, 16, 19, 27, 33, 34, 50, 51, 53, 56, 57
Bell, Julian vii, viii, 27, 51, 69, 143, 144, 146, 198
Bell, Vanessa (*née* Stephen) 16, 22, 24, 29, 33–4, 50, 51, 55, 56, 57, 58, 66, 70, 72, 73, 142, 195, 200
Bentley, E. C. 13
Berlin, Isaiah 10, 169
Bethmann-Hollweg, Theobald von 97
Bloomsbury district 4, 29, 34, 60
Bloomsbury Group 4, 5, 51, 70, 71
  Cambridge 15, 16, 17, 19, 21, 22, 24
  influence of G. E. Moore 25–6, 192
  nicknames 16
  retrospective image 199–200
Booth, Charles 85
Booth, Imogen 85
Brailsford, Henry Noel viii, 95, 97, 98, 99, 111, 137, 167
British Empire *see* anti-imperialism; imperialism
Bryce Committee 88
Bryce Group 97, 101
Buddhism 35
Bunin, Ivan 67
Butler, Samuel 19
Buxton, Charles Roden 100, 118, 120, 167

Calvocaressi, Peter 201
Cambridge
  academic performance 17–18, 28
  Apostles 17, 18, 19, 20, 21–3, 26, 33, 50, 84, 86, 97, 133, 169, 190, 192, 197
  entrance examination 14, 15
  King's College 15, 17
  Magpie and Stump 20
  Memoir Club 24
  Midnight Society 19
  Shakespeare Society 20

Cambridge (*cont.*)
  Sunday Essay Society 20
  Trinity College 14, 15, 16–18, 28, 190
  X Society 20
Cambridge Review 27, 70
capitalism 137, 154, 161, 170, 176, 180
Cecil, Lord Robert 96, 136, 165
Ceylon 28, 109, 200
  civil service 30, 31, 38, 41
  correspondence 30, 32, 33, 34, 35, 38, 39–41, 110, 161
  Hambantota District 36, 37, 41, 42, 109
  Jaffna 30, 31, 33
  Kandy 34–5, 110
  official diaries 41
  pearl fisheries 32–3, 44
  revisited (1960) 130–1
  riots (1915) 110
  salt trade 41, 42
  Stories of the East 43–4, 52, 84
    "Pearls and Swine" 43, 44, 66
  Tamil minority 124
  (The) Village in the Jungle 42, 45–6, 47–8, 52, 54, 55, 83, 84, 128
  voyage to 29, 30
  Yala National Game Sanctuary 36
Chamberlain, Neville 150
Charity Organisation Society 85, 161
Chatto & Windus 69, 75, 201
Chesterton, G. K. 13
Churchill, Winston 146
Clarke, Arthur C. 45
class war 164, 165, 176
classical Greece *see* Hellenism
Clifford, Sir Hugh 36, 42, 48
Cobbett, William 173
cold war 156
Cole, G. D. H. 13
colonialism *see* anti-imperialism; imperialism
communal psychology 169, 173, 174, 175, 176
communism 148, 149, 166, 170, 183
Conrad, Joseph 43, 45
conscientious objection 134
Contemporary Review 99, 135
Conway, Sir Martin 167
Cook, A. M. 13
cooperative movement 164, 165, 166

Co-operative News 86, 162
Cox, Ka 59
Creech-Jones, Arthur 126

Darwin, Charles 177
Day Lewis, Cecil 69
de Jongh, Henriette (grandmother) 3
de Jongh, Marie (mother) 4, 7, 30, 54, 57
de Jongh, Nathan (grandfather) 3
democracy 170–4, 176, 181
Dickinson, Goldsworthy Lowes (Goldie) 22, 88, 97, 98, 116, 175
Dickinson, Violet 34, 84, 135
disarmament 137–8
Disraeli, Benjamin 4–5
Dostoevsky, Fyodor 67
Dreyfus trial 12, 27, 84, 98, 195
Duckworth, George 51, 57
Duckworth, Gerald 51, 57
Durbin, Evan 146

Eliot, T. S. 66, 67, 99, 194
Empson, William 69
Erasmus, Desiderius 195
Etchells, Frederick 57
Eugénie, Empress of France 35
Everest, Louie 76

Fabian Research Department 86, 87, 89, 126
Fabian Society 86, 87, 95, 96, 106, 111, 118, 121, 126, 129, 134, 153, 154, 158, 162, 165
Fascism 72, 92, 137, 139, 142, 143, 145, 146, 148, 150, 170, 178, 180
feminism 162
First World War 133–6, 168
Fisher, Geoffrey 185, 189
Fisher, H. A. L. 162, 167
Fisher, Mary 57
Fisher, Rosamund 184
Forster, E. M. 17, 21, 45, 52, 71, 77, 201
Frazer, James 18
French Revolution 169, 172, 173, 176
Freud, Sigmund 67, 169, 177
Fry, Roger 17, 21, 51, 57, 61, 66, 70, 85
Fyfe, Hamilton 66

Gaitskell, Hugh 146
Garnett, David 24

Index

Gandhi, Mohandas K (Mahatma Gandhi) 124
Gilbert, W. S. 161
Godwin, William 173
Gollancz, Victor 10, 136, 148–9
Gorky, Maxim 67, 68
Grant, Duncan 13, 24, 50, 51, 57, 70, 72
  conscientious objection 134
Greece *see* Hellenism
Greenwood, Leonard 21
Guild Socialism 164

Hallam, Arthur 21
Hammond, J. L. 103
Hampshire, Stuart 181
Hardie, Frank 138
Hardy, Thomas 19
Harrison, Jane Ellen 18
Hebraism 14, 178–9, 188–9, 192, 199
Heine, Heinrich 141, 188
Hellenism 11, 14, 24 , 178–80, 181, 188, 192, 199
Henderson, Arthur 99, 100, 101, 102, 106
Henderson, Hubert 99, 103
Hill, Christopher 173
Hitler, Adolf 106, 136, 137, 138, 139, 140, 142, 143, 146, 147, 150, 151, 155, 180
Hobsbawm, Eric 201
Hobson, J. A. 98, 111, 112, 118
Hogarth Press 18, 54, 59–70, 72, 74, 75, 100, 103, 135, 143, 152, 163, 169, 200, 201
  New Signatures 69
Holocaust 196
homosexuality 22, 23, 24, 51, 69
(The) Hours (movie) 60
Huxley, Elspeth 128
Huysmans, Camille 99

Ibsen, Henrik 20, 161
immigration 5, 122, 123, 125
imperialism 37, 38, 43, 45, 46, 83, 84, 85
  (*see also* anti-imperialism)
  paternalism 110, 120, 127
  racial stereotypes 115, 128
Independent Labour Party 98, 162, 164, 165

international arbitration 90–1, 93, 94, 102, 105
international law 90, 93
international organizations 88–9, 92
International Review 99, 135
internationalism 104–5, 137
Isherwood, Christopher 69
Israel 126, 130, 185, 194

Jackson, Henry 18
Jacobson, Dan 194
Jay, Douglas 146
Jebb, R. C. 18
Jews
  anti-Semitism 5, 6, 7, 9, 10, 13, 53, 55–7, 95, 125, 140, 190, 191, 193–4
    Nazi persecution 139, 146, 153
    Quack, Quack! 139–42
  Dreyfus trial 12, 27, 84, 98, 195
  fictional depictions 7, 52–4, 58, 62–3, 84, 147–8, 193
  Hebraic values 178–9, 188–9, 192
  Holocaust 196
  immigration 5, 125
  Israel 126, 130, 185, 194
  political groups 6
  position in English society 4–6
  trades and professions 3–4
  Zionism 125, 130, 185
Jowett, Benjamin 12, 15
Jowitt, Gladys 35
Joyce, James 65

Keynes, John Maynard 17, 21, 22, 23, 24–5, 50, 98, 99, 100, 103, 147, 177
  Economic Consequences of the Peace 71, 101
  marriage 70
Kipling, Rudyard 45
Korean War 183
Koteliansky, S. S. 67

Labour Leader 99
Labour Party 96, 100, 106, 112, 135, 144, 145, 146, 154, 157, 165
  1922 General Election 167–8
  colonial policy 118–21, 123–4, 126
Lamb, Walter 51
Laski, Harold 103, 148, 149, 175

Index

Lawrence, D. H. 24
League of Nations 89, 94, 95, 96, 101–2, 104–6, 119, 136, 137, 138, 143, 144, 145, 152, 168, 182, 200
League of Nations Society 97, 169
League of Nations Union 97, 116, 121
Left Book Club 136, 148, 149
Lehmann, John 68–9, 73
Lenin, Vladimir 98, 150
Leys, Norman 118, 167
Liberal Party 103
Liberalism 161, 167, 171
Llewelyn Davies, Margaret 86, 98, 134, 162, 166
Lloyd George, David 168
London School of Economics (LSE) 103, 111
Lopokova (later Keynes), Lydia 70, 147
Lushington, Charles 42

MacCarthy, Desmond 17, 21, 31
MacCarthy, Molly 57, 85
MacDonald, Ramsay 98, 99, 101, 110, 120, 167
Mackenzie, Compton 10, 11, 13
Macmillan, Harold 122
Mansfield, Katherine 65
Martin, Kingsley viii, 70, 103, 104, 138, 156, 182, 183, 184, 185
Marxism 150, 161, 166
Massingham, H. W. 99
Maynard, Sir John 124
McTaggart, J. T. 22
Memoir Club 24, 70
Midnight Society 19
militarism 105
Mill, J. S. 171
Miller, Jonathan 10, 22
Monks House 70, 71, 72, 76, 151, 197
Montaigne, Michel de 13, 141, 195, 199
Moore, G. E. 20–1, 22, 26, 161, 162, 177, 192, 197, 201
Principia Ethica 23–4, 25–6, 192
Morel, E. D. 98, 118
Morrell, Lady Ottoline 71
Morrell, Philip 110
Morris, William 61, 62, 166
Mortimer, Raymond 103
Muggeridge, Malcolm 199
Murray, Gilbert 162

Murry, John Middleton 65
Mussolini, Benito 138, 143, 150
mysticism 18–19

Namier, Lewis 125, 175
Nation 97, 99–100, 102–3, 104, 135, 169
nationalism 104–5, 137, 154, 171
Nazism 72, 125, 136, 138, 139, 140, 142, 146, 147, 150, 153, 155, 180
Nazi-Soviet pact 149
Nehru, Jawaharlal 124
New Statesman viii, 43, 70, 86, 88, 89, 93, 98, 103, 104, 118, 120, 135, 137, 142, 151, 175, 181, 182, 194
Nicolson, Harold 69, 142
Noel-Baker, Philip 96, 102, 138, 167
nuclear weapons 156, 157

obscenity laws 66
Olivier, Sydney 112
Omega workshops 57, 61
Orwell, George 45
Ottoman Empire 95
Oxford Union 138
Oxford University 15

pacifism 106, 134, 135, 138, 143, 182
Paine, Thomas 173
Palestine 117, 119, 124–6, 156, 157
Parsons, Ian 75
Parsons, Marjorie (Trekkie) Ritchie ix, 75, 76, 78, 130, 198
Partridge, Ralph 68
paternalism 110, 120, 127, 161
Pease, Edward 129
Pericles 4, 50, 172, 179, 180, 197
philanthropy 161
Political Quarterly 103–4, 145, 147, 157
Priestley, J. B. 172, 195
Pritchett, V. S. 195

racial conflict 122–3
racial stereotypes 115, 128 (*see also* anti-Semitism)
Rajk, Lazlo 182
rationality 7, 19, 25, 27, 91, 179, 188, 195, 197
Ritchie, Alice 74
Robson, William 103, 104, 106, 157, 196
Rosenbaum, S. P. 18, 27

Index

Rowntree, Arnold 99
Rowntree, Joseph 87
Russell, Bertrand 22, 23, 174, 177, 194
Russian Revolution 98
Rylands, George "Dadie" 68, 103

Sacks, Oliver 10
Sackville-West, Vita 60, 69, 73, 75, 182, 190
Sargant-Florence, Alix 111
Second World War 150–7
self-determination 154, 156, 168
sexual aggression 53
sexual freedom 51
Shaw, George Bernard 19, 20, 87, 89, 103, 147, 161
Shelley, Percy Bysshe 77
Sheppard, John 21
Shoreditch Care Committee 85
Sidgwick, Henry 22
sin 6, 7, 9, 59, 178, 179, 188, 189, 192
Singer, Charles 141
Sissinghurst 69
Sloan, Pat 149
Smallwood, Norah 75
Smillie, Robert 99
Smyth, Ethel 193
Snowden, Philip 164, 165, 167
social class 7–8
social conditions 85
socialism 86, 98, 99, 161, 162, 164, 166, 167, 171, 185
Socialist Review 99
Southorn, Wilfrid (Tom) 30–1, 36
Soviet Union viii, 129, 130, 139, 145, 146, 148, 149, 150, 153, 154, 156, 157, 166, 180, 181
Spanish Civil War vii, 144, 145
Spender, Stephen 69, 137
Spotts, Frederic 196
St Paul's School 7, 9–14, 28, 56, 109, 179, 190
Stalin, Joseph 98, 148, 149, 150, 180
state socialism 164
Stephen, Adrian 17, 34, 50, 72, 152
Stephen, Katherine 16
Stephen, Sir Leslie 16, 191
Stephen, Thoby 16, 19, 20, 29, 33–4, 198
Stephen, Vanessa *see* Bell, Vanessa

Strachey, James 67
Strachey, John 148, 149
Strachey, Lytton 7, 15, 16, 17, 19, 22, 23, 27, 40, 59, 98, 99, 100, 192
 Ceylon correspondence 30, 32, 33, 34, 35, 38, 39–41, 110, 161
 conscientious objection 134
 death 70, 198
 Landmarks in French Literature 162
 proposes to Virginia 39
Suez conflict 126, 183
Swanwick, Helena 143
Swift, Jonathan 77
Swinburne, Algernon Charles 19
Sydney-Turner, Saxon 15, 18, 19, 21, 23, 27, 33, 56, 57

Taylor, A. J. P. 181
Tennessee Valley Authority 154
Tennyson, Alfred, Lord 21
Thompson, E. P. 173
Tolstoy, Countess Sophia 67
totalitarianism 142, 151, 168, 196
trade unions 162, 165, 167
Trevelyan, G. M. 22, 23, 26
Trevelyan, R. C. 84
Trevor-Roper, Hugh 181

Union of Democratic Control (UDC) 98, 101, 171
United Nations (UN) 155, 156, 157, 158, 200
Upward, Edward 69

Vaughan, Margaret (Marny) 85
Verrall, A. W. 18

Walker, F. W. 12, 14
Wallas, Graham 175
War and Peace 98–9, 135
Waterlow, Sydney 51, 96
Weaver, Harriet 65, 66
Webb, Sidney and Beatrice 6, 61, 86–9, 93, 96, 99, 100, 111, 112, 118, 120, 129, 148, 162, 167, 193–4
Weizmann, Chaim 125
Whitehead, Alfred North 22
Wigram, Ralph 142
Wilberforce, Octavia 72
Wilson, Peter 110

Wilson, Woodrow 96, 97
Women's Co-operative Guild 86, 96, 162, 169
Woolf, Bella (sister) 7, 19, 28, 30, 31, 34, 40, 50, 54, 191
Woolf, Benjamin (grandfather) 3, 4, 188
Woolf, Cecil (brother) 7, 65, 134, 198
Woolf, Edgar (brother) 50
Woolf, Herbert (brother) 9, 50
Woolf, Isabella (grandmother) 3
Woolf, Leonard
  After the Deluge 121, 134, 136, 169, 171–7, 195
  anticipation of German invasion 56, 72, 152
  anti-imperialism 109–31, 151, 156
  Economic Imperialism 116
  Empire and Commerce in Africa 111–16, 119, 121, 128, 163, 169
  Imperialism and Civilization 121–3, 124, 163, 171
  Mandates and Empire 116–17
  paternalism 110, 120, 127
  antipathy towards religion 194–5
  atheism 189
  attack on Christianity 173–4
  autobiography vii, viii, 6, 7, 18, 71, 181, 200
    Sowing 3, 8–9, 22, 25, 26, 28, 77, 190, 191, 192
    Growing 33, 38, 42, 109, 110
    Beginning Again 54, 62, 88, 103, 133, 134, 162, 166, 190
    Downhill All the Way 103, 117, 124, 133, 136, 142, 143, 166, 167, 168, 175, 189, 194, 195, 196
    (The) Journey not the Arrival Matters 77, 133, 146, 147, 189, 190, 191, 198–9
  Barbarians at the Gate 149–51, 163, 166, 176, 180, 196
  BBC talks 127, 169–70
  (A) Calendar of Consolation 77
  Ceylon *see* Ceylon
  civil service exams and appointment 27–8, 29
  considers marriage to Virginia 39–40
  Co-operation and the Future of Industry 163–4
  correspondence with Kingsley Martin 182–4, 185
  courtship 50–1, 53, 54–7
  decision not to have children 58
  disputes with publishers 163
  early years 3–14
  education
    Arlington House 9
    St Paul's 7, 9–14, 28, 179
    university *see* Cambridge
  elitism 172
  enjoyment of sports and games 9, 13, 15, 31, 34, 71, 76, 77, 109, 200, 201
  essay on mysticism 18–19
  fatalism 3, 7, 8–9, 25, 48, 74, 77, 190, 198
  final years 198–201
  first sexual experience 32
  First World War 133–6, 168
  founds Hogarth Press 59–70, 135, 200
  (The) Future of Constantinople 95
  General Election (1922) 167–8
  Hellenism 11, 14, 24, 178–80, 181, 188, 192, 199
  honeymoon 58, 84, 85
  (The) Hotel 70, 147–8
  income 55, 72, 83, 88, 89, 100, 103, 201
  indifference to wealth and popular esteem 196–7
  insider/outsider 4, 22, 31, 84, 190
  intellectual heroes 195
    G. E. Moore 20–1, 22, 23–4, 25–6, 161, 162, 192, 197, 201
  (The) Intelligent Man's Way to Prevent War (introduction) 136
  International Government 89–97, 102, 111, 112, 135, 162, 163, 169
  invited to visit Russia 129–30
  Jewish identity 3–7, 8, 11, 12, 28, 53, 54, 56, 84–5, 133, 190, 191–4, 197, 199
    Hebraic values 178–9, 188–9, 192
    love of the Book of Job 15
    Quack, Quack! 140–1
  journalism and reviews 83–4, 86, 98–100, 102–4, 135, 145, 146–7, 157, 162
  Labour and the Nation 104

Index

letters to Virginia 55
love of animals 33, 36, 45, 77, 200
love of gardening 75, 76, 151
(The) Modern State 170–1
pet names 60
pets 29, 31, 33, 60, 76, 142
photographic portraits 79, 80
physical health 135, 146
poetry 27
Principia Politica 8, 161, 169, 171, 172, 177–81, 189
Quack, Quack! 138–42, 150, 180, 191, 196
rejection of cruelty and injustice 195–6
relationship with Trekkie Parsons 75, 76, 78, 130
return from Ceylon 50, 83
Second World War 150–7
secretary to the Advisory Committee on International Affairs (ACIntQ) 100–2, 106, 110, 112, 117, 121, 126, 135, 144, 145, 157
short stories 52, 66, 84
"Pearls and Swine" 43–4, 66
"(A) Tale Told by Midnight" 43–4
"The Three Jews" 52, 58, 62–3, 84, 193
siblings 7, 9, 15, 19, 28, 30, 31, 34, 40, 50, 54, 56, 65, 134, 191, 198
Socialism and Co-operation 165–6
spiritual anxiety 191
travel abroad in later years 129–31
(The) Village in the Jungle 42, 45–6, 47–8, 52, 54, 55, 83, 84, 128, 130
visits Germany and Italy (1935) 142–3
War for Peace 133, 134, 151
wedding 57
(The) Wise Virgins 7, 44, 52–4, 56, 75, 84, 85, 193
work habits 33, 38, 84, 88, 109
Woolf, Marie (mother) 4, 7, 30, 54, 56, 57, 189
Woolf, Philip (brother) 56, 65, 134
Woolf, Sidney (father) 4, 7, 8, 133, 161, 188, 189, 198

Woolf, Virginia 4, 7, 39, 40, 48, 98, 111, 147, 149, 163, 172, 188
affair with Vita Sackville-West 69–70
anticipation of German invasion 56, 72, 152
anti-Semitism 55–7, 193–4
Between the Acts 73
courtship 50–1, 53, 54–7
death 73, 74, 151, 197–8
decision not to have children 58
diary 87, 175
flirtation with Clive Bell 51, 53
founds Hogarth Press 59–70, 135, 200
honeymoon 58, 84, 85
income 55, 67, 71, 72, 83, 85, 103, 201
introduced to Leonard 16, 22, 29, 33–4, 50
Jacob's Room 67
jealousy 66–7
Kew Gardens 66
Leonard's socialism and 166–7
"(The) Mark on the Wall" 62, 64
mental instability 58, 59, 60, 71, 72–3, 83, 85, 86, 88, 129, 135, 146, 197
Night and Day 67
Orlando 69, 103
pet names 60
pets 60
photographic portrait 79
proposed to by Lytton Strachey 39
reputation and literary legacy 158, 197
sensitivity to criticism 68
suicide attempts 58, 59, 72, 85, 133
suicide notes 73, 74
To the Lighthouse 103
(The) Voyage Out 27, 52, 67
wartime 151–2
(The) Waves 198
wedding 57
(The) Years 146
Wright, Maurice 135

Young, Hilton 51

Zimmern, Alfred 96
Zionism 125, 130, 185

The manufacturer's authorised representative in the EU for product safety is Oxford University Press España S.A. of el Parque Empresarial San Fernando de Henares, Avenida de Castilla, 2 – 28830 Madrid (www.oup.es/en or product.safety@oup.com). OUP España S.A. also acts as importer into Spain of products made by the manufacturer.